Cloud Cover

a memoir of perseverance
and transformation

Margot S. Milcetich

Brahmrishi Yoga Publications
Ravenna, Ohio

Publisher: Brahmrishi Yoga Publications
www.brahmrishiyoga.org

Date: October 2013.

Printed in United States of America

Library of Congress Control Number: 2013949384
ISBN: 978-1-4528-2467-3

for my father

who loved story

A man who is his own mystery is a disaster.
It is for God to be a mystery, God and the lives of others.
Frank Gaspar "Stealing Fatima"

Perseverance brings good fortune.
I Ching, 39 Obstruction

Introduction

Brahmrishi Vishvatma Bawra told us, "If I tell you the sun exists, hearing alone is not enough. You must learn to see the sun with your own eyes."

I wanted to tell the story of my teacher as I knew him for twenty years. Guru means teacher, one who removes darkness and reveals the light—a teacher of knowledge, self, presence, and truth. A guru teaches us to be a master of our own self. My Guru's teacher would end his discourse with "Okay, my dear, I have told you what I intended to say. It is my duty to say these things to you, but I have no right to compel you. I am your guru, not your ruler, your king. I can only give you knowledge. In the end, your life is in the hand of God."

The story is also about language. As a child, I had learned to trust what I saw, not what I heard. Learning Sanskrit was wholly different; I trusted it because I felt its vibrations as truth. Returning to English as a felt language was how I integrated a sense of self. As an adult, I let my younger self speak with me and together we crafted this story.

1

This singing art is sea foam.
Rumi

My ordinary life is suspended when I fly.

The ground vanishes within minutes as my weight is pulled back in the seat, my ears are filled with the hiss of the air system, and the craft raises to the wide realm of light, space and white, rhythmic layers clouds. I have no fear of flying, but rather an inordinate sense of trust.

That same feeling came to me as I was lying on the floor of an old bread van—a feeling of space and suspension. It was 1976. I was headed to my mother's home in Philadelphia, Pennsylvania from college in Fairfield, Iowa, where I had gone to study meditation. It was a cool July night at the end of my second year. A few students were sharing the ride with a couple who owned the delivery van. The interior had been gutted so it felt even more top-heavy and less travel-worthy. A shag carpet fragment was spread on the floor and some kind of bed was built into a side wall. We drove all night, taking turns at the wheel, adjusting ourselves to the loud pitch of the engine by not speaking much. The winds are strong in the plains, so we drove below the speed limit, 55 mph in those days. During my short turn at the wheel, my hands grew stiff from gripping, straining with the unfamiliar stress of the wind and the passing trucks.

After my turn, I thought sleep would come with the swaying of the vehicle. It did not; I lay awake on the thin fibers of the carpet and felt the metal floor of the van under my back—aware of the space moving under me, around the van and out into the space of the starry sky.

Space in Iowa was vast. Storms blew in with thick banks of clouds crossed with lightning displays. Sunset and moonrise were both visible at once in an orange sky bringing a soaring feeling of living on a turning globe. My eyes were closed as I lay back. I could not see out, but I could see with a kind of inner eye. I was filled with a sense of expansion, clarity, and peace. My meditations had never been as deep as this. They were filled with thoughts—superficial thoughts of what to eat for dinner in the cafeteria, and fantasies about coming up to a farmhouse.

The van broke down in Gary, Indiana, on a Sunday morning. As no mechanic had showed up at the truck stop, another girl and I asked around and found a truck heading east. We hauled ourselves up into the cab; I sat by the window. The sensation of space had diminished. Sitting up high, I merely felt watchful. Using his cab phone, the driver found a ride for my companion where the road split: Route 80 to New York, and Route 76 to Philadelphia. So we pulled off at a truck stop in Youngstown, Ohio.

I went inside the lobby to find a restroom.

"Young lady!"

I looked around and saw a woman behind a window in a booth, staring me down.

"Yes?"

"Don't even think about it. You are not getting back on another truck," she said.

I stared back. She had red hair piled up on her head—easier to look at her hair than listen to her. It was late Sunday afternoon, and she was here doing God's work.

"You find a hotel, and take a bus in the morning."

"I'll be fine," I finally said.

"No, you will not get on another truck."

She got up, and came out through a door next to her desk. She took a firm hold on my arm, looked into my eyes and repeated herself.

"Okay," I shrugged.

She let me go. I did, in fact, know people in Youngstown—a married couple—and I guessed there might be a Transcendental Meditation center. We had been told that all centers were open to us as teachers. At a pay phone with a phone book dangling on a wire, I found the TM center in the Yellow Pages.

"Hi, I'm a teacher traveling through. Could I spend the night?"

"Who is this?"

I said my name.

"It's me, Teddy Altman. I live here. Where are you? Can I come get you?"

I was beginning to feel that the lady at the dispatch cage had really done her job well. I knew Teddy from MIU.

"Sure. I'm at a truck stop where Route 80 and 76 come together."

Teddy was not a student. He had health problems, so he had lived on campus and had joined in the healthy lifestyle of whole foods. MIU had imported the California lifestyle of carrot juicing, whole grains, vegetarian casseroles, fruit and salad bars to the quiet town of Fairfield. Teddy ate at the dining hall only infrequently—he had a juicer in his dorm room. It was the atmosphere he needed, unusual in 1976. His car came up to the station after half an hour, and he took me to the center, talking about his diet the whole way. This made me feel comfortable as if some of my life in Iowa had moved to Youngstown ahead of me. This was how I knew him: he always had a new recipe for his Champion Juicier. Once we arrived, he told me to take the empty room on the third floor.

"We've got a full house on the third floor. There are four rooms. There's a graphic artist you'll never see. He works all the time. Then there's a teacher couple who share a room, and a single guy, named Bill who is training to be a teacher. Go across from the stair to the right. You'll find a room with a mattress and a sloping ceiling."

The bed was made up with sheets. Outside the window, there were tall trees lit by a streetlight. I went to bed and slept well.

When I came downstairs in the morning, I made my way to the kitchen. It was a galley kitchen with a small table at one end by a door to the drive at back of the house. A dark-haired guy stood at the counter, dressed casually in black khakis and a blue denim shirt. He had olive skin and his thick hair was brushed back from his face. He captured my attention with his look. It was as direct as his question.

"You want fresh-squeezed orange juice?"

"Sure."

"Toast?"

"No, thanks."

"I heard you spent the night. You a teacher? Do me a favor." He went right on, "I took care of my friend's kids yesterday, took them to the circus, and today I promised them ice cream. I have to go get them from Sharon in Pennsylvania. But I'm supposed to check some peoples' meditation today. Could you help me out?"

3

Checking meditation was a standard practice that teachers-in-training could do for new meditators. We guided them with instruction, sat for a while, and then fielded questions.

"Sure."

He handed me a glass of juice and went out the back.

I had no reason to move on from the house quickly. I had no plans in Philadelphia. I checked the folks' meditations, then went to visit with my friends, Thoraya and Ross. When Bill returned, he joined us; he was close friends with Ross. He talked most of the time, discussing some practical concern he had with them. From there, Bill gave me a ride home, and upon our return, I went to my room to sleep.

But I couldn't sleep. The same experience of space that I had felt in the van returned. I felt the space beyond the house with my eyes closed, a vast galactic space filled with stars.

I had chosen meditation as a path five years before. The idea of meditation was not easy to find in the States but an opportunity came for me to travel to Taiwan with my Uncle and Aunt and their four children. My uncle was developing a college department of Asian studies in Vermont. He was taking his sabbatical in Taiwan with his family, and my mother was seeking ways for me to be gone from home in the summer. On the trip to Asia we first stopped in Japan, where I saw the Great Buddha of Kamakura that stands ninety feet tall.

I drew the figure on a sketch pad. In the middle, the flow of robes revealed the space of an open heart slightly caved by the restfulness of a long span of sitting. Below the serene brow and the eyes with their inner focus was the softest feature, the lips, carved with a smile of knowing. As I was drawing, I had to stop—a kind of magnetic pull made me close my eyes. Sitting below this symbol, I felt a sensation of quiet—a loud silence and a palpable expansive feeling.

This feeling came again in the house in Youngstown—a sudden expansion that made the house appear to have no walls.

Then, abruptly, in my mind's eye there was a window and a man and a woman next to it, looking at me. He turned away and flattened into a cardboard cutout, a ghost of himself. She turned to me and pointed an angry finger.

I sat up quickly, feeling uncomfortable with the stillness. I went to the window first and looked out and up beyond the trees. The sky was clouded over.

4

"Curious," I spoke out loud to myself. There had been a universe of stars in my vision, but when I looked there were clouds. My next thought was to talk with someone. I had a friend at MIU who stayed up late playing guitar, and when I wandered the campus unable to sleep, I could knock on the door of his room and talk with him. He would stop playing and pull some milk from his little fridge to have with cereal. Restless, I went out into the hall, and stood looking at the closed doors.

The room by the stair housed the married couple. The one across from them belonged to the graphic artist, whom I had met only briefly. Teddy was downstairs. Bill was in the room across from mine.

I went over and knocked.

"Who is it?" His voice was abrupt.

"It's Margot."

"What do you want?"

"You want to go out for a walk?"

"Let me get dressed." He spoke from behind the door.

We walked to a neighborhood park and swung on tall swings, pulling on the cool chain link. Streetlights stood on two sides of the park. The street was behind us. Bill's face was mostly in shadow, so I could make out his dark hair but not much expression. His voice had a direct tone.

"Do you think you need organized religion to find God?" he asked.

"Well, no."

"Being raised Catholic, I feel strongly that we don't need it."

We talked a short while, maybe fifteen minutes, after which time he seemed satisfied. Back at the house, I went quietly to bed. I never mentioned my vision. The next day Bill was to drive Teddy to the airport; and I asked to go along. From the airport, Bill said he was headed to the country, to his family's place. I asked him if I could go with him. This was bold, but Bill felt like a friend, and I remembered how excited I had been in Iowa, when I had stopped at a farm where cows were wandering in the dirt drive. I mostly contained my emotions, so my burst of pleasure upon seeing the cows was unusual. It felt important to me to visit the county. Bill agreed, reluctantly.

"I'll be your little sister," I said. "I like the country. I like cows. You have cows there?"

"No, it's the double house, where I lived during college. My grandparents lived in the adjoining apartment, but they've passed away.

My father is remodeling it. It's empty most of the time, but I still have a key to my apartment."

I adjusted my expectations but still wanted to go to the country. The setting of my family home was among Angus cattle farms; I longed for some connection with that part of me. My parents had divorced and both were remarried then; our childhood house was sold.

When Bill and I arrived at his family homestead, and I saw the house from the outside, it looked like one I had seen in my meditations, an image of a house in the country. I told Bill not to go in until I told him the floor plan.

He just looked at me. His eyes were deep brown, sharply defined beneath black brows.

The rooms were laid out as I had imagined. When I was in school at Rochester, before MIU, I consoled myself with a vision of this house and the name of "George." Bill said his grandfather's name was George. That made me pause. I would expect Bill's name to be George, not his grandfather, though his grandfather seemed important to him.

By then it was dark. The part of the homestead I had seen in my mind was under construction, so we went to the apartment side where Bill had lived in college. He pulled a mattress into the dining room for me to lie on; he pulled out a mattress for himself in the living room.

Lying there, I began to have visions of a deity. I had not liked Hindu deities. They were too stylized for me with their round cheeks, colorful robes, and multiple arms. I did not understand them. Here was one dancing in front of me: a female goddess with many dark-skinned arms and red robes. I was awake. From the other room, I heard Bill's voice.

"Want to walk?"

Outside in the dark he gave me a tour of the garden. We sat in a swinging chair—painted thick with white paint—that hung crookedly but was fine for rocking gently with feet in the dirt. His grandfather had made it. He pointed out the outdoor brick oven he had made as well, shadowed in the starlight. Then we walked further down the gravel drive to a cobbled brick street lined with old maple trees, spotted with a few lights that threw shadows up toward the dark sky. Space opened again, this time with a stretch of time beyond my lifetime.

"I think we are supposed to be together," I said to him.

Bill looked at me without saying anything. His wavy hair and cut sideburns were looking even more familiar.

6

"I feel like we have been together two thousand years."

I went over and held his hand. I was slightly taller, but he felt larger than me.

"All right, I'll tell you now," he said. "I knew we would be together from the first night. In my meditation I heard a voice telling me to marry you."

This felt right.

Yes, I had been looking for the man I might marry. I was willing to accept that Bill was he. Though I hardly knew him, the sense of space and expansion that I had been feeling was the affirmation I had been seeking.

"I have to tell you about my meditations," he continued. "When I used to live here, one evening I went outside and sat on the lawn. A ball of light descended from the night sky and filled me with white light. It overwhelmed me with an incomparable happiness and wholeness, but I had no way to explain it. I did not know what was happening to me. And this altered experience kept returning, especially when I went for a walk in nature. It was crazy; it was confusing."

He realized he was telling me a lot. We had resumed walking on the brick road toward town. So we stopped and rested on the grass under the night shadow of a maple tree. No cars came past.

"I was seeking a meditation path. TM was what I found. Things have sorted themselves out some. Lately when I sit, I go directly into white light. The light takes on the form of a woman-like goddess. She mutates into an orange-robed man."

I played with the grass between my fingers. This was a lot to take in.

"I think of him as God. It's like I'm rapping with God."

The night of my arrival, this orange-robed figure told Bill to marry the woman who had showed up in the house. This was upsetting to Bill as he had decided to be a monk. Bill had been sitting in his room in meditation, arguing with this inner voice. He wanted to end the disturbance when I knocked on his door.

"All right if you want me to marry her, have her knock on my door right now!" Bill had said to the voice.

Thus, my future husband was cornered.

That night, we went for a swing in the park where I passed his one test: I would respect his inner path.

Two nights later, after agreeing to marry, we returned to our separate mattresses and went to sleep. I stayed on in Youngstown for ten days. On a rainy evening, in the park with the swing set, we stood quietly sharing the shelter of an umbrella. His touch on my back softened my anxiety, gently tethering me to my body.

For the moment, all was calm.

2

He is carried on, even against his will, by prior practice.
Gita 6/44

Meeting Bill and becoming engaged in three days was not normal. I was agreeing to marry a man I did not know. This was a big risk. The little knowledge I had gained from my study of meditation about the value of an expanded sense of self, free from fear, led me to believe that our marriage might be successful. But I was beginning to have doubts; our decision to stay together had been quick. I had simply wanted to be married—to someone.

We decided marriage was logical, because we lived in different states, with Bill in Ohio and my home in either Pennsylvania or Iowa. We were out in a restaurant, a lunch buffet with a selection of Italian food and salads, when I voiced my doubts about our decision.

"Bill, I wanted to get married before the end of 1976. And it's July. It's almost just crazy."

We had decided on a wedding date, December 20, right at the end of 1976, the year I determined I would be married. Bill had chosen the date.

December 20th was the birthdate of Swami Brahmananda Saraswati. We knew this man by name and by his picture. He was a Shankaracharya of the North of India, meaning he carried authority as a teacher within the Indian culture. He was the guru of Maharishi Mahesh Yogi, who founded Transcendental Meditation, a simple meditation technique that was gaining ground in the West. The date felt significant. We were both lapsed Catholics, but we retained a feeling for the significance of a holy day.

"Margot, to not get married would mean the voice inside me means nothing."

I agreed with that, but I was not sure what it meant for me yet. Affirming his reality seemed more important than not. I had been restless my last semester at Maharishi International University, also called MIU. It was time to choose a major. I had been consciously looking for a husband instead. I needed a family. I needed to recreate some stability for myself.

I thought the decision to be married might make me feel better, but I was moving away from the familiar.

Student life had suited me. The routine and the group setting were comfortable. I could hide in the rows of seats and not confront myself. I could write papers and go for walks, eat at a cafeteria and find comfort in the routines. I had attended two colleges before settling on MIU where meditation was structured into the curriculum.

With Bill, it was the experience of expansion that had captured me. I was not new to this feeling, but each moment, however occasional and brief, came with such a profound relief that I relived those moments and tried to recapture them. They guided my sense of destiny—though I did not understand them.

When I first committed to studying Transcendental Meditation at a one month intensive called the Science of Creative Intelligence, I traveled by bus to upper New York State from Philadelphia. I intended to go from there to Iowa. MIU offered intervals of two months traditional coursework that alternated with a month of meditation and study similar to the Science of Creative Intelligence. I had dropped out of Brown University to commit to this and I was anxious about my decision. Brown was a good school, I had transferred there from Rochester, also a good school, and I was straining the expectations of my parents, and their guilt about the disturbance of their separation on my brothers and myself. They separated when I was in my last year of high school.

At the bus station, hauling a small green duffle of clothes on my back I was looking for my bus line in a large open building with a linoleum floor. People were passing on all sides, when a voice came through the murmurs and footsteps—again and again repeating something that sounded like "Holy! Holy!" I looked over and saw an impoverished black man standing perfectly still, pointing at me, his arm and finger tracing the arc of my path. His eyes looked into mine. It was only for a second. I looked away, but I had felt something. My rational voice told me he must be mentally ill, in a psychosis that made him able to see my aura. I did my best to forget it had happened. I have told myself many times since then *he was not pointing at me*. But it makes no difference. I still see him pointing at me in my confused state, and feel the suspension of his affirmation—

spacious and quiet among restless movements in the station. I felt affirmed for heading in the right direction. Destiny, if there was such a thing, was at work. I smoked my last cigarette on the bus, and threw the rest of the pack out the window.

Here was a man who was agreeing to marry me after three days for unusual reasons that felt right, peaceful, and impulsive. I was trying to move away from my ordinary dysfunctional family, where feelings were not handled well, or at all. I saw through my own eyes but without a spoken language to match my reflections. I could not speak simply and truthfully. I stopped saying much at all. My father abandoned his life with us when I was seventeen, my two brothers in college and I still at home. Dad started a new life with another woman and her two young children. Our family dissolved, out of my control, dramatically and suddenly. This juncture propelled me into anxiety and fear. I was losing my family and I could do nothing to prevent it. I had no control of them or of my feelings. Ironically, here I was rashly engaged with a man to create stability in my life.

We drove to my mother's new home that belonged to her husband, Pete, a surgeon who was near the end of his career. He had a 19th Century summer house, since annexed into the city of Philadelphia, with a wide veranda and an artist's apartment in back with tall panes of glass open to the northern light. I had told Bill nothing of my background. He was taking me home in his blue Dodge Charger, leaving it with me while he went to France for three months to complete his training to become a TM teacher. We arrived at night; Pete and Martha were out. Bill went to bed, a little shocked by the grandeur of the house. A house trailer could have fit in the front hallway. We agreed to not say anything about being engaged. That is not what happened.

I waited up for my mother and told her I was going to marry the guy who had brought me home.

Bill awoke the next morning before me, went downstairs for breakfast and was interviewed by Martha and Pete, who were waiting for him. They ended their questions with:

"If you could travel, where would you go?"

"Probably to India to sit in a cave with my guru."

Bill and I went over all this later.

"Bill, how could you say that? You don't even know if you have a guru."

11

"Yes, but that is what I think."

I smiled. "Well received, huh?"

"Margot, I did not know what was happening. I came down for toast and juice. They grilled me!" He paused. "You spoke with them last night."

"Yes."

"We agreed not."

"I know, but I could not help it."

Bill had his doubts now. I calmed him by saying it was my mother's second husband's house. I had not grown up there. I was anxious and excited, and needed to talk with her.

We decided to formalize our engagement with a ring. I had a broche of a Satyr set with a tear-shaped emerald and small diamonds that had belonged to my Grandmother Biddle. I was her namesake, so I had received some unusual items. I sketched out a setting for the stones and we went to a jeweler up the street. The estimate was a hundred dollars.

"I don't have any money left," Bill said. "I just don't have it. After paying for teacher training, my bank account is down to almost nothing."

Bill had always earned his money. He had a paper route as a child and he mowed lawns. He was proud of the fact that his father once took a loan from him to build a porch. He was the third of six children who went to Catholic school.

"Maybe Pete needs some work done," he added.

Bill painted a white picket fence along Rex Avenue that spanned the length of the circular drive. I had the ring set and drove with it in Bill's Dodge Charger back to MIU in Fairfield, where I showed my friends and told them my last name would be "Milcetich."

"Milcetich?" One friend wrinkled up her nose. "No way. That is unpronounceable!" I wanted to leave my past behind by taking a Central European name. The conventions of my upbringing were losing significance, but taking a new name was one I would keep. Since I was living in Iowa up until the time of the wedding, I let my mother handle the arrangements.

Bill wrote short and inspiring letters from France, returned in November, flew to meet me in Iowa, and we drove to Ohio to decide where to live. We were married in Philadelphia on a cold and rainy December night. Mom invited family and friends. I felt resigned. I had never fantasized about a wedding. I had no expectations. She was happy to host and suggested the church of Our Mother of Consolation with pink interior walls, and an officiating priest who was a personal friend. Few of my friends came. I had lost touch with those from high school, and friends from Iowa lived all over the country. One coming from nearby Downingtown got lost coming into the city on the dark, slick curving roads that had once been carriage trails. He never made it and although I felt disappointed, it felt about right. Only my maid-of-honor, Marge from Minnesota, made the trip.

I chose a white wedding dress with a sleek material that flowed down from under the bust. It had a scooped neck, long sleeves, and a train that swept the ground if it were not tied up. I had the train down while going into the church, ready for the wedding march. Leaving the car, it dipped in a large puddle. I did not care. The church was lit by a series of candelabra, old-fashioned tall stems holding multiple candles in glass lanterns to hide the pink walls. In the dim lighting, the mud on the dress went into shadow. Then Bill stepped on the train when we shifted to exchange the rings. That felt about right, too. The wedding was sufficient. We were married in a traditional setting, and in the service, Bill and I included five minutes of silence and mysterious quotes about "bliss."

3

*Your deepest presence is in every small contracting and expanding,
the two as beautifully balanced and coordinated as birdwings.*
Rumi

My family life had fallen apart in 1970, when I was seventeen. Though the practice of meditation was helping me, I had much ground to cover. Meeting Bill initiated a new stage. The previous time of chaos was barely behind me.

Six years earlier while I was in Taiwan, I received a letter from my father. He wrote that he felt dried up like a raisin. His words were confusing. I did not understand them as a warning that he might leave, but his letter had made me cry.

Returning from Taiwan, the jet landed in New York, where a young man in the airport wearing a top-hat and tails over his jeans was a sharp contrast to the subdued culture of Taiwan. I shook my head. I had forgotten it was 1970, the Vietnam War had disturbed my generation and marijuana was at work. I had culture shock upon returning to the States, feeling how we cultivated differences and glorified personal expression. I had almost forgotten the conflict over the war and my brothers' fear of the draft. Tired and alienated, I caught the connecting flight to Philadelphia. In Japan and Taiwan, I understood that quiet could be a cultural value. By contrast, the Western culture had an inbred compulsion to think, talk, and do out of fear of self-annihilation. In Taiwan, I found affirmation within the insignificance of our shared human life and the long drama of survival. As I walked in the old hills behind the house my Uncle and Aunt had rented, a spirit of quiet and simplicity visited me. I walked in complete innocence and looked out through the delicate foliage of trees. I saw centuries-old tiers of rice paddies contained by walls of stone into narrow levels, worked by countless hands and feeding countless mouths. In Taiwan, mountains kept time. Human life was tiny and spanned untold generations.

My mother and brother Chris were waiting for me in Philadelphia. We stopped for sweet corn at a roadside stand. I asked where Dad was. "He's in New Jersey."

I looked at both of them carefully. I felt distant.

"Helping another family."

I knew something was wrong. "What do you mean by helping?"

Chris gave a long complicated answer about neighbors where he had been staying in New Jersey. I did not really listen. I was pretty sure Mom and Chris were lying to me. This made me angry, but even irritation with them felt out of place, so I just waited for them to say more. They also appeared to believe what they said. I was confused, knowing something was wrong.

"Would fresh corn taste good?"

I nodded. What could I say?

When we arrived at the house, I was certain that Dad had moved out. He came home days later in his green Volkswagen Beetle to pick up his belongings. After watching his car go down the long curving drive and over the small bridge that crossed our stream, I lost my memory for two weeks. There was no discussion of anything with my mother. She neither asked me about my journey to the Far East, nor did she offer to help me feel anything with my father gone. She was gone in her own way. She spoke with visitors in the living room. Not with me. I found myself sitting in study hall in my senior year of school, not sure of how I had gotten myself there, and then dropped out of courses and sports. I spent the next summer moving between both parents' homes, feeling even more confused and unmoored. I stayed with a family friend for a month, and made it to my first semester at the University of Rochester.

Winter in upper New York State settled in with bitter, cold winds, and by March, I was ready for a change. I saw a poster on a tree announcing a course in meditation. The picture was of a brown-skinned man in white robes, Maharishi Mahesh Yogi. The practice was Transcendental Meditation. I attended the lecture given by a thin, young blonde man in a suit who had left his center in California to travel and teach at college campuses. I paid thirty-five dollars, witnessed a *puja* sung by the teacher and received a mantra. The practice did not take hold in me.

After the first year of college, I returned home, disoriented to myself and the world around me. I felt alone, unsupported, overwhelmed by a profound grief and a racing mind. I did not know how to feel; intense emotion was making concentration on my courses impossible.

I went to a psychiatrist who prescribed a medication that stopped all feeling, all motivation and learning. I no longer felt distressed; I felt nothing. I tried to draw.

"What is that?" she asked.

I had a small pad of paper in my lap. Talking with the psychiatrist was not helping. I sat in an easy chair feeling uncomfortable most of the time. I had tried to draw in that session.

"Looks like a sword," I said. I was ambivalent about drawing. I just wanted some help and she wasn't helping. I scribbled a little more, and held it up for her to see.

"Looks like a flower now," she said. "Good, isn't it? There's a change."

That was not helpful. Her remark was obvious. I felt critical of myself, ashamed that I had dropped out of college. Our silence made her uncomfortable. She talked and I found out more about her marriage and work. Her nails were painted bright red.

On medication I could not read or comprehend a magazine. I tried a waitressing job and could not remember the price of a hamburger, which was $.65—now I remember, because I went back to the restaurant later to see what my problem could have been. Anxiety and a racing mind overwhelmed my ability to cope at all. Then I was depressed. I had trouble understanding what people were telling me. I heard different words. I lived in a pharmaceutical strait-jacket, home alone with my mother.

Over Christmas, when the psychiatrist was out of town, my mother and my brother David were enjoying playing Telemann duets. She was on piano, David on flute, and they were ignoring me. He was home from college in Hiram, Ohio.

I had watched with jealousy and anger, but I was not allowed to express anger. I did not know how to feel it. I lay on the floor in spasm—my body had odd contractions that pulled my head to my shoulder and made me hyperventilate. My psychiatrist had left instructions for my mother to call the psychiatric unit if I had any difficulty. She called them. Mom and David drove me into the city where, legally, I had to sign myself in. The presiding doctor asked me to answer: *Why should people in glass houses not throw stones?* I gave a literal answer that was a completion of the metaphor: *Because they will break the glass.*

I understood that they wanted me to elaborate on the meaning by saying something like, "One should be cautious and understand the circumstances they are in before acting rashly." I was angry that I had been taken into the facility and not simply held and comforted. My answer was rash, but the words came quickly out of my mouth. That was their basis for determining I was suitable for the ward: a literal answer to a symbolic question. I felt coerced into signing; my mother would not speak with me. She left me in the hands of the doctor. I was shuttled to a smaller waiting area where I asked the attending male nurse if he thought that was fair. He backed up the doctor by saying: *They know their job.*

So I resigned myself by signing my name and entered a locked ward, where cigarettes were a currency for survival among the patients who bragged about their *elephant doses* of anti-psychotics, when they were coherent.

The priest who would later marry Bill and me came to visit. We got permission to go to a courtyard where we sat on a park bench and he told me about himself. I was still not talking.

"Life is hard for me," he said.

I wondered if he was talking about his celibacy.

"So much of life we have to tolerate and not even understand."

I gleaned that he did not understand his choices when he made them, but he learned to live with his faith, even if it faltered.

I was grateful for his visit. My family did not come. I conformed to the routines and was released after four days. There were two results. I had to keep my emotions as if frozen so that I could move ahead. Cigarettes helped. And I forged an acute determination to find another way to live. I had suffered from flight of ideas and paranoia, the doctors said. My breakdown was termed "a psychotic break with reality."

In March, three months after this incident, I resumed my TM practice. It worked. I had one moment of complete calm sitting with two friends who visited and were also practicing TM. We sat in circle of three back-to-back on a small dock by a pond. I felt calm under the open sky—no thoughts, no dread, no fear. That experience launched my daily meditations. I stopped taking medication that same month. TM meditation was a technique that quieted the mind with mantra meditation—no meaning, no breath, just simplicity of sound. It worked.

I found a job in the early summer landscaping an overgrown garden for an older woman, who praised my pruning, comparing it to a Japanese garden. This made sense. I was returning to a feeling of who I was. While in the Far East, I had traveled on a tour bus from the ship, without Uncle Nicky's family, to a Japanese garden and silk store. The rest of the tour group went quickly through the garden and into the store. I had been left by myself. With each step, every angle of vision was complete with pine, rock, moss and water. Light reflected on the pale cotton trousers of women, barely visible and lightly audible, sweeping soft grass brooms. Perfection was revealed beneath their touch. The textures of moss and stone, the shapes of the pruned trees, the angles of water falling over rock, every gaze reached into silence. I walked slowly, seeing, not thinking but feeling the inner place opening. My feet felt tiny, way below me on the earth, and the trees and plants in their spaces felt vast. I had no way to explain my experience to myself, so I left any need to place language on it. The memory of that quiet returned while I gardened. This experience was possible in the garden, but not easy to maintain.

The blissful expansion that had initiated Bill's and my union was not my steady state. Keeping anxiety at bay was my normal state, and living with him without the schedule I had at MIU, I was at a loss. In Iowa, the regularity of wholesome vegetarian meals, the simple dress code, group meetings and classes helped me. I had long nights of high anxiety where I walked to calm myself, and found friends who were similarly sleepless. Occasionally I saw an aura—white light off Maharishi's forehead when he bowed to a gymnasium full of students. I felt relief out among the cries of Red-winged Blackbirds in the broad cornfields that met at every intersection of roads outside of Fairfield. The meditation technique and the lifestyle helped me sustain a feeling of simplicity and order, but my heart was not at peace.

My body had pain, too. It started with constant pain in my arches in high school and then my knees. By the time I made it to Iowa, sharp, shooting pains in my knees would awaken me at night. The pain in the body was easier to manage than anxiety. It was acute, unlike the free-floating, unanchored mental state. I tried jogging to free myself from anxiety. But after one good run, I had ten days of fitful sleep. Only long walks were possible. So out in the wide lands and open sky, I cultivated a habit of fasting on fruit and juices and walking to quiet my mind. Meditation alone was not enough.

I had boyfriends in Iowa, but none with Bill's intensity and focus. I had never lived with anyone. I was not serene upon waking in the morning; I had discomfort stepping into ordinary life. There was so much that Bill did not understand about me and I did not know about myself. I had not really left home. I had left my distress behind and I was trying to manage it with meditation. I was hoping that marriage would provide some stability. I had lost my family. Bill knew nothing of how challenging it had been for me to make the decision to go to MIU. I could not tell him. I was surviving. Leaving MIU to be with him was just as difficult.

4

Racing, chasing, hunting drive people crazy.
Lao Tzu

A mental health diagnosis of a brief psychosis is both damning and freeing. The old rule book is thrown aside. Conformity and non-conformity are tossed into a new light. Passing as normal can be easy, if you lie low. I tried to, but I was college age, and college did not suit me.

As I recovered from my psychotic break, I paid visits to my father, his new wife and her two children. They seemed good for each other. My mother had returned to college to complete a degree that had been deferred by her hospital volunteer work at the end of World War II. By fall, I returned to college as a transfer student at Brown University in Providence, Rhode Island. While at Rochester, I had applied to Brown, thinking that my lack of adjustment was because Rochester was the wrong college for me. Brown was an excellent school. I should have been proud of myself, but the change in college was not enough. I was not interested in any intellectual pursuit. I wanted to feel better; I needed more.

I purchased a copy of Wilhelm's *I Ching* an ancient Chinese text, based on some blend of Confucian and Taoist thought, translated as "The Book of Changes." The philosophy espoused in the text advised both when to act and when not to act. Advice, such as "It furthers one to cross the great water," means move ahead. "Keeping still is a time of building character," means the opposite. Reading the text was instructive. But you could also roll three pennies to find an oracle, a specific reading that would address your precise situation. First you held an open question in mind—one that asked for what attitude was best for staying with the problem at hand. I felt I had no one who could help me make a decision about college. My father was preoccupied with his new life. My mother was adjusting to her life without him. So with "The Book of Changes," in

20

front of me I rolled three pennies twice and based on whether I got heads or tails, I would mark down a straight or broken line until I had a stack of six, called a hexagram. The broken lines were changing lines, so they were predictive of what was coming into form. So in addition to a general reading, there were six possible ways the situation could move forward, and the appropriate attitude in each case.

The *I Ching* kept bringing me the message: *Youthful beneficent folly*. My fate was prompting me to study meditation, and I was receiving a warning that I might regret my decision later. But at this juncture, folly seemed like a good choice.

I left Brown after one semester. For my final exam on South American Colonialism, I wrote extensively in black ink in my little blue exam book why I was not going to answer the questions since that was merely parroting, but would the professor kindly give me a passing grade so I would not waste my mother's dime. I wrote that I sincerely believed there was another way of integrating knowledge; I was already thinking of heading to Iowa to study meditation at the college level. I was the first person to hand in the blue exam book. Very anxious about my choice but certain it was authentic, I went into the lobby and lit up a cigarette. The professor gave me a "C."

Leaving Brown was not an easy decision. I had rolled the *I Ching* many times and always got the same reading about youthful folly—one out of sixty-four hexagrams. What were the odds? I went with it. I packed all my belongings into my small VW Beetle, and traveled home to see my mother.

I was making an impulsive decision to go home and see my mother. I had not planned to go home; the plan was to go directly to upper New York State. But after listening to Joni Mitchell one more time, and smoking one cigarette too many, I settled the stereo components on top of my suitcases, and barely shut the lid of the green VW Beetle trunk. My three roommates were also transfer students to Brown, and one of them was on valium for anxiety. They wished me goodbye while joking about my going off to get a degree in selling flowers—their way of wishing me good luck with what they understood of meditation: flower power and the peace movement. I did not care. Once you have lost all sense of dignity by living on the inside of a mental institution, where four days turns your life completely inside out, it is possible to have a sense of pride in making any kind of decision, right or wrong. I had no idea what I was doing. I had a

21

determination to pursue something I did not yet understand. I drove south from Rhode Island to see my mother and arrived home just as the phone rang. It was the hospital. My mother had been admitted after a car accident and she was calling to inform the graduate students who lived at our house to come and pick her up. Her car was totaled.

"Margot?" she said in surprise as she recognized my voice.

"Mom?"

"I did not expect you home."

"I did not expect to be home." I felt a shift inside—a small moment of freedom, a small *yes, I did the right thing*. I went to fetch her from Bryn Mawr hospital. She was lying in a bed waiting, with a bandage between her eyes.

"I fell asleep at the wheel."

And awakened the third eye, I thought to myself. The third eye is the point of concentration in meditation. When you close the eyes to meditate, you can feel the eyes soften and turn and begin to feel like a single eye. Sometimes people see a blue light there. I thought that my mother's injury was significant. I waited to speak with her at the farmhouse.

Once she was settled on the couch I carefully taught her the rudiments of meditation. I told her the accident was some kind of sign. Her solution was to be tested for hypoglycemia and carry a can of peanuts with her in the car after that. She carried a scar on her third eye for some time.

The significance was mine. How I managed to start on the six-hour drive from Rhode Island to Philadelphia, Pennsylvania before the accident and show up precisely when she called for a ride home was the more noteworthy event. I felt calmer about my decision to leave Brown. I was headed in a new direction that I could not understand. The non-ordinary was feeling comfortable. Ordinary life made me anxious.

When Bill and I settled into our first apartment on Summit Street in Kent, I had a dream of the interior of a house with white walls. I was standing by the stair noting how completely empty it was of things and people, and quiet in a way that made me fearful. I was alone.

Bill grasped for ways to help me. In our first fall together, he pulled quickly off to the side of the road stopping by a wooden table piled with ripe tomatoes—on sale. I had long since given up smoking. Bill was instinctive about things. He knew that working with the hands might help me.

"What are you doing?"

"Buying all these tomatoes."

"Why?" He was already out of the car and my voice barely reached him. I slowly got out and walked over. Bill was fingering one in each hand. There was a note to leave money in a mason jar.

"They're good." He cleared the table into a waiting bag, and left some money.

"Now we'll stop at Kmart and get canning equipment."

Jars with lids, a big pot and a wire rack—I got started. I learned to can and make pumpkin pie. It helped to be busy with my hands. I could accomplish small tasks and feel momentary comfort, some satisfaction building skills for our new life. Bill could make bread—he taught me how to knead the dough and let it rise. He had a saying he liked: "See the job, do the job and stay out of the misery." Work was helpful, but our commitment to the daily meditations was the centerpiece of our lives, and my biggest adjustment was his comfort with silence.

For me, silence was loaded with tension. In our house chatter and noise were a way to avoid feeling anything. I had been raised in the arts, music, painting, theatre, literature. I was used to my father's chatter, music from the stereo, Belefonte to Bach.

Bill returned to Kent State University to complete his degree in accounting and finance. He had started college at the Salem Branch and enjoyed philosophy but now he was deciding how to make a living, and he was content with concentration. His silence made me fret. Silence left me with my feelings. I could not differentiate one from another—they were blended in one high pitch of discomfort living in my own skin. Bill thought that he and I should be able to communicate through silence. One of our on-going arguments as a couple was that I could not hear his thoughts.

"You don't love me enough," he argued. "If you did, you could."

"That doesn't make sense."

"Okay, what I really mean is, if you are settled inside, you can tune in to the other person."

"Well obviously, I am not settled." I agreed, but I felt dismayed.

He claimed he could hear my needs and my thoughts—irritatingly incessant and irrational. Anxiety is just that. Bill had no experience with my kind of fear. He would come out of the bedroom into the kitchen addressing my thoughts, countering my inner state with logic.

I criticized him for addressing what I was trying to keep to myself, adding, "You don't talk enough." I wanted to hear him talk about himself out loud. I wanted to hear his thoughts as a distraction from my inner state.

My concern was what to do with my restless self and what to study in college. Bill would preach to me that the future was created in the present. Just listen in the present moment. I could recognize his good advice and I could see him peacefully waking up ready for the day to unfold. If we needed a bookshelf, he might bring one home from the curb where students left their unwanted furniture. It was easy for him, which made it all the more frustrating for me.

Our attempt to resolve our differences was often not peaceful. When we were heated in argument, he would shout,

"I am leaving for the Himalayas."

That silenced me because it was so incongruous to hear him blurt that out in our overheated third-story hilltop apartment in cloudy, Northeast Ohio. Why the Himalayas?

On the other hand, his looks brought me a deep sense of being in the right place. I would turn to him when we were driving in the car just to gaze at his profile.

"What?" He would say with his characteristic minimum of words. Sometimes he would only nod.

"I'm looking at you." That would end the conversation.

Or, he might say, "Why?"

My replies: "Because I like to," or "You know, I like to," or "Just because."

From grade school into high school, with black pen and white paper, I had traced the lines of a man's profile—a chiseled Roman nose and dark eyes, sharp brow and strong chin with dark hair that lifted up off his brow like a warrior. That face was Bill's, nothing like what I had seen among the East Coast families of British or Northern European descent. I would joke that his Croatian, Italian and Romanian family was spiced by the Mongolian hordes riding through. Bill had a fierce, handsome look that made me toss the pen aside, feeling my destiny as an artist fulfilled. Some other destiny waited.

24

5

Among benevolent men, four kinds worship me Arjuna,
the distressed, those who desire wealth,
those who desire knowledge, and the man of wisdom.
Gita 7/16

It was a big deal to me to go around the world before I was seventeen and to find a sense of peace and order that could be a part of daily life. So when Bill and I married in December, 1976, I put my conviction into the lifestyle we had chosen: a vegetarian diet and twice-daily meditations as the TM organization advised.

Choosing how to complete my education at Kent State University where we first lived created spinning thoughts. I changed my major four times and then quit trying to find a solution. Bill suggested we have children. I readily agreed, thinking it would relieve me of the burden of making sense of my mind. With me I still had the copy of the first six chapters of the *Bhagavad Gita,* translated with a commentary by Maharishi Mahesh Yogi. Deciding on a major was impossible, but I had studied that book with concentration. It was a consolation. The opening chapter of the *Bhagavad Gita* is called the yoga of despondency. Arjuna was having difficulty with the problem of how to avoid the civil war in front of him. As Krishna gave his teaching of the eternal self, Arjuna had the natural question we might all have, "What if I turn my attention to this spiritual quest, fail to address the world on its terms, and then fail in my spiritual quest?" Krishna assured him:

> *Here in the yoga of practice, no effort is lost, nor is any loss of progress found.*
> *Even a little of this discipline protects one from great fear.*　　　*Gita 2/40*

At the teacher training in France, every day I labored on the essay in my room adding more verses from the *Bhagavad Gita* that indicated the

25

tradition was of the heart, not the head. I was seeking a link with emotion to make TM more than a technique. The *Bhagavad Gita* has been called the Bible of Hinduism, but it is not a Bible. It is a teaching of a way of life. The essential teaching is that a spiritual vision of wholeness can sustain us even under all circumstances. There are few situations worse than a civil war.

A few verses had consoled me.

Weapons do not pierce the embodied self, fire does not burn this, water does not wet this, nor does the wind cause it to wither.   *Gita 2/23*

This cannot be pierced, burned, wetted or withered; this is eternal, all pervading, fixed; this is unmoving and primeval.   *Gita 2/24*

I was consoled by the idea that if I followed this path I would find some stability inside myself. I loved the imagery of a place that cannot be touched by the senses—a completely transcendent place like the sky. I wrote my philosophical treatise during afternoon rest time for much of the training. I decided to read what I had written to a friend who had let me use some of her lemon-scented Jean Nate bath gel.

I knocked on her door, on the other side of our shared bathroom. She was a short person with long, bushy red hair. I was tall with long, straight hair. I tied mine back to keep the stringy feeling off my face. She tied her hair back to keep it from bushing out to the sides. The main difference between us was her palpable comfort with herself. She was happy. I was not. I sat on her bed, and after asking if she had a few minutes, read my paper, hand-written, re-written a few times. It took about twenty minutes. After finishing I looked up. She was staring hard at me. Then she said, "I don't know anything about philosophy, but you are very strange. After all these hours of study and memorizing who would write a paper on philosophy?"

The look in her eyes was one I had seen before. When I had been depressed the last year of high school, a veteran English teacher had handed me a copy of *The Varieties of Religious Experience: a Study in Human Nature*, written by the Harvard psychologist and philosopher, William James. She had given me the look. She said, "This will help you understand who you are and how you think."

Again, another high school English teacher, and two college professors, took the time to speak with me and gave me the look that said, "You are not normal in your understanding." I sat before a statue of the Buddha in the Memorial Art Gallery of the University of Rochester, and wrote about the halo surrounding his head as a depiction of self-reflection. The South Indian Asian Art History professor had said, "There is no way you can know this." At the time, I caught his implication of past lives, though I had not given the idea much thought.

I was committed.

I sought peace with enormous determination. When pregnant with Paul, I meditated three hours a day, morning and afternoon. Six hours a day for a period of four months was the practice I carved out for myself. It was a necessity. Normally, when I calmed the body, I remained busy with thoughts. Rarely would I reach an elevated state. When I did, the veil of fear would lift completely. Normal human feelings were replaced by an expansive ripple that passed through me and into the beyond—the shape of peace that made all things perfect. Once, during a six-hour stint, a single drop of water from the leaky faucet landing on the stainless steel sink inspired the perfection of the Japanese garden. In our confining rental apartment subsidized by the university, the vibration of the drop resounded as the center of all space.

I understand now that the powerful need to alleviate fear was driving a sense of destiny. Without the severe anxiety and the break-down in my past, I doubt I would have chosen this new path. I was moving away from my family of origin. But, as I gradually came to know, we can't leave our past. It came with me.

The unusual accompanied my birth. My mother says she felt something distinctive at my birth. I was the third child; two brothers came before me in quick succession—we were each seventeen months apart. Since she did not medicate herself into unconsciousness with me as she had with them, I was special to her. My brothers, David and Chris, fought before I was born; Mom viewed my arrival in Boston, Massachusetts in May of 1953 as a consecrated peacekeeping mission. I am here because the Pope's method of birth control had failed, making me a part of an even higher plan.

Our mother took us to Catholic Mass. By the time my brothers and I were in grade school, we were skipping breakfast, fasting before taking the consecrated host. In church I learned to follow the missal. The red ink was the mysterious mumblings of Latin. The black ink, English. I would often begin to faint from hunger before the consecration of the host, between the *mea culpas,* when we professed "through my fault, through my fault, through my most grievous fault." As my mother would beat her breast with her right fist, bowing her head to receive the blessings of redemption, I would tap her on the shoulder with "I'm getting dizzy," having held back until well after the nausea had crept in to my neck.

"You know what to do," she would say. I would get her permission to put my head down low and be different from everyone else.

At MIU, where I studied and meditated for two and a half years, there were an inordinate amount of lapsed Catholics. People used to say that the trappings of Catholicism, the ritual and the prayers in Latin, fasting before church and the celebration of holy days made us comfortable with the meditation that came from the Indian culture where Hinduism was a dominant tradition. In the winter of my second year at MIU, I completed the teacher training course with a three-month stay in France, where I had written the essay on devotion.

Maharishi Mahesh Yogi was not present during the training until the end where we each met with him individually before leaving France— briefly raising the ghost of Catholic confession. He checked my mantra. I told him the sound I used in meditation, he gave me another sound. I had seen him only once before when he lectured to the full student body at MIU. In France, we watched video tapes of his lectures and senior teachers fielded discussions. And we practiced the *puja,* which was part of memorizing the steps of instruction for meditation.

Puja is a traditional Indian ritual ceremony. Ours included a long chant that honored the tradition from which our meditation came. After chanting the *puja* and making small offerings of fruit, flower petals, water and rice over a small flame of camphor, we would instruct meditation. It set the mood. It appeared to the one being instructed that we would cognize a mantra for them to use in meditation out of a state induced by the trance of the *puja,* but we had a simple system for determining the particular sound we would give.

I loved the *puja* and learned it quickly. The sounds of Sanskrit were music, even without the melody. I loved the names of the flower, *pushpam,* and to offer, *svahah.* I savored the names of the teachers in the tradition, Brahmananda Saraswati Guru and Padma Padam, which means lotus-foot. The lotus flower is an image of how we can best be in the world, our feet in the mud and our consciousness lifting above and shining. In the tradition, we bow to the feet of the teacher. The feet are revered as a holy place. Padma Padam was a man who gained enlightenment while sweeping the floor of the ashram where he lived. He listened to the teachings around him, did his practice quietly and rose above.

Our mother had taught my brothers and me a life of rules and discipline that I was bringing to this new tradition. We did homework on Saturday mornings, piano lessons, and chores. In the summers I swept the wide porch that wrapped around two sides of our Pennsylvania farmhouse. My comfort lay in the folded white of my mother's linen closet where bleached and ironed sheets and pillowcases were stacked, hand towels counted. Above in mothballs were woolen blankets. My head would lift as if in church where rows of votive candles illumine waxy stands. A silent inventory, a virtue honored before I gently moved my hands over the tops, white and smooth. Mom trained us to be faithful to the church. We celebrated all holy days with special meals, including Jewish holidays like Passover—a full repast with leg of lamb, a white table cloth and candles, and matzo crackers.

Our parents' antique double bed was another altar. It had slender, fluted posts and a horsehair mattress that bulged to a great mound in the middle. The bed squeaked and sagged and made a faint rustling sound when it moved. When my brothers and I were small we would swing around the posts in the early morning and lumber over to the lumpy middle between our parents. During grammar school, we would kneel around the bed still wearing our blue uniform blazers, mine with pencils and pens lining the inside pockets, and offer novenas to the Virgin Mother. My mother would say a phrase of *Her glory* or beseech *Her mercy* for our long list of ills, and we would respond with *Mother Mary, pray for us*. Often after his bath, Dad would stride around us toward his closet on the far side of the room, the steam trailing off his red-tinged body, smelling fresh. His presence was part of our ritual as though he were circumambulating a holy place.

From my mother I learned discipline. From my father—something else. During the Catholic Mass when I started to faint and hung my head between my legs, I was his daughter. I was not supposed to turn around and look at the people in church, not allowed to stare. But I could fold completely forward in my seat and look behind upside down at everyone's shoes. My father was not Catholic, but Episcopalian, and not a church-goer. He made efforts to be a good father. He scolded us well, did projects in the yard, and he marked his path through the house with bursts of high tenor. He sang ballads and ditties, painted cartoon-like paintings, and tossed us about on his knee as he played word games.

In France, I did as I was told. I memorized the *puja* so well that I was asked to check others' *pujas* to see if their memorization and pronunciation were correct. We were a group of a few hundred and there were only a few checkers. The *puja* was about ten minutes of Sanskrit, and I listened to a succession of people for two days when we were not meditating, sleeping or eating. I saw about fifty people.

After the second day, the *puja* sang through my head as I lay in my dark room waiting for sleep. Syllable by syllable, I heard *Guru sakshat parambrahma tasmai shri guruve namah, tasmai shri guruve namah.* This was a line of appreciation for the lineage of teachers, a humbling of oneself to the teaching that had come through the ages. As I listened to the sounds in my mind, I saw corresponding shapes come in front of my eyes—a long line along the top, around which circles and flares, dips and simple right angles appeared with the sound. If the sound vanished into space and silence, there was no corresponding visual note. As the chant continued, the visual dance scrolled in front of my eyes with precision. It was alive like the little bouncing ball in the old movies that marked the words of the songs. I was in some cosmic sing-a-long with Sanskrit.

I got off my pillows and on to my knees on the bed. I bowed down to space itself, hoping someone was there to listen, and vowed that I would learn to read Sanskrit someday. I felt funny as though I was making the vow outside myself. I felt no personal connection to Maharishi or his teacher Brahmananda Saraswati, but I could not imagine how all this was happening by my own volition. I bowed to the saffron robes of Brahmananda Saraswati, whose picture was on my dresser, just to have a place and a connection with a human form. I needed some anchor for the large space through which I had felt the sounds move. Space was alive with sound.

This was not an experience I could share—it made no sense at the time. Ultimately I would not receive enough support from the TM organization to help me grow. They stressed conformity. I wanted something more heartfelt, alive, something that would bring me out of my constraints, not keep me hemmed in with rules; although there was no doubt that the rules had helped. Like my mother's discipline, the rules gave shape to my days. The quiet ordered my thoughts.

Now Bill and I were preparing for a child. I was taking the daily discipline of a meditation practice into motherhood, with some idea it might help me.

6

Hollowed out, clay makes a pot.
Where a pot's not is where it's useful.
LaoTzu

A year after our marriage, our first son, Paul, was born in our apartment within Kent State's married couple's housing.

Having a child at home was prompted by me. We met with friends of Bill's near Salem who were expecting a child, and had a home-birth doctor. I immediately felt I would be more comfortable at home. My experience with the psychiatrist and the mental institution made me mistrustful of the medical profession. I wanted to avoid any memory of that complete loss of control while bringing my babies in the world. I insisted on no crib as well—just the family bed. The home-birth doctor had a successful practice of 40 years. He was located in Salem about an hour from Kent.

I went into labor with Paul 24 hours before he was born. I had gone for a walk on a winter evening and slipped on the ice. Falling initiated contractions every five minutes. Dr. Vance made a house call. He told us to visit people the next day and be easy. It might be false labor. In the morning we went on a road trip, visiting Bill's parents and friends near Salem, ending at the Doctor's office after 22 hours of easy contractions every five minutes; he told us to go directly home. He would follow. I was almost in transition.

Transition happened in the car during a white-out snowfall. The pressure of the baby inside made me shrink in deep concentration. I could not speak. In TM we had learned to do *samyama*, which means placing your concentration on a point. I placed it on the cervix. I pressed my feet into the floor and gripped the door handle. Bill wanted to stop for eggs.

"No," I said. The easy time had passed.

He missed our exit off the freeway and was heading to the next.

"No, no, no! Back up!" This was the safest option for me.

Bill still did not understand what was going on. I was not talking. When we got to the apartment, he announced:

"I'll just head up and get the mail." The boxes were on the next flight up.

"Bill! No you are not! Take off my boots!"

I could not lean over. This was it. I went to the bedroom, lay back on the bed in extreme discomfort, put my full attention on the cervix, and calmly determined that I had fully dilated. Someone had to decide. I squatted on the floor by the bed.

Bill said all the right things when I was on the bed, reading from his notes. I did not notice the notes. I valued his help. The water broke and baby came in a water-slide into Bill's hands. The baby cried. We were stunned.

Bill called our midwife from the kitchen wall phone. We had been coached by the mid-wife but made no plans to have her help at the birth.

"The baby came! The doctor did not make it! What do we do?"

"Put the baby on the belly!"

Bill cradled the phone against his chest and yelled out to me, "Put the baby on the belly!"

I put the baby on the belly, and we waited for Dr. Vance.

He came an hour later, stomping snow off his boots at the door while mumbling something about a lot of patients and a lot of snow. He cut the umbilical cord, sat back and said in his usual slow and measured manner.

"If you want the doctor to attend the birth, don't squat."

The night Paul was born I sat him up on my belly. I looked into his little face and my mind rocketed out to the expansion of the turning stars. Uncanny and all that I could hope for—all that I wanted to be real.

In April of 1978, when Paul was three months old, we moved from Allerton Housing in Kent to a rented house in Washingtonville, Ohio where Bill had his first job in a loan company. We moved back to Kent after two years, but our first real home was in Washingtonville, southeast of Kent and Akron, a small sleepy town near Salem, closer to what had been a coal and coke oven area among thriving truck farms and orchards. Bill's grandparents on both sides had immigrated to Ohio from Central Europe in the time of world hunger before World War I. This was a land-of-plenty for those who worked hard, and the children could go to local schools. The small town was working class; I was an anomaly. I set to learning to cook. I became more serious about diet. Homebirth and vegetarian diet were rare items.

I had purchased an attachment to my Kitchen Aid mixer that was a small grinder. Into it, you could pour about a cup of whole wheat berries and grind them fresh before making bread, a loud and time-consuming task that could not be done when the baby slept. The berries in the receptacle diminished slowly with a loud abrasive noise as they were pulverized by circular metal teeth. In design, it was a small grinding wheel, similar to the ones found in any town in America fueled by the waterwheel or turned by the beasts of burden.

I began grinding grain the first year, when Paul watched from his baby seat up on the kitchen counter. Placing a baby up high is against the rules now, but my generation had few rules, fewer lawsuits. We had no car seats. Tidy umbrella strollers were folded out of the way into corners, and making whole food was time-intensive. The bread was great and an acquaintance asked if I would make some for him. I set a high price—ten dollars a loaf. I knew he would back down. This was for my family.

Yogurt was easy to make. Boil and cool to the right temperature, add a bit of yogurt for a culture, cover and set it quietly aside overnight. I placed a bowl on the hot water heater. Bill and I went to nearby farms to buy raw milk. In those days—easy. The baby went from my lap in the car to my hip. Enter the milk chamber smelling moist and warm, scoop what you need, listening to the quiet echo of liquid off the cement and white-washed walls. Leave a few dollars.

We brought home drinking water as well. The ground water in Ohio is often bitter with minerals and sulfur. Going north out of the town of Washingtonville, there was a pipe by the side of the road where an underground spring was diverted; anyone could stop and fill gallon milk jugs. The dirt pull-off was often busy, with empty milk jugs lined up waiting to be filled.

More difficult to cook were vegetarian burgers. I made mixtures of cooked beans, grains and sunflower seeds. No matter how much oil I added to the pan, they still stuck, and no matter how long they were cooked, they were a gummy failure.

I cooked to stay busy when home with Paul. I remained anxious even though I was content with him. In meditation my inner tension suspended. I felt quieted by nursing my child. Rarely did I have a deep meditation. Once, when Paul was a year old, asleep in our shared family bed, I was in meditation on the floor in the adjacent room when a single, thin asparagus fern leaf dropped on the cover of an old typewriter next to me. It landed with a heightened sound that propelled my consciousness into a suspension of time and expansion of space. This moment kept me meditating in spite of the incessant demands of a toddler. Bill and I took turns meditating. He got up early. I waited for naptime.

Cooking made me happy. My hands were busy. I needed challenges. My most time-intensive venture was making tofu. We could not buy it. Cleveland Tofu Company was just starting up, but we lived 80 miles from Cleveland and the neat plastic tubs had not made it to our grocery stores or bulk food stores. Whole food stores sold foods in bulk. Whether Iowa City, Iowa or Kent, Ohio, the early health food stores served up unprocessed foods in large bins. Barrels of flour, beans, rice rested on the ground and scoops and bags were set nearby for handy packaging. Whatever you needed, you measured out and purchased by price per pound, often leaving a small trail of flour or beans on the floor. The clerk would peek inside, confirm verbally what you had in there and tape it shut with masking tape. These were grassroots stores.

I kept up with exercise to quiet my mind. Paul and I took long bike rides with him strapped to my back. His little feet hung below my windbreaker. In the winter, we took long walks with him bundled in the umbrella stroller.

Making tofu was character-building. There was no varying the procedure or recipe. You needed raw soy beans, nigari, lots of water, a blender, cheese cloth, a colander and a huge pot. Nigari is magnesium chloride, a Japanese coagulating agent, naturally extracted from clean ocean water by solar evaporation. It could be purchased through special order. Tofu was new to the States but not to Japan where spare amounts of the soy cheese were part of a traditional diet.

There were three steps: making soy milk from raw soy beans, curding the milk, and then pressing the cheese. I soaked the beans overnight to make milk. Placing raw soybeans the next day in the blender at high speed was another noisy venture with a baby. Paul adapted. He sat in his plastic rocker up on the counter kicking his legs and making tight fists with excitement. Then I poured the mixture into a colander lined with cheesecloth and squeezed the cloth. The milk went into a bowl underneath that was set aside, and bulky bean scraps were thrown in the mulch pile. Then, heating the milk to a boil before adding the nigari required a big pot. There is nothing difficult about boiling soy milk and making curds. It is easy to strain off the milk, and wrap and press the curds for hours as the liquid seeps out of the cheese. The pot that boiled the soy milk was hard to scrub clean—worse than milk scum. Paul was often content as I worked, but if he were impatient and fussed as I cleaned, he matched my mood.

In the spring, bike rides were with Paul sitting behind me, strapped in a plastic orange seat with a knit sweater and hood that peaked in a tassel above his round cheeks. No bike helmets for him or me. They were not made yet. We went up and down tall hills through apple and peach orchards and pick-your-own berry fields. And I meditated twice a day, every day.

Bill started a new job with the Internal Revenue Service in Akron. I was pregnant again. We spent weekends looking for starter homes near Akron. We settled on a small cottage on the crest of a hill overlooking the forty acres of Brady Lake, just outside of Kent. The lake held the sky feeling I craved inside. I persuaded Bill that living by water would help me live in Ohio. It would help me live with me.

Near Brady Lake were two lakes owned by the City of Akron, Lake Pippen and Lake Rockwell. Towner's Woods along the shore of Pippen is a refuge of walking trails that I had already hiked, and strolled, while expecting Paul during our first stay in Kent. The oaks grew to cathedral height and the mosses around the stony banks were smooth and green even in winter. Along the southern shore of Lake Rockwell, Ravenna Road borders a high causeway of grass. The road there had graffiti that made me feel I had come home. In 1980, there were large maples shading the road at regular intervals and the words were written in similar intervals in block letters on the tarmac so you would ride in your car over one word at a time. The words were in spray paint—each one 30 feet from the next, except the last, which was double the distance. As you rode along, the words scrolled one by one under you. I wrote them in a small journal I was unsuccessfully keeping. It was the only entry. Read from the bottom of the page up it went:

NONE

BIRDS

HAPPY

NO

ARE

THERE

This poetic philosophy cheered me. Someone ahead of me had realized the same thing. Happiness does not lie where we expect. I had all the makings of happiness, but it still eluded me.

Our cottage needed serious re-modeling to turn it into a home. Bill set to learning a new skill set. He tore out interior walls, the entire kitchen, and added a new entryway, in between three and six-week trainings in Cincinnati for his new job. I stayed at the house with Paul. He was two years old, so long days by the water and in the sand made it easier to care for him. It was a cool summer. We had a small fireplace where I lit small fires to take off the chill. But I was lonely.

7

No purifier equal to knowledge is found here in the world;
he who is perfected in yoga, in time finds that knowledge in the Self.
Gita 4/38

Our second son, Matthew, was born in October of 1980 in our Brady Lake cottage that was only partially remodeled. While pregnant with Matt, we arranged for Dr. Vance to come to the birth along with our midwife. He was attended by his physician's assistant and her husband. Paul was present, too. There were plenty of them. They deserted me to talk politics in the next room.

I called them in when I determined I was in transition. Paul was there. He checked my belly with a stethoscope. The birth was peaceful. Matt's birth brought a feeling of motherhood that was distinctly different from Paul's. With Paul's birth, I became as if part of the world. When I held Matt on my belly, he did not cry, he stirred space with his fingers as if wondering about air, different from the watery womb. I felt an intimacy with him that helped me feel softer—my life was not easy. Bill was hard at work.

The first winter with our new baby and our three-year-old, the studs and electric boxes were exposed and the mice were my most frequent guests. The original wall board had been torn off in the kitchen and living room, and a musty green shag rug covered the floor until we could resume remodeling in the spring. There was no beauty; it was pure pragmatism. I cut my long brown hair and settled into a practical life wearing old jeans and caring for babies. I had shifted to the simplicity I witnessed in Taiwan. I was seeking peace, and I was living counter to the familiar comforts of even clean, painted walls and carpets. Naturally the demands of our life were a strain.

With a second child, and our new cottage home by Brady Lake, sustaining a meditation practice was not easy. I had been meditating for nine years; Bill, a few less. Bill and I both found the rules of the TM movement superficial and conformist—a benign cult. We were not supported by an organization that required us to return to their facilities for month-long intensives, and the price of the intensives was increasing. This was not for growing families. Our TM friends were up-scaling into middle class neighborhoods, while we had been subsisting on Bill's Vietnam era GI bill money, and then a small salary. I had received a small trust fund from my parents that went into buying our new home. I was poised for deeper practice. Bill was discouraged.

The winter of 1981 was long; people call it "the kind of winter we don't see anymore." My car, the "white whale," a used Buick sedan, was unmovable. It stayed beached in the snow at the top of our steep drive. The sun was out only a handful of days; the sky, a deep gray. Snow blew across the windows, pushed by winds off the lake in front of our house. In the company of a baby and a small child I remained isolated day after day. Loving my children did not feed my need for social contact. And no matter how much I tried to find a place in meditation where I felt complete, the feeling was fleeting.

An Indian swami was visiting Cleveland in early March of 1982, staying at various houses where he presented lectures in the evenings. A TM friend introduced us. Bill went first without me. Returning, he was excited. He intended to see him the next day to receive a mantra. He asked me to go with him. I was uncertain.

"What do you think of this guy, really?" I asked Bill.

"You'll want to meet him."

"What about the kids?" I felt Bill's certainty, I was ready to go but if it were a TM function, children would not be so welcome.

"We can take them. We can go during the day. He meets people during the day." He paused. "I asked him about us."

"What do you mean?"

"How we met. I asked him if he saw you coming."

"What did he say?"

"He said, 'no.' He said your own Godhead brought you there. He did not expect you."

That made me feel special, even though I did not know what it meant. We knew nothing of our teacher's humility. "What else did he say?"

"Well, I said I wanted to be a monk, and why didn't he let me be a monk? He said that people in the West need companions. So you came along and you are my companion."

Something was happening here that felt different. As Bill talked I began to feel agitated: excited that this teacher might make sense of our lives, but scared of any change. I remembered how early on Bill would suddenly announce his departure for the Himalayas. He liked this monk.

"You will like it there. It is an Indian couple's apartment, and this swami made sure I had a meal with them before he spoke with me." Bill was happy.

On the next day, we went with the children to take turns playing with them and meeting with the swami. We entered an apartment on a gloomy day in March. No lights were on inside, showing our hosts were modest people. The couple was busy cooking in the kitchen; guests stayed in the living room and visited the swami upstairs.

Bill went upstairs first. His stay was brief. He must have simply told the swami I had come. It was my turn. I carefully made my way up the dark stair, and at the top found the guru's door ajar. I tapped lightly, and hearing nothing, slowly opened the wooden door. My first view of my teacher was by the oblique light of a window to his right. He was leaning against the wall with his legs tucked up, sitting on the carpet covered by a sheet that served as a bed. A box of Kleenex and a scattered range of used tissue surrounded him. He leaned forward as I entered and then the room settled back into stillness. I sat on the floor, unable to break the silence. Finally, he asked me a few questions followed by silences. He was either very pensive or slowed by his head cold. Then, he motioned with his hand that I should go downstairs where he would join us.

I sat waiting on the floor with Matt on my lap. My husband sat on his heels next to me while Paul played somewhere behind us. My feelings had become intense. Was it because I had seen that this man could be sick and vulnerable? Maybe that realization had opened me to how vulnerable I felt. I felt a surge of energy. From what I had read in the *Bhagavad Gita*, I knew that a deeper state of happiness existed. But the circumstances of life invariably overwhelmed this inner state. I wanted to know why the inner state could not be maintained; it was supposed to be a state not dependent on circumstances.

We were quiet as he descended the stairs, and he took his place on the floor. Then it was I who began, "Why does the experience of meditation not last? What is wrong with what we have been taught?"

He did not reply at first. His legs were crossed as he simply leaned forward, extending his spine to its full height. I could almost see the thoughts building in his mind as he turned the full light of his consciousness toward both my questions and the presence of our family in front of him. He began with a steady flow of words that seemed to respond to my mood rather than reflect his quiet state.

"You need proper knowledge to sustain experience. The experience of a higher state of consciousness cannot be maintained without clear understanding."

Then the swami went on to delineate the knowledge that I lacked, glancing at me with a flash in his eyes as he spoke. His cold and sickness had disappeared. It seemed to be a mirage, like my suffering, something that could be there but have no substance in face of something much more real. At the time, what was most real in me was my longing, my readiness. What was real in him was his knowledge. I understood from my reading of the *Bhagavad Gita* that a real teacher is alive with not only the experience of wholeness but an ability to impart the teaching with knowledge. He could help me walk the path.

"You must understand that you have five sheaths: body, senses, mind, ego and intelligence. And when you sit to meditate, you need to search out in which sheath you sit, because your practice will begin from there. And wherever you are, go deeper. So if you are attached to the senses and dwelling in sensual experience with the eyes closed, then move to mind; watch the sensations of the senses and the play of the mind in response. Then go deeper to the I-am behind the play of experience."

He pronounced his words carefully. As he continued, I began to feel a shift in me. Like a long-awaited meal, his assurance that I could tread firmly on the path eased some of my intensity.

Here was a real teacher, not just a video-tape and my imagination. Since it was not possible to put the knowledge into practice just then, I continued asking questions about what I had been taught, to which he patiently responded.

Bill and I and our two children returned to Cleveland every night for the nine-day celebration of the *Ramayana*. Here was another text, new to me—the story of Lord Rama who is separated from his consort Sita while

41

living in the forest. His search for her and her faithful longing for him exemplify our souls longing for the divinity that is lost to us. We listened to lectures in Hindi. The children played with other children. A buffet of Indian food was served in every home, and we went home with handfuls of sweets, fruit, nuts and raisins. On his last day in Cleveland, Swami Bawra, whom we called "Swamiji," said that he would return in the fall and would divide his time, staying one month at our home in Brady Lake, and one month in Medina at the home of another TM couple who had decided to follow his teaching.

Later, Bill explained what had happened with him when he was with the guru. This swami gave him the same mantra that Bill had received in meditation years before. Bill did not need confirmation that this was his Guru. I was not sure. Bill insisted that I cease the TM method and follow Swami Bawra's teaching. This meant I would need to align breath with mantra and meaning with breath. Each pulse of internal sound should be attended with focused awareness.

Even though TM was not taking me forward, I was uncertain. I had no awareness of how difficult my rigidity was for Bill and how much he wanted a partner who could share more of his elation. We were going to host this swami, and Bill needed me to be on board.

I was sitting on the couch of our half remodeled living room, facing the only view to the lake. Bill had let me know what he needed just as simply as stopping to buy tomatoes. For him, it was a way forward. All I could think was "Damn."

8

One practices to bring the Way into oneself as rain falls on the earth.
Deng Ming-Dao

Bill lay on his back looking up into the fireplace, chiseling out space for the stovepipe insert. His hands bled. He cussed as dust and chips fell on his face. We were converting the fireplace flue to insert a woodstove.

When pregnant with Matthew, Bill and I had torn out the kitchen and bedrooms, a wall between the living room and a sun porch that had the only direct view of Brady Lake. We patched the living room together. The kitchen was still in studs, and our master bedroom was temporary, until we could remodel the attached garage the next year.

As exhausting as the remodeling was, it was giving me a sense of place again. When I was two and a half, my family had moved to an old stone farmhouse in Pennsylvania. This place came to hold me more securely than my parents. Built in the 1700's, our house was originally two millhouses that shared an inside wall. The homes were for laborers and their families, who worked on a saw mill about a mile away at Darby Creek. The walls were built two feet thick, using a dry mortar technique that left the structure vulnerable to erosion. A flat stone etched with "1852" had been placed high up under the eave facing the driveway. The date commemorated the remodeling of the two houses into one, when a third floor had been added. The third floor seemed larger, especially Dad's art studio in the largest white room where the sills were littered with lifeless black flies. Coming to the top floor, I'd feel a lifting inside as if I were as insubstantial as the debris of flies. I would push them to the ground with a sweep of my little finger to feel their absence of substance. But outside the house, every window was guarded with deep green-black shutters, as if to contain us all. They were fixed open with a curve of iron that rotated in a pin driven in the wall. Inside, the windows had deep sills,

43

painted white. By the time we moved there in 1955, hot water radiators stood under the windows; my father "bled" them every fall with the turn of a key on a valve, releasing a strong hiss.

Good fortune placed me in the lap of fireplaces. I learned to feel comfort from the crackle of kindling as the fire was lit, the warming stone and the lingering smells of ash. The stone farmhouse had one in each room. Wide chimneys flanked both ends of the house and angled in near the roof to form narrow stacks. When Dad started a fire, he balled up a wad of newspaper and clamped it with fire tongs before igniting it with a wooden match—releasing a roar inside the flue. He would wave the tongs back and forth high in the flue to heat the brick and encourage smoke from the hearth to go up, and not in the room. The sparks rose harmlessly above the wood shingles of the roof. When I needed to feel the rightness of things, I would imagine the tall rectangle of the stone house and roof, its walls whitewashed to prevent the crumbling of the dry mortar and the wide chimneys on the outer walls.

When I was nine-months pregnant with Matthew, Bill and I stacked the wood from an oak tree shading our garden area. Paul helped. We layered the cords outside the room we designated as Matt's, where he was born on a mattress on the floor.

With the swami's visit pending, and with Matt in a baby carrier on my back we were remodeling the living room. We had torn out the ceiling, so the inside was open to the roof rafters. When we added back the drywall ceilings, I held wall board over my head as Bill screwed it in. The board is extremely heavy, so we used props of two-by-fours. I had told Paul to be sure to let me know if he needed attention. Coming in from the sandy play area outside, he paused watching us manipulate and strain against the board.

"I need…'ttension," Paul said.

He was a mirror. We all had tension and we all needed attention. We looked over at Paul and did not want for him to feel that way, but we could not move. Remodeling a home together meant Bill was mastering his learning curve of how to do construction, while training in his new job position, while becoming a father.

If Bill found paint on sale one dollar a gallon cheaper than what we already had on hand, it was simple.

"Margot, tomorrow return those five gallons of paint and pick up the semi-gloss interior white on sale at Kmart."

"Bill, the paint has to be returned to Akron!"

"Just do it."

Our marriage was strained. I both admired Bill and felt put off by him. Our conversations were practical or we escalated into unresolved feelings. If he heard confusion or strain in my tone, he would cut me off with, "Okay, that's enough." I would fall into a compressed and conflicted silence. Left with my own feelings, I waited. I needed to watch my speech. I spoke little with the children around, avoiding conflict, and waited until night to express my feelings with Bill. Keeping him awake made him tired and miserable. I imagine the more he wanted to quiet me, the more I was critical of him. It is hard to remember exactly. The arguments went quickly as we leaped past each other's assumptions and hurled insults like the dry cut ends of lumber kindling a fire.

He was resourceful. We had ripped out floor and door molding from a house that was being torn down in Stow, and had stored the strips of wood along with three interior doors in the garage attached in back. When the time came to push for the swami's visit, Bill rushed the completion. He was taking vacation days as he earned them, unusual for a new employee, and he was still behind schedule. He asked another carpenter to help. At a pause in the work, the two of us were taking a moment to admire the view of the lake. Bill was trimming one of our reserved doors to a smaller height to fit the bathroom opening. We heard him cut with the circular saw. Then we heard a string of cusswords.

A door flew sideways past the window.

We looked at each other and went back to talking. We heard another buzz of the saw, another round of cussing, and another door flew past. Third cut, no cussing.

"Trouble with his temper?" Our friend smiled, his thumbs tucked in his tool belt.

"Maybe," I reflected back his understated manner of speaking. We both smiled.

"But he must have used three doors...Bill, what happened?" I shouted.

"I cut the bottoms wavy! Wasted two doors!"

The excitement of finishing the master bedroom and having small bedrooms for our children and their growing collection of toys was supplanted by the need to finish by September. I still found moments of exhilaration. Roofing was one. Leaving Matt on the ground to play, I climbed up to the lower level of the new roof just over Paul's bedroom where all of us were currently sleeping. I was gazing over the expanse of shingles—large for a small cottage—when Matt's face with a blue hood appeared at the top of the extension ladder.

I refrained from startling, so he would remain calm. I grimaced and cooed, and carefully went over to place him on my hip. We took in the view together and then tenuously descended. I was shaky, upset, and amazed by his agility. He was barely walking, still nursing. My family was everything to me.

How would we host a swami? I felt some smoldering questions about how this would go. But this was another choice-less choice that I made by first agreeing to live with Bill. How could I say no? The meditation practice that had saved my sanity was now shifting. I went along.

The work was constant. I awakened in the morning and finished painting base molding while still in my bathrobe, Matt moving behind me, and Paul outside playing in the sandbox. After the swami arrived, which I don't even remember, I was simply exhausted. I was both the cook and program director. He rested during the day and lectured at night. I balanced listening to the lectures with keeping the children quiet and getting them to bed. I liked sitting in meditation and loved the philosophy but I could not concentrate well. I cooked for about 20 people every afternoon—bean soup, vegetables and rice with my own spices—in between caring for the boys and checking on the swami. I called him, "Swamiji," when I addressed him. The "ji" ending is one of respect and endearment. I left the garlic and onions out of the spicing to suit his diet. They are not part of the yogic diet. Guests came and sat on sheets spread out upon the new living room carpet.

The swami liked to serve the food himself. I did not know why, but assumed it was his way of taking care of everyone with his own hand, like giving a blessing. We placed the pots of soup and vegetables around him, where he sat crossed-legged, and watched bits of food trail off the ladles as he lifted his arm high over the pots to reach the plates and bowls set off to his side. I had invited my few friends, some people we had met in Cleveland during his last visit, some neighbors, and I posted flyers in the local health food store. A few couples from the TM movement joined us. A couple from Medina, Frank and Evelyn, had three children whom they brought with them for meals.

During the meal, our boys sat on either side of me. They knew enough to be quiet with guests around. Evelyn's daughter leaned into her.

Their children were older; her two boys were more independent. There was not much any of them liked to eat. Evelyn asked me if I had any salt. I went to get it and sat down between my boys again. We all waited through the long ritual of Swamiji sitting carefully, folding his square skirt of orange cloth into his ankles, and only then beginning to inspect each pot, lifting lids and naming each dish in Hindi.

"*Subzi...dal.*" Looking at the boys, he continued in English, "Rice...and yogurt."

Then he doled out a plate for each person with a big spoon. We waited in silence for the last to be served when he would chant the Sanskrit mantras that sent energy through the body and out the head. The vibration of the chant cleared my mind, leaving me peaceful and satiated. The silence was full, but the boys were impatient.

"Food is not for the body, you know," he said, very distinctly. "It is for the mind."

We chewed in silence.

"Do you have any peanut butter? You know this food is not right for her," Evelyn said. She glanced down to her daughter.

I got up, went to the small galley kitchen, found what she wanted, and sat down again. It seemed simpler than asking her to help. My tone of voice would not have been pleasant. I needed to watch myself.

After the meal, the swami instructed us to get up quickly without lingering, which suited Matt and Paul, their round bellies stuffed with rice. They had been looking at me, pleading, impatient for the sticks and dirt waiting in the yard. Paul went out. The swami, the guests, and Bill who had been at the office all day, stood and planned to walk by the lake. Bill was headed out of the kitchen after setting his plate on the counter. Matt was pulling on my leg.

"Bill?"

"I'm going with them. I've been gone all day."

"What about me?" I felt the heat of anger rising.

Besides cooking, it was also my job to do the swami's laundry, the pieces of cloth that he left in a bucket after his bath. One piece was a long faded loincloth, the other an orange rectangle that he pulled around his waist and tucked in to itself. Faded orange was the traditional saffron color of renunciants. His clothes were varying hues from saffron to bright orange. He sometimes wore a square shirt—two pieces of cloth sewn together with openings left for arms and his head. I had rinsed them and hung them from the line that ran under some cherry trees out back overlooking the lake.

"Bill, what is this? Are they all going with him?"

"He asked them to go."

"All right, but I'm not happy." When I was not happy, I would keep him up late at night talking. He was already short on sleep.

"What can we do? I am not staying behind tonight."

I understood Bill wanted to be with Swamiji and the group. I had been with the swami all day, even though it was awkward to be alone with him. And now, I was exhausted, and sullen.

Finishing the dishes, I lifted Matthew on my hip and went outside to finger the orange cloth flapping on the line like prayer cloth. The cotton was stiff, cleared of moisture by the breeze that rolled up the hill from the water. As my fingers touched his shirt my awareness shifted up to the tops of the wild cherry trees above me. I unfastened the clothespins with a soaring quiet inside. I was content in spite of myself. I had plenty to keep my hands occupied: children, tasks, and now more tasks. We had visitors; I was less lonely. I sighed.

9

It furthers one to cross the great water.
I Ching

"Why are we so busy helping you? We have no time to sit still. Others come and sit. You don't ask them to do anything, give anything..." Bill was complaining for both of us.

I was imagining Evelyn's nicely coiffed, blonde hair. I had no time for myself. I wanted a walk.

It was near the end of the month, midnight again. Everyone had gone home. Our children were in bed and we were enjoying our time alone with Swamiji. Bill and I were exhausted and yet uplifted by an unseen energy that coursed through the air around him. He was wakeful at night and liked our company as he drank the warm milk that I prepared for him before bed.

He did not reply at first, which helped us become quiet and attend.

"My dears, you know, in India, we make *ghee* out of yogurt. *Ghee* is a very pure form of butterfat. You know *ghee?*"

We nodded.

"You know *yogurt?*" He was checking his pronunciation. We barely understood him.

"Yes, yogurt," Bill and I chorused loudly, feeling somewhat empowered by helping our teacher with his English.

"Okay, yogurt." Swamiji repeated carefully. He leaned to one side, adjusted the orange cloth around his feet and then rocked back to the center. He lifted his hands to make the shape of a medium-sized pot.

"When you make yogurt, you put a culture into the warm milik." In his language all consonants have their own life.

"Milk," we chorused under our breath.

"And you set it aside. It sits quietly for some time." He raised his eyebrows and smiled.

Like meditation. Swamiji nodded as he saw our comprehension. "It stays quiet for some time, but it is not yet pure. To become pure, to make *ghee*, first the big bowl of yogurt is taken from that quiet, warm place, and it is put into a churn. Churn?"

"Churn," we repeated.

His hands shifted back and forth as if moving the paddle of the churn in a bucket. He raised his eyebrows.

"Yes, it's called churning butter."

"Yes, and in India we have a special process of churning butter from yogurt. The churning, churning separates out, the how you say, curds from whey?"

We nodded.

"You have this butter then..." He held out one hand as if there were a weight of butter in it. "...that is not yet pure. It needs more. So it is put on the fire, where it is heated so that it bubbles, and more separation occurs. On the fire, what bubbles from the melted butter is some kind of stuff." He wrinkled up his nose to express distaste. I had made *ghee* so I said,

"Yes, some residue."

"Residue and some water come out." He continued carefully. "Then you have pure *ghee*."

"So," Bill said, "Margot and I are churning, and these people are sitting like yogurt?"

"And we can look forward to the fire?" I added.

Swamiji laughed and slapped his thigh.

Quieting the mind was not enough; I would need to learn to observe the mind outside of meditation under challenging situations. Then the experience of feeling whole would become more fixed and could be felt while engaged in action.

Bill had asked me to take a leap. I remembered how my brothers dared me to leap off our shed roof. The landing hurt my feet and knees but I kept quiet. I resented that Bill pressured me to make a choice, but now I was seeing it would be okay. I did breathing exercises in the morning before the boys got up, and I meditated late into the night when they were sleeping. I could feel a deeper quiet developing.

The swami's lectures were simple and clear. The philosophy he would give to us over the next twenty years was laid out simply in these first few times of sitting with him: nature and spirit, analysis and practice, knowledge and devotion, the focus of every moment of our lives into an integrated reach toward divinity. Bill comprehended everything. Swamiji lit up when Bill entered the room, spoke the philosophy directly to him, and praised him for his comprehension. I was uplifted and gradually convinced.

Before leaving the area to return to India, Swamiji put his hand on my shoulder and said, "Be happy."

In that moment and in his words, I felt understood by him.

Happiness was illusive, simple, almost impossible…and exactly what I needed.

10

The essence of strategy is to know when and how to apply force.
Deng Ming-Dao

For the Swami's first visit, Bill and I had purchased pounds of Brazil nuts, almonds, walnuts, and dried raisins. I had carefully washed them all and had them ready for the ritual of *prasad*. At the end of each evening of chanting and lectures in Hindi at the Indian family homes, Swamiji had scooped his right hand into bowls of nuts and dried fruit and placed them into our cupped hands, along with some ripe bananas, apples or oranges. Sometimes squares of *burfi* with pistachios and small rounds of *peda*, both variations of cooked dairy sweets were placed on small paper plates and passed around. The sweets were eaten before the meal of *dal*, vegetable and *puri*, the fried bread.

Having participated in this tradition, I thought that we should at least serve the nuts and dried fruit to the guests who came to our home for lectures.

So, after the worst of the dust of re-modeling had settled, I laid out trays of washed dried fruit and nuts on cookie sheets to dry for about a week. Then I put them in jars, ready for a month of lectures and people. Handfuls of people from the TM movement and the community came up our narrow drive to find a place to park and sit for an evening. A few neighbors came. Other neighbors stayed away; they watched the orange cloth dry on our line, and the Swami walk down the street in the afternoon or evening in his orange skirt and wooden sandals, while speaking with his followers. The nuts diminished slowly. By the end of September, the Brazil nuts were fuzzy with mold.

"You can just serve fruit. We don't need all this," Swamiji said, wrinkling his nose in a friendly way. I relaxed, feeling foolish but my efforts were noticed.

Swamiji not only stayed with us on his visits, he continued to live in the homes of a few Indian devotees, and give lectures to the community in Hindi. Bill and I were with the boys at a *satsang*, the first of the new season, in a living room crowded with Indian families. I sat, eyes closed, in a narrow hall that ran back to the bedrooms. There was a playroom for when the children became bored. I was sitting with no boys in my lap.

By this time, Swamiji had affirmed that Bill and I had been married twice before. In the Vedic system, the commitment of marriage is made for seven lifetimes, at the end of which enlightenment is assured. This idea explained how when we had just met, we felt we were continuing together. The idea was neither binding nor liberating, it was simply a perspective. From hearing this, I understood that enlightenment is never easy. The friction of two people spending that much time together could bear an unusual fruit. I cannot call it a belief, merely a viewpoint that casts light on a possibility.

When an Indian woman innocently asked if we enjoyed Indian food, Swamiji laughed, saying we were more Hindu than they were. For him, a Hindu was one who lived a way of life developed along the Indus River. A Hindu practiced a pure lifestyle, dedicated to doing no harm. Our commitment to meditation and a vegetarian diet was exemplary, and we were raising our boys the same way. His statements made us self-conscious. Rarely were we affirmed for our choices. We were innocently comfortable sitting on the floor eating freshly cooked aromatic food and enjoying their hospitality. His intended effect was for the Indian families to feel uncomfortable with their choices if their lives did not include spiritual disciplines. It was awkward. We were an example.

Swamiji was chanting the end of the recitation of the nine days of *Ramayana,* which had been going on for a couple of hours that evening. Each day, after the completion of a section of the book, the final prayer, *arti*, was chanted in front of an altar with pictures of deities in the living room. It was like Catholic communion in that people waited in line for a turn, but when they come forward, they did not receive but instead took into their hands a dish containing a small burning flame, which they moved in large circles to pay homage. It felt to me as though they were giving their particular spin on the devotion, their offering of love and delight to whatever deities were present on the altar. The deities varied in every house.

I felt a breeze go by me, swirling like a flock of migrating birds winging down the hall—so full of energy, and yet soft. I glanced up and saw a small orange figure go past, tossing the end of her sari up on her shoulder. The breeze lingered in me, and a sense of presence.

I moved into the living room then, to watch the close of the chanting. The altar had been set beside the couch where Swamiji sat elevated so we all could see him. For the celebration of the *Ramayana*, pictures of Rama and his consort Sita were placed at the center of the altar since they were the subject of the scripture. Kneeling at their feet was Hanuman, the monkey-god, and standing beside them were the three other brothers. Two brothers have dark-blue skin, as though their flesh is a window to the deep night sky, and two brothers have more human flesh. They are paired: one dark, one light, like the balance of day and night. Wherever Rama is featured, Shiva is also there. According to the story of the *Ramayana*, each keeps the image of the other in his heart in meditation. On this altar Shiva sat in a deep trance at the top of a mountain, legs tucked, a topknot of hair on his head, adorned with a tiger skin and a necklace of skulls, while the river Ganges sprouted from the top of his head. If Shiva is present, he is accompanied by Uma, or Parvati, two separate incarnations of his consort, the Mother Goddess. And the altar is not complete without the god of auspicious beginnings, the elephant god Ganesha, son of Shiva and Parvati, with his belly, his pen, and focused eyes. Off to the side was Shiva as the statue of Nataraja, Lord of the Dance, the one who dances just outside our seeing and hearing but whose flame of purification we cannot escape. I was asking questions of the families about their altars, and learning more.

The chanting ended and the woman who had passed me in the hall spoke in English for a few minutes. Then I then remembered Guruji had told us he had invited another teacher to come live with us. She spoke well in English. I wanted more explanation of the *Ramayana*, but she simply offered a few well-chosen words on philosophy. She had a master's degree in Sanskrit and spoke English well. People called her Didiji which means beloved sister. Her full name was Krishna Kanta Didiji, which means Reverent Sister, Beloved of Krishna. Her orange blouse had long sleeves and her sari was wrapped neatly around her shoulders as she sat still and straight.

Then many hands offered the circle of light, as *arti* began. I watched the bowed backs as worshippers stooped to offer the dish of light low to

54

the base of the altar and humbly up to the crowns of the deities. A line of people waited patiently. Finally finished, everyone sat back on the carpet. A few women in saris cut fruit onto plates on the floor while sitting in front of the altar, and a few others piled fruit, and the denser sweets, *burfi*, and *halva*, on napkins, ready for each person. The first distribution of food after the chanting and lecture is always sweet, reminding us of the nectar of divinity. The second would be a full meal. To receive the sweet food, we each went forward to bow, *pranam*, to the swami and receive a touch on the head, his blessing. His touch opened a special feeling as if a channel were opening to the ocean. Some touched the didi's feet as well; she held her hand open over each head but did not touch.

Kanta Didi came back to our house with Swamiji, who motioned toward the kitchen. He told her to teach me to cook *chapatis*. Swamiji had told us he invited her to come teach us in English. So I was confused by this new assignment. I was too literal, perhaps. My first teaching from her began with fresh bread. Bread is called *roti*. The meal is called *roti*. Bread is the heart of the meal.

"In Northern India, we eat *roti*. In the South, they eat rice." Didi rolled her "r's" as she spoke.

She is five feet tall, while I am five feet ten inches. We stood side by side at the sink pouring water over fine durum-wheat *chapati* flour that we had measured into a steel mixing bowl. Didi swept the end of her sari up over her shoulder. She deftly mixed the flour without getting any moisture or dough onto her clothes.

"Here, try this."

I put my hands into the dough and began to press. It was very sticky.

"Your hands are strong," she laughed.

I was confused by her laugh, and must have looked puzzled.

"Good hands for *chapatis*."

I nodded, understanding the work that awaited me.

She asked for an iron pan, and we set it on high heat. I kneaded the dough until it was less sticky and more pliable.

"Rolling pin?"

I pulled a French pastry roller from the base unit by our feet.

"So long?"

"I have a thicker one somewhere, a bit shorter."

"Never mind, I can use this. Now watch." She fingered a round of dough from the container and rolled it in her palms until it was firm.

Then she poured some more of the fine flour onto the counter and dipped the round of dough carefully into the flour.

"This rolling pin is large. In India, they are quite thin." She struck the "th" sound with her teeth, so that "thin" sounded thinner. She artfully rolled the dough into a round shape, picked it up and slapped it between her hands, back and forth. "This gets rid of the extra flour, which burns in the pan and makes black spots on the bread." She flung the round shape right to the center of the hot pan.

"Now you try."

My shapes were not so round. She called them maps of continents, and laughed. Hers were the whole earth. She would tap my hand if I touched the cooking dough before it bubbled. I waited, flipped the *chapatis* only once and then waited again to see the bread puff. Puffing signaled us to press on the cooking flatbread with the end of a towel to force more heat into it. Then it would pillow and rise. The trick was not to tear the thin bread, which would let air escape. When the bread puffed, it rose up from the pan like an orb about to take off. A *chapati* was best when it inflated well, without adhering to itself, like a good meditation. I felt a kind of freedom when the bread lifted off from the hot pan. Mine rarely did. Teaching me cooking was liberating. No more guessing about food by preparing too many nuts and raisins. I could relax and learn with her training.

Swamiji asked us to find an ashram for his mission, so he or Kanta Didi or any other of his preachers could stay there. It did not have to be a big place. He wanted a setting where people would feel free to stop and visit. Bill and I volunteered to help remodel a house that another TM meditator had offered for their use. A wall was removed to create a small hall downstairs. There was a modest kitchen and one bedroom, also downstairs. A sister of one of the other didi's from India came to stay there with her little son. This was good for Kanti Didi because she would not be alone when Swamiji returned to India.

The sister sat for hours with Swamiji, comfortably resting with her knees out to one side and leaning on her hand. Her son played quietly. She spoke occasionally in Hindi. The guru would respond with patience, and then irritation. Each day I arrived, she would be sitting with him. Once he said loudly in English:

"So you think that because you eat only a little food, that you need only do a little work! That is not the case. Others think of all the work they can do and what they eat, they eat."

I paid close attention, hearing the essence of *karma* yoga—simply offer your work to life. Do not think of what you should gain in return. He was observing that some might think they are taking up little space or have few needs, so they can work less.

My life was always busy, so I felt sure I would not be scolded in the same way, though I was reluctant to keep working as hard as I had. I was happy that the work had shifted to another house.

I also was there when this same woman helped Didiji in the kitchen, cutting vegetables for the meal. Didiji asked Bill to install a lock on her bedroom door.

I came by the ashram alone; the children were with Bill.

"Let's see your new lock, Didiji."

We walked to her room. I looked around quickly to see if the other woman was following us. She was not. Inside, I pulled the latch shut.

"Ha! There now, privacy!" I said defiantly.

Didiji threw her head back and laughed. She slapped her leg, and then touched my arm. I knew I had a friend.

The ashram did not last. The American disciple asked Didiji to vacate the house. The complete reason was never clear. It seemed he could not afford to donate the rent, and the mission could not afford to pay it. The ashram was closed and Didiji spent a few winter months in our house before returning to India. So the work returned to my house. I was not unhappy. I found Didi companionable, and she was not asking us to set up programs. She wanted to study and teach more quietly. She played with the children, dressing Paul as Rama's brother, Lakshmana. Matt would sit with her, in his little room, and ask to learn meditation.

Didiji stayed in Matthew's room, as Swamiji had done. Matt was again sleeping with his brother. It felt alright to teach them to be flexible this way. At night when my children were quiet, I would go to her room to listen to her talk. I asked her what our teacher's name meant.

"Ah, his full name has much meaning. He is a very high guru, very high, very great."

It felt as though she was talking about our Guru and Bill and myself at the same time. How was it possible that we had such a great guru? I had certainly no way of verifying that he was high, or if I were deserving of such a teacher. I did not know if Kanta Didi was doubting or affirming us.

Our teacher's full name was Brahmrishi Vishvatma Bawra.

"His first name is a title meaning seer of *Brahman*," she said. "*Rishi* means seer, one who sees and knows. *Brahm* is *Brahman* the primordial Oneness, the supreme source of life. One who has a vision of the whole is a seer of *Brahman*—the highest title."

I was impressed.

"*Vishvatma* is our Guru's spiritual name, his given name, often given at the time of taking one's vows to be a monk. *Vishva* means universal. *Atma* is soul. One with a universal soul is able to be a spiritual father and mother to all his followers. We feel that in him—he is universal and for all, like water or fire. We all derive benefit from him equally."

Kanta Didi moved her head side to side in what I was coming to understand was an emphatic "yes."

"*Bawra*, his last name, is a nickname that he received as a young man. When he first began practice he was crazy for higher realization."

As she spoke, her voice gradually pulled me inward, and I felt like closing my eyes. And I did, since closed eyes were a kind of compliment. There was nothing for me to say.

"You should know," she continued. "A swami is one who has mastered himself. A swami is one who has self-mastery, not mastery over others. A guru is always a swami first. Our personal guru helps us remove our darkness, so we can be free inside."

I felt an inner expansion and elevation. Then I had a question.

"Didiji, you say 'go deep,' and to me that means to dive down. When I close my eyes, I go up."

"Can't you say, 'go deep' and mean up?" Hers was an honest question about language.

"I suppose so, but I get a little confused with the instruction."

She closed her eyes and sat a moment in quiet. I watched her. She quaked a little and then opened her eyes. "Deep is up. No problem."

I remained quiet.

"You go up and it creates a kind of heat." She put her hand to the top of her head and pressed. "It is hot." She took my wrist and placed my hand toward the top of her head.

"Press," she said.

I pressed and felt heat in the small bones of her skull.

58

"You know, when babies are born, there is an open spot there."

"The fontanel."

"Yes, and it closes as the baby matures. In meditation it opens back up."

I sat with my eyes closed and felt a deeper elevation.

"That is the place where the soul enters the body, and it is from that same spot that the soul merges back to the source."

11

The vitality of a tiger is pure energy.
Deng Ming-Dao

That first winter in 1983, when she stayed with us, Didji started a Sanskrit class for a few people. We met once a week in our living room. She sounded out each symbol of the alphabet, after which we repeated it and wrote it down, filling the lines on the paper with one at a time. We learned two symbols a week. I counted the scheduled remaining weeks of her stay and realized I would learn only a third of an alphabet.

"Didiji, I want to learn the whole alphabet."

"And then you can chant the *Ramayana*." This was the text they were chanting in the nine-day celebration where we had met. I did not know it then, but chanting the book was considered a way to purify the atmosphere and our souls at the same time. Chanting was a practice that Didiji encouraged.

So I went ahead and learned about five characters a day, remembering my uncle writing Chinese characters on his notepad, seated at a little table on an ocean liner slowly crossing the Pacific. A minimal reading vocabulary is 3,000 characters. There are thousands more and they are pictorial. Sanskrit and Hindi are written in Devanagari script. It is entirely different from the English alphabet, but it has a mere fifty letters and they are pronounced phonetically, so my task seemed easy.

Seeing Sanskrit dance as if alive in my mind was not a conscious memory. I had forgotten the experience on my teacher training course for TM, but it had created some kind of readiness. After a month, I had mastered the fifty syllables enough to read the *Ramayana*, which I did daily, without understanding the meaning.

Didiji rushed my attempts to chant out loud, then teased me if I chanted a sound incorrectly. She said I chanted like a child. She seemed affectionate, but I felt shame when she pressed me to perform beyond my ability. Feelings of shame were a problem for me. Shame came with a bodily sense of distortion, feelings of inferiority, and wanting to hide. Didi was using shame as a method to make me conform. I guessed it was more cultural than particular to her, so I tried to be unreactive. It was a struggle.

I did not want to be on display in the Indian community, though as it turned out, Bill and I were. When Bill and I went to Indian functions for lecture and *arti*, we were later told that while Swamiji spoke in Hindi, which was most of the time, he was holding us up as models of Hindu lifestyle—vegetarian diet, raising our children with a vegetarian diet, and daily practice—and we had not been raised Hindu. But I loved the sounds of Sanskrit and classical Hindi, and chanted during these gatherings of the Indian community, eventually proud of my accomplishment.

Guruji had taped the prayers that were chanted at the ashram in Virat Nagar by the whole community, including himself. He led the series of chants and mostly women voices responded. I memorized the series to help with my pronunciation. While chanting, I felt the vibration of the sounds in my own body, and I liked the meanings. I understood vibration; I could feel meaning. *Nityanadam* meant pure, *achalam*, unmovable. The simple words helped me shift inside. I learned that sound was related with space—it moved through space. This is obvious—science tells us how sound waves move through space—but Sanskrit helped me to feel spacious.

The same year that Didi stayed with us and I learned Sanskrit, Hindu deities would vividly appear in my mind when I was resting and I would find myself dwelling on their meaning in meditation. The experiences were unbidden, and I attributed them to her. I pondered the image the first time without saying anything to Didi, but then it happened again, and a third time. I asked Swamiji about the visions the next time I saw him and he stated that when the chakras clear, visions can come. But I did not believe the visions were mine. I did not believe that my psyche, left to itself, would create Hindu deities. Each time, I would be lying in bed in the dark next to Bill, close to sleep, when a deity, a vision of a form would appear in my mind. With it came a feeling. It was odd to have a felt experience of an unfamiliar image.

Naturally, my curiosity about the Hindu pantheon grew. I dwelled on my thoughts before speaking with her.

"Shiva is there for all people, like Christ." I said.

61

Didi nodded in agreement. We were sitting at the breakfast table in our little house. The floor slanted so Didi sat at a slight angle with one foot tucked under her on her chair. She was used to sitting cross-legged on the floor. Her dangling foot did not touch the floor. She held the handle of her cup with the tips of her fingers. I was becoming familiar with the shape of her skillful hands and the copper ring on the third finger.

"I read in our translation of the *Ramayana* that he wore a necklace of skulls, and when he came for his marriage to Uma, he was followed by a train of vagrants—kind of like a hippy."

Didi went along with me, saying nothing.

I began to feel excited that Christ and Shiva are no different. They are both figures on whom we heap our own meaning to console ourselves.

"There is no difference," I said.

I knew that Krishna, not Shiva, was compared to Christ. Krishna and Christ are both teachers. However, Krishna was not scorned. Shiva was an ascetic, and did not care for the company or opinions of others. It was Shiva's unconventional nature that appealed to me. Rama and Krishna, both incarnations of Vishnu, are expressions of divine sustenance—the love of God. Shiva was called the destroyer and Brahma the creator. The destroyer is the destroyer of ignorance. I felt Shiva as one who loved all beings and defied convention. The blurring of meaning was helpful for me. I needed to come to my own meaning, my own conclusions. And in the next month, February, I had another vision.

In my meditation I saw a tiger—roaring in my face. This was the vehicle of Mother Goddess. All deities ride a vehicle. Ganesha, the elephant-headed god of auspicious beginnings, rides a rat. Shiva rides Nandi, the bull. The significance of the vehicles eluded me. I had to ask.

"Why would I see a tiger, Didi?"

We were again at breakfast, which she took at about eleven in the morning after meditation, bathing, and prayers. Paul was at preschool. Matt was playing in the back in our large bedroom. She took a sip of tea and wiped her mouth on the end of her sari. She placed the mug on the slanting table.

"You saw just the tiger?" Didi looked up at me and then away, as if she were hiding something.

"Just a tiger—and it roared in my face."

"You know, Mother Goddess rides a tiger," she said.

I nodded.

"And if you see the tiger, it is good."

I understood that seeing the goddess was very special, but I stayed quiet. "Mother Goddess rides a tiger, and this shows her mastery of the tiger. So what is the tiger? There is a verse in the *Gita* that we have not five senses but six—and the tiger is the sixth sense—the mind. As a tiger roams in the forest looking for prey, the mind roams among the senses looking for experience. A roaring tiger is good."

I was left to decipher my experience. I had the feeling that the good part was that I had a vision. The not-so-good part was that my vision was roaring at me, perhaps trying to get my attention. I sipped my tea.

"So, we must try to master the senses, not be their slave. The senses are nothing. The mind is the problem," she finished.

I began to feel exposed. I had struggled for some time with the confinement of young motherhood. Now I had a didi to take care of as well. My spirit was beginning to soar with her there. Our late-night talks, learning Sanskrit, meditating—now with more assurance—were boosting my sense of purpose, of being in the life I was meant to lead. I was finding a path that I liked—a feminine presence in my house, sharing the kitchen with her, learning Sanskrit.

But I longed to walk freely outside in the woods. That was my kind of freedom, not just meditation. I decided then to take Didi for a walk on the lake, when I was sure it had frozen.

I would watch for the ice fishermen's small tents to let me know it was safe. Then I would take her out under my sky.

12

Listening means listening to the soundless; looking means looking at the formless.
The Secret of the Golden Flower

Swamiji returned to stay with us each September for a few years. He occupied Matt's room off the living room, barely the width of a bed under a narrow window. We had turned the garage into a large master bedroom, and each boy had their small room. When we had our guests, Matt had to share with Paul in bunk beds placed at the end of Paul's narrow bedroom, previously a back porch. Matt complied by lying back and beating the upper bunk with his feet. Matt did not say much; we understood. He was adjusting.

One warm night in late fall, our windows were open to crickets' song breezing in with the balmy air. The boys were finally asleep. The neighbor's dog outside in his pen howled from time to time. At midnight, Swamiji, sat leaning against the window on the low bed we had made for him. As usual, our Guru was wide awake and we were tired. He had just finished a snack of nuts and dried fruit, washed down with warm milk with ginger and *ghee*. The dog began howling in earnest. Swamiji leaned forward cross-legged, his hands pressing into the soles of his feet; we saw he was preparing to speak.

"This is a very difficult path, not easy, but not impossible," Guruji said. "And there is a great consolation we must keep in mind. You know if you set out to travel from here to Pittsburgh and your car breaks down, you fix it where you are and continue on your way. You do not have to return from where you started. Practice is the same way. We travel so far, and we never have to repeat that portion of the journey. It is complete.

"You know, when you reach the stage of *samprajnata samadhi,* then you can understand the howl of this dog. You will listen to the sound and know what the dog is saying."

Bill and I sat still, looking out the window past his head into the dark, and waited for him to continue.

"A guru's job is a difficult one. People do not necessarily like a guru. You see, his job is to remove the power of the ego. And the ego is like a bone." He paused here, to see if we understood the word, "bone."

"Yes, bone."

Swamiji looked at each of us. "If a dog has a bone stuck in his gum...you know, 'gum?'"

"Yes, gum."

"It is very painful, but he wants to keep chewing on the de-li-ci-ous taste of the sharp bone." He pronounced each syllable as if to make the word itself taste better. "If you try to remove that bone, he will growl and snap at you. So the bone is like the ego." He smiled. "That is cutting, but no one wants to release it. My job is to take that bone away. That is causing pain."

He called the ego the I-am, a term that does not imply possession. Mind consciousness, he would say, is the cause of "me and mine." The ego itself is not the cause of possession, but when the ego projects into the world it moves as waves of mind. As the ego moves in the world perceiving through the mind, attachment causes possessiveness and grasping. If the mind can settle back into the ego and let go of attachment and craving, it settles into the pure I-am.

I loved these ideas. I felt the beauty of the little I-am as a direct connection with divinity. He used to say that the I-am is a child in the lap of two parents, energy, the mother, and consciousness, the father. With proper use of energy, we come to know consciousness. Practice was about coming to understand nature, not to separate ourselves from nature. Our detachment is only from our identifications. I had no idea that Swamiji was thinking of me when he described the dog and the bone. I knew I had been hanging on for dear life, but I did not understand how to surrender my control. In time, he would add that the ego must be strong to surrender. We find the I-am, appreciate the gift of I-amness, and then surrender back to the source. This philosophy was making sense to me. Much more than a simple technique, here were ways of defining self and going deeply in meditation. The philosophy was no longer coming from a book or a video but from a guru in our living room.

My Guru was not a slight man. He was six feet tall and had been a wrestler in his youth. His arms were strong; his voice was husky. In India, where he had lectured to crowds as he wandered from village to village for twelve years, he had spoken without a microphone and chanted the *Ramayana*, drawing audiences in the hundreds. In those years, he had no home. He ate by going to two houses each evening and begging for alms. Whatever he received was his food. I was more comfortable listening to him lecture than I was speaking alone with him. When Bill was at the office, I had the children and the meals to prepare, but I would steal a few minutes to sit with him. It was awkward because I tried to be thoughtless. I was trying to let go of self and please him by respecting his silence. I felt a kind of purity. He said that I had purity: I could sit alone with him and be comfortable not speaking. But it was not purity. I fasted a great deal to subdue my feelings. When I ate less, I felt quiet and any emotion I had was reduced. I tried to be humble for my own good in the face of raising children in relative isolation and now hosting the flavors and scents of India.

Swamiji would go in to the front bathroom by the lake, the placement of which we could not change because the house was constructed of brick building blocks—an old-fashioned construction of interfaced brick mortared into larger blocks that were then mortared into thick walls. Bill had cut into these thick red walls to replace small windows with larger ones, grinding a thin red dust that penetrated every fiber of clothing and bedding. The bathroom blocked much of the view of the lake in front of the cottage. We contented ourselves with one modest picture window next to it. The swami would disappear into the front bathroom, with a large plastic cup, the kind that we kept around because of raising children, and he spent an hour there, loudly splashing, and would emerge in his spare loincloth. The bathroom was floored with simple linoleum, and in a block house by the water, it retained the damp. After his stay that year, I cleaned a small crop of mushrooms out from behind the toilet.

The swami's apparent love of water was comfortable for me but we still did not know what he was doing. As Bill and I went to sleep at night, we discussed if we dared ask the swami. Bill must have asked. I could not have spoken so plainly. Swamiji replied that he did a complete round of *neti* and cleansing exercises, clearing out all the openings of the body. We did not pursue his answer with any more questions. He appeared content after the cleansing and he would stand in the living room swinging his arms, breathing with an exhale that had enormous force and an audible texture of sound. Then he would hold out for a long time and then in, and then exhale through one nostril, the other held shut tight with his thumb. The holding was called *kumbhaka* and when he held the breath out he shaped his body so his stomach flattened and his chin was tucked, which made his long beard angle forward. After the cleansing and *pranayama*, his postures were brief. Our experience of meditation practice did not include this athletic morning routine before sitting. I did not yet know that he sat for hours in the night. In the morning he cleansed the body of impurity and prepared the mind to think clearly. The mind was clear because the intellect was keen and the mind was uncluttered by distracting thoughts.

After this practice he would wrap the rectangle of orange cloth around his waist, fitting it like a knee-length skirt, and sit with his sturdy legs tucked in and ready for the day. I then brought his breakfast of boiled milk with honey, grated ginger and *ghee* that he also took at night before sleeping. He ate one meal of vegetables, grains and beans in the mid-afternoon, although while with us he often waited for Bill to come home from work. I put most of my effort into learning to make *ghee*, how long to cool the milk, and took care to clean the nuts and dried fruits before serving him.

When we met our Guru and I was expected to feed dozens more, stand over a hot stove making *chapatis* until my back was sore and my fingers were singed, I was okay with it for a while. But I did not love cooking for others. Bill finally took over the job of cooking food, after the children were in middle school and high school and into their college years. I was busy in the first long stint of figuring out food combining for good vegetable protein, and creating dishes they liked. For a vegetarian, complete amino acids are not found in single sources as they are in meat, so eating several sources of protein at once, like a peanut butter sandwich on whole wheat bread with a glass of milk is complete protein—any one, eaten separately, will not give complete protein nutrition. We were not vegan—we were ovo-lacto-vegetarian. The swami suggested we omit the eggs. But he encouraged dairy to help soothe the nervous system.

An Indian woman suggested I learn to make *peda* for Swamiji. He liked the round sweets made with roasted milk and sugar with cardamom seeds. Roasted milk was a new idea. Cultures that center their diet on a few foods learn to cook them in a variety of ways. Corn in the American Southwest becomes tortillas. Chickpeas in Indian cooking are made into flour for flat bread. Here milk is turned into a solid sweet. I was game. You start with cans of Borden's sweetened and condensed milk that you open and pour into a pot, add crushed cardamom seeds and stir on low heat. It takes a long time to thicken the already thick condensed milk, and it is easy to brown, giving the *pedas* an unappetizing color. To keep them a light, milky color it has to be a low heat.

I stood and stirred with a flat wooden spatula that made a swishing sound as the air hit the base of the pot near the heat. To the back and forth of the spatula, I added the mental repetitive sound of my mantra. This was a new practice for me and it turned cooking into meditation. Any activity could become a moving meditation with mantra and conscious breathing. The sweet smell and the mild heat created a slightly silly feeling—a pseudo-enlightened pleasure. There was always the added tension of small children at my feet and needing to attend to them. I don't know how I found the time. My legs would get tired. And just when I was ready to quit, the milk would be thick. Then, to thicken it more, you add powdered milk, and stir until you have a paste. The paste is like malleable cookie dough that you roll into small balls and press with your thumb making a pleasing shape that can be popped in for one large mouthful. I did not taste the sweets, only smelled them. If you are going to offer food to others, tasting defiles the food. The guest or God must eat first. Swamiji loved them, especially the ones I filled with mantra: one silent mantra with each thumb press.

Matthew liked them too; we had few sweets he liked. He did not like cookies, just blueberries and strawberries. He did not like pie, just cherry tomatoes. But he liked *pedas*. Bill and I would not feed him *pedas*. I only made them when the guru was around and if Matt wanted one he had to take *prasad* from the hand of the guru. I did not like serving something so sweet to my children. But the fact that Matt liked it at all and that it was given as a kind of blessing, tempered my intemperance. Paul had no sugar until after age two. Matt was eating sugar-packed *peda* when he could first walk.

Matthew was shy. He said little in the company of others and spoke not at all with our teacher. But when he wanted *peda* he had to ask. He asked with his body. He had to walk to the teacher and hold out his hands, the left hand tucked under the right as was traditional. He learned to do this after lectures in other people's homes; I always ushered him. In his own home, he mustered his bravery. When Swamiji was sitting eating *peda* with his milk in the late morning, in Matthew's room, Matt approached him alone. Even seated on the bed, Swamiji was much taller than Matt's standing height, and he had long muscular arms. Larger than his body was his presence. You could not hide near him. It was as if his consciousness was a bright sun, and you could feel it. There was no way to squint and avoid the intensity of his awareness of you. So Matt ducked. He got on his belly and slid along the floor using his elbows. Then with his head buried in the carpet he lengthened his arms so Swamiji could place *peda* in his hands. He got a few more than usual for this new effort. I watched from the door. The Guru laughed. Matt stood right in front of him and stared down in his hands, pleased and happy. In India, this is called a full prostration—a complete surrender. It worked for Matt.

Sitting with my Guru and his comfort with silence made me ponder Bill. I really did not understand Bill. The kinds of conventions I was raised with were not important to him. He did not care to indulge me at all. If I needed a coat or shoes, we went discount shopping and found the least expensive item that served my purposes. The lack of style fit my sense, at this point, of dull rebellion. I was barely conscious that I longed for the kind of aesthetic that I had been raised with. I was emotionally surviving still, seeking to calm my inner state by adhering to Spartan personal values that suited our modest income. We had been married for five years before we met our Guru, and I still did not understand Bill. I had dismissed the first sign of my ignorance. When Bill and I stepped into the farmhouse where we first held hands, where I saw Indian deities dancing in front of my eyes, and where we decided to get married after three days, he had sat on a couch and looked back at me—completely impassive. He was a sitting wall of dispassion. He had nothing to say. He was prompted by none of the usual markers of insecurity that I was familiar with, the small flits of memory or irony that prompt us to speak with one another. He simply sat.

My Guru was like this—he sat, impassive, within himself. Perfectly content, perfectly happy. But my Guru was happier when Bill was home. Bill's presence sparked these late night talks, when we were both tired. Another talk was on the nature of the mind. This is how I remember the story. In English, our teacher's speech was halting and brief. He filled in the detail with his eyes and gestures—we filled in the rest with our imagination.

A poor man picked a bottle up off the street. The glass was blue, but dusty, so he rubbed it with both hands and felt the smooth glass shift under his palms. A genie flew out of the top of the bottle and stood next to him.

The man was surprised, not only by the genie, but by his size. He was enormous, three times the size of a normal man.

"I am here to grant your wishes," the genie offered.

"Oh, I am so honored. You mean three wishes?"

"No," the genie replied, "All your wishes."

The man began to light up with interest, and was instantly overwhelmed by the thoughts that rushed forward in his head. His wife had been complaining about their bed. Now he could buy her a whole house, more than a house, a palace with servants, cooks and all the food they could eat.

"All my wishes?"

"Yes, but there is one condition."

"What is that?"

'That you keep me busy. I have a great deal of energy. I like to be busy, and if you fail to give me a task, I shall return to devour you, for I am as hungry as the day is long, and no amount of work or food can satisfy me well."

Now this man was not stupid, though he was poor. He had had some bad luck. He wanted to be cautious. So he asked the genie if he would kindly wait. The genie nodded his big bearded head and the man went off.

The man went to consult his teacher. The teacher looked at his disciple and thought maybe he had not yet learned enough lessons. So he told him to go ahead with this plan with the caution that he must have a great number of ideas ready. He asked the man:

"Do you think you can keep him busy?"

"Oh yes, master."

"Then go, but beware of his hunger."

So off he went back to the genie and found him waiting in the street. He was sitting with his chin on his hand, patient for such a voracious being.

"I am ready!" the man cried. "First, build me a palace of many rooms north of here, near the foot of the mountains so that it will be cool in summer."

The genie went off. He returned one minute later.

"What do you want?"

"I am finished, my master, and I am hungry."

70

The man was surprised. "Oh, so soon? Now find good loyal servants and once they are in place, fetch my wife and take her to the palace. You have to find good, loyal servants. Make sure the cook is a fine one, and the palace is well stocked. And find a half dozen gardeners. She likes flowers." The man thought that perhaps searching for the right people would take time. He was anxious but he settled himself thinking he had been clever. And he went off to his old home to see what was there.

After five minutes, before he had come near to his old home, the genie returned to his side.

"Done. And now?"

The man was upset. He asked for twelve lakes, stables for horses, wheat fields and rooms for the farmers, and bulls for pulling plows. And then he ran quickly to his guru.

His guru was sitting quietly and when he saw his disciple rush in he smiled. He was not surprised.

"So?" he asked.

"Oh my master, I am in trouble. The genie is so quick. He will be back here in minutes. I need your help or I will be completely ruined. Please my master, it takes him only minutes to perform tasks that should take months or years." He fell at his feet and sobbed in fear.

"Very well, I have an idea," the teacher began. The man lifted his head.

"You see that ladder in the corner of the room? Take it. Give it to the genie, and tell him the following: Climb the ladder, and when you get to the top, come down, and when you have come down, go up again."

The man ran out with the ladder, delivered the instruction to the genie, and sat down in relief to see the giant climb up and come down the ladder, climb up and come down again and again.

Our Guru continued speaking with delight. He explained that the story illustrates the use of mantra to help calm the mind and free us from its insatiable hunger for experience:

"No man has ever fulfilled his whole desire. It is not possible. We tame the mind with the use of a sound that is pleasing. Then we can be calm and continue our journey for true happiness—happiness is not dependent on obtaining the objects of our desire. The mind is either the master of the senses or the slave. It is for each of us to choose."

I finally understood the difference between Transcendental Meditation and this teaching. I could say my mantra all the time and ease the feeling of longing for something. I knew things would not satisfy me, and I hoped meditation someday would. But now there was no need to wait. Every day, all day, anywhere, anytime I could hear the sound inside like a ladder that would keep me safe from harm. My whim of placing mantra in *pedas* was a good one.

13

To truly listen is to perfect ones own virtue.
Deng Ming-Dao

So now the harder work began. We had a teacher and a teaching, I had made a new friend in Didi, and the daily-ness of applying the teaching was in front of me. I was determined to feel better. I was attempting to quell the power of fear and diminish the power of cravings. The sense of separateness and isolation was lessening—problem of the ego—and a basic darkness and melancholy that lived with me in spite of my love of our children were beginning to lift.

I refused to wear a sari for my Guru, as he suggested I might. I had a rudimentary need to become somebody. I was not ready to surrender myself. I did not have a self. Resistance was helpful. I told him that other Americans might think it was necessary and they would imitate me. I rationalized my thinking well. I did not think the philosophy of yoga was about our dress. I did not think I should indulge his cultural prejudices. He basically shrugged when I told him so and did not bother to change my mind.

Practice takes a long time and much revisiting. Likes and dislikes that make up our identity are locked in place by comparison of ourselves with others. We like the familiar and we dislike the unfamiliar—the root of prejudice. On the yogic path we strive to keep the valuable near us and let what is harmful diminish in importance. Attraction and aversion are transformed into what is valuable for growth and what is not. I was determined in meditation practice, but the experiences of wholeness I had gained were not enough to keep me stable. I lacked continuity of experience. I had left behind a familiar life that evidently had failed me, and I carried a sense of shame about my past.

My early love of my childhood home had been lost as a result of my parents' divorce, and I moved on to a new life with Bill in Ohio, remodeling a past I did not want to remember. My early fear followed me into my adult life. I was vulnerable to moments of complete collapse where I felt fear, shame, and fatigue and all by abilities to manage life fell as if through a trap door. I now know I was suffering from post-traumatic stress disorder due to the strains of my childhood and the sudden loss of my family of origin. My balance was tenuous. I had agreed to a life of simplicity and work that Bill was offering, but I was struggling to find my sense of self within it. A sense of self comes with what we want to keep close. Certainly my children were special to me, but the world in which I was raising them did not feel entirely mine. And as I attempted to hang onto something, anger and resentment were easy to feel.

I sewed a few dresses with wide skirts so I could sit on the floor and nurse Matt. The dresses were frilly and old-fashioned; that phase lasted only a year. After that I went back to buying inexpensive clothes, loose tops and pants that were acceptable around my teacher. I had an ascetic leaning of my own that fit with Bill's frugality, and a real love of philosophy that made me want to live as simply as I could just to see how it felt. I retained the habit and friends started to give me clothes just so I could be more presentable. That reinforced my austere leanings. Waiting until someone handed me new clothes rather than buying them was a practice in letting go of desire and letting life meet my needs. I wanted to be detached so I cultivated this brand of detachment. By contrast I could see how easy it would be to revert to cultivating a sense of style and taste to reflect a self-concept. My approach was minimalism and I made it part of the new me.

A neighbor came to visit the swami and spotted his wooden sandals outside his room.

"Nice sandals," she said to him with a mixture of irony and acquisitiveness. Since she lived in the house next to ours, she had seen his meager supply of saffron loincloth and skirt drying on my line. Her remark mostly sounded wrong given his simplicity.

"Not for you," he quickly rejoined.

I felt pleased that he and I had never had this conversation. I felt superior to her. I did not think his sandals were for me. His wooden sandals were thick and flat with a peg that he gripped between his toes as he walked. The sandals were for mendicants, not for householders chasing after their chores.

But I liked my Guru's shawl. I watched him wrap his shawl around his head as he headed into Matt's room for his afternoon nap. The idea that he napped puzzled me. Was he truly sleepy from the exertion of his morning *pranayama* and yoga poses and an evening lecture? I heard the Indian communities talking about his powers. Swamiji had been seen in two places at once in India. The swami had visited a man in a hospital across the sub-continent. No time to travel by conventional means.

"Have a nice visit." I said quickly as he swept his arm up and around to pull himself under the wool cloth. By then I knew he must have seen me coming to meet Bill in Youngstown, but he would not take any credit. He told Bill my own Godhead brought me there, giving me the power and making me look favorable in Bill's eyes.

I took a risk saying anything out loud, assuming he would know what I meant. He smiled and shut the door. I felt clever and affirmed for being a little bold. I needed that kind of affirmation to feel better about myself, and I liked shawls. Bill found a few yards of cloth at the local Jo-Ann Fabrics store for both of us. I sewed the ends and meditated under the draped enclosure.

In meditation the shawl provided an outer skin—a quieting effect of less air and sensation on the skin. This kind of acquisition suited me. It was a symbol of my new life and it was soothing.

I was most interested in *malas*. Didiji and Swamiji wore simple orange clothing, but they had *malas* around the neck and a wrist. The wrist *malas* were bracelets, but the ones on the neck were removed and held in the hand while sitting quietly and doing *japa*. *Japa* is the repetition of a holy name to purify the mind and intellect so that God can be felt. They used the language of "God" but I preferred the language of the self. I cared about God if God could help me feel myself. Self is to God as a ray of light is to the sun. I needed a self and I wanted a *mala* to help me. There was something about touching the hard dark-red *rudraksha* beads, each one a lumpy seed with a natural hole in the middle. One hundred and eight beads were strung and knotted on thick thread, tied at the end with one extra bead and a tassel that hung over the heart.

As a Catholic, I was familiar with the tradition of saying the rosary while holding the beads in your hand—a prayer for each bead. I was not interested in the rosary or the crucifix, any more than in saying prayers, but in this tradition I liked my mantra, and the warmth of the *rudraksha* beads. Bill brought me back a set of beads from his first trip to India in 1984. I took them to Swamiji when he was staying in Matt's little bedroom, and asked for instruction.

"Can I use these for my meditation?"

Swamiji had been reading and he set his book aside. It was early afternoon. No one else was around.

"You have beads?"

"Yes, Bill brought these for me."

He nodded.

"You can say one mantra with one bead, moving the beads with these fingers." He held out his thumb and ring finger. "One breath, one mantra, one bead."

I looked up at him as if to ask, "Is that all?"

"Or," he continued, "If you want to purify with the holy name of *Ram*, then before sitting quietly, inhale deeply and on the exhale, go quickly through the beads saying one holy name on each bead." He leaned forward so I could place the beads in his right hand. "Complete one round with one exhale."

I smiled.

"Watch." He settled the beads into position without using his left hand. He flipped them around, deftly catching the first bead next to the thread tassel. He sat tall and adjusted his feet by tucking them under, which made him sway once from side to side. He inhaled deeply and exhaled with a humming noise coming across his rapidly moving lips; he repeated the holy name 108 times with one breath as his thumb and ring finger glided through the beads.

Back in the privacy of my bedroom, with its window that overlooked the lake, I sat with the beads in my right hand, awkwardly training my ring finger and thumb. After a few minutes I inhaled deeply and began a rapid repetition of mantra. My lips were well ahead of my fingers. My mind was distracted, competing with my body. I decided that he had given me a task to meet my restlessness, one that I would soon quit and simply sit in stillness—no moving beads or lips, just stillness and inner communion with sound.

Once in a while I did *japa*, the repetition of mantra, with one breath and one bead, but it was short-lived. I normally sat with a handful of beads cradled in the palm—one palm under the other, facing up the center of my body, stabilizing the inner core of silence. The beads reminded me of my Guru.

Bill received one practice. He repeated one mantra per breath, per bead, as long as that took—about twenty minutes—twice every day. Then he would set the beads aside, which made a light clicking sound, after which he would wake up his legs and then rise to go off to work or to bed. He continued with this one practice for years.

I did five rounds of deep breathing while standing, twenty breaths each round, then exhaled for a *rechaka kumbhaka* where I held the breath forcefully outside the lungs by flattening the belly up to the spine. When I could no longer hold that, I inhaled deeply for a *puraka kumbhaka*, a hold with the lungs filled, the chin pressed down and the pelvic floor lifted, which often made me so dizzy I had to touch my hands down on the floor to avoid toppling.

Occasionally, I fainted.

I learned to breathe in a rhythm measured by the length of the *gayatri* mantra—a chant of twenty-four syllables. It was not easy to learn the mantra, and then align it with breathing while keeping the meaning within the mind.

I cooked for the family without tasting the food, as Didi taught me. Food was offered first to God, then to others, and then finally eaten by oneself: the remnant of sacrifice. Tasting while cooking would defile the offering. Often I cooked for my family while on a fast, never eating at all.

I fasted on fruit and yogurt or milk one day each week.

I chanted the *Ramayana* and the *Bhagavad Gita* after I meditated for thirty to forty minutes, sometimes even a blissful hour at night when the boys were in bed and Bill asleep.

Bill's only practice was to sit quietly, using his set of beads, for twenty minutes each morning and evening. I thought he was not doing practice. He thought I was not doing practice. I was irritable about the simplicity of his and not satisfied with my own.

I was caught in comparison with Bill though I shared a feeling with him that was below the surface of our relationship. No matter how much I chaffed at life and made it about him, I felt an undercurrent of stability in him that I cherished. I had little experience with inner stability; my parents were both anxious. But I had been given discipline.

As a child in Pennsylvania, my mother had taken my two brothers and me to a well-attended Irish Catholic Church, where I learned the steadiness of perpetual repetition. This was early training in the "no expectation" of meditation: just go through the motion, and it will pay off someday. Once coming out of the church to the light of the blue sky, I felt completely elated for no reason. It was after confession, and the priest had instructed the usual litany of *Hail Mary's* and *Glory Be's*, so what caused the thrill was not the ritual itself. In that moment I wondered if I had faith. Seeing the sky, I felt spiritually alive. It felt simple.

There was once a boy in church with whom I experienced simplicity. I had taken a seat farthest from the aisle, away from my mother, but next to him. He was in Catholic school clothing of a white shirt and dark pants. He might have been ten years old and I was about eight. I kept glancing at his rosary. The beads were dark mahogany linked with silver chain. He held them interlaced in his fingers while he followed the missal. He noticed that I noticed him, glancing at me with the indirect look that is allowed in church and only with people next to you.

He handed me the beads without a word. Just like Bill. I looked at him in surprise and then continued to hold them through the service.

At the end of mass, I moved to hand the rosary back to the boy. He indicated *no* with a shake of his head. I looked over at his parents who had started to move out of the pew toward the sidewall. They glanced back and nodded their heads affirmatively. The boy held his hand out with the palm down indicating that I keep the beads, but it felt like a blessing of peace. I felt acknowledged, comforted and warm. Something in him awakened something unknown in me. His action was genuine.

I realized that my *mala* and *japa* were kind of phony. Bill's practice was real. Mine was a complex of behaviors necessary to make me feel that I was doing something—something to quell the fundamental disharmony that made me work to gain short intervals of peace.

During this early time with Swamiji, I met yoga teachers from other traditions, and heard about *bij* mantras that corresponded to chakras along the spine. So I sat again with my Guru in Matt's room and asked for instruction in *bij* mantras. At this point, I knew Swamiji a bit better and realized he was humoring my impatience for progress. Only time would help me, but I needed stuff to do.

"You can use the beads for these *bij* mantras," he said, as if knowing I was looking for ways to justify my attachment to the beads. I wore them around my neck all the time except in sleep, in the bathroom or while showering.

"Do one round of each *bij* mantra with each chakra before you sit to meditate. This helps to clear the chakras." Then he carefully recited and spelled each sound, which I wrote down, beginning with the base chakra and ascending toward the throat.

I memorized them and said them with my *mala*, but I was uninspired. This was clearly not a core practice. There was no magnetic pull, no vision—nothing like the simple touch of his hand on my head. Then I felt an immensely soft and sweet expanse spread through my being, relieving all tension and confusion. During this particular visit, I learned to accept his grace. I cannot say that I surrendered, but I felt safer with him—safe enough to ask more from him and to accept his teaching. Each day, I felt more of the substance of peace, contentment, and elevation.

Slowly, slowly.

About this time, we started calling our teacher Guruji, respected and beloved Guru. I had made the transition to trusting life more, trusting my teachers, while Bill's settled state of being remained incomprehensible. Didiji and Guruji valued him, his opinions, and his dedication, but I still did not know him. I was not steady. I would feel safe with him, then disturbed by our lack of clear communication, and sometimes when in silence with him, frightened. I did not understand I was placing what I did not want to feel onto Bill. I was doing a simple psychic maneuver of turning him into the bad guy in order to manage my inner lack of well-being. But I could not face myself until I was more stable.

A nice contradiction was building: I was learning practices to help me surrender my ego and at the same time I needed to make myself stronger. I was surrounding my sense of self with new values and new behaviors that were helping me and I was putting onto Bill all those feelings I did not want to feel. I was still not out of suffering. Yoga philosophy calls my suffering "the miseries" or *klesas*. They had their hold. Fear, likes and dislikes were present. I was caught in comparison, I was restless, and my sense of self felt separate most of the time.

But I was ready to work.

14

Having hands and feet everywhere, eyes, heads and faces
everywhere, having ears everywhere,
that stands enveloping everything in the world.
Gita 13/13

He laughed and slapped his thigh, and we laughed with him. Our Guru was encouraging us to find our own way. Our way of life in America was very unlike India. We found out later that our teacher never intended to leave India; his Guru had sent him to the West to find his disciples. While here he was openly teaching to whoever came in front of him. In 1983 in Portage County, Ohio, there was not much frame of reference for a guru from India. Some came for one lecture and left, some stayed a while. Some were close to him like Bill. He did not care; he taught the same divine truth to everyone, shouting his divine message above the busy clamor of our minds.

His unexpected laughter came from a story he was telling about a mantra he chanted at the Indian homes. He encouraged us to chant together. On this trip he brought us an audiotape of the evening chanting at his ashram in India. On the recording, Guruji was the lead vocalist, calling the chants and accompanying the music on a double-headed drum. Women's voices responded. Harmonium filled out the sound. The harmonium is an instrument in a rectangular box with bellows and keyboard that release the sounds of metal reeds. The organ-like tone blends well with the human voice.

Shri Rama Sharanam Mama, Shri Krishna Sharanam Mama means, "Oh Glorious Lord, you are my shelter."

The story was of a man who sought a guru. In those days the teachings of yoga were secret. It was not easy to find a guru. A student had to prove himself a worthy vessel for the teaching by waiting. In the

80

Upanishads, the ancient teaching of the *Vedas* that is a compilation of the direct teaching and distilled wisdom of many teachers, a disciple might approach a master only to be told to go away. The student needed to think more about their own question, for a year, or even six years, before returning. Once again in the presence of the guru, after waiting for him to open his eyes and be ready to speak, rather than receiving an answer, the student might be posed another question by the teacher, such as, "What is the essence of life?"

One persistent student received the mantra *Shri Rama Sharanam Mama, Shri Krishna Sharanam Mama* from his guru. His guru insisted upon two conditions: one was to repeat the mantra day and night, and the other was to keep the mantra a secret. The man agreed, humbly bowing his head with his palms pressed together.

One day the guru was in meditation when another disciple came in and bowed to his feet.

"What is it?" The guru asked without opening his eyes.

"Oh my teacher, you must come and see," he replied.

The guru sighed, whispered the name of God into the space around his seat and got up. He put on a shawl and sandals and set off down the street following his disciple. The disciple took him to a tall tree. Its branches spread over a busy roadway. High in the tree was the first disciple melodiously chanting the mantra in a loud voice. He was holding the branches. His eyes were lightly closed in apparent bliss.

The guru lifted his head higher and called above the sounds of the street.

"What are you doing, my dear?"

"Oh, my guru," the man began, opening his eyes. "I am chanting the name of God."

"Do you not remember what I told you?"

"Yes, you told me to repeat the name of God day and night. I am doing so."

"What else did I request of you?"

"That I keep the sound to myself."

"Yes, and are you doing that?"

"Oh no, my dear master, I could not keep this sound to myself. When I started to chant the holy name I became so intoxicated with Divine love that I was inspired to share it with everyone."

And so our teacher was sharing all that he knew with us.

In our early years with Guruji, he took the time to instruct us in the postures and breathing of hatha yoga. One evening in 1982, he told us to come early to the house where he was staying, to take a bath and eat nothing.

"Come with empty stomach," he said.

He meant for us to come in the morning before eating, and I knew from my TM days also to bring fruit as an offering. We were going to receive instruction. Instruction is always given in the early part of the day when the mind is fresh and the body is rested. We arrived and waited. Our boys were with us; they were always welcome. Someone watched them in another room. A few other disciples joined us in the living room.

"Now line up on the floor on your back." He began abruptly.

We did.

"And make an aisle in between where I can walk." He motioned side to side with his right hand.

We slithered away from each other and readjusted our clothing.

"Close your eyes and mouth and breathe, inhaling 'so,' with long 'o' sound. You are inhaling from a vast, infinite source of energy suspended in space in the form of oxygen. Now exhale 'ham,' surrendering your little I-amness back to the source."

I was baffled by the simplicity of the instruction on the hard floor. I was familiar with sitting to use mantra. Receiving a mantra while on my back was a new experience. But his husky voice was certain. With my eyes closed, I felt the vibration of his speech fill the room.

"Now breathe deeply."

It was uncomfortable to breathe deeply on the floor with the legs outstretched.

"Breathe more deeply, long and smooth and with no interruption. If you become relaxed with the new oxygen—keep going—never mind relaxing now. Make the lungs like bellows."

I pushed my breath and listened to its sound—a distant surf rolling against the ocean shore. I heard Bill's breath beside me as I watched myself breathe. I began to feel bored but reluctant to reveal any distraction of mind. I kept going.

"Okay now, lift one leg and look at it and hold the breath in."

We did.

"Breathe fully. Exhale carbon dioxide. Inhale oxygen. Fill the body with fresh oxygen and discharge carbon dioxide. Repeat the long sound of

'*SoooHammm*' with breath. Keep the eyes closed and watch the breath inside." He paced back and forth in an open lane of carpet beyond our heads. "Breathe fully."

After a few minutes, my back was starting to feel sore.

"Now raise the other leg. Lift the head to look at it and hold the breath. Now exhale down slowly."

A deeper calm came over me as I relaxed toward the floor.

"Inhale up and hold on the other side. Look at the toes. Lift your head."

A sense of space in my body began to expand as my awareness of the others near me diminished.

"…and exhale down slowly."

After a number of repetitions on the back and then on the stomach, I began to feel there was nothing else in the world besides breath, legs, and floor, and the vibration of his voice that was fading from my hearing.

Turning on my back again, I heard an odd sound, like feet moving. In my mind's eye, dancing feet were rubbing on the carpet and releasing puffs of air. I was certain there was no actual breeze from feet on the floor, but I was feeling one, and why was the swami dancing? I tried to avoid the distraction of my thoughts and continued to follow the breath—inhaling and exhaling deeply, fully, completely—as he instructed.

Suddenly a kind of magnetic charge coursed through my body in a current from the toes to the top of my head.

"And come down slowly."

It was as if a door had opened and a stream of energy had come through me, followed by a river of light moving from both the inside out and the outside in.

"Inhaling, receive oxygen from the space around you. Exhaling, surrender carbon dioxide and toxins from the body back to the space."

I understood breath, then, as never truly voluntary. Guruji was asking us to use a voluntary breath, and I had been breathing deeply, but at this point I could detect no effort. While inhaling I was receiving, and while exhaling I was surrendering. My body was breathing, and my sense of self was more of an observer than a doer.

He continued to speak with us as we practiced. "The purpose of breathing deeply is to attenuate the ego and quiet the mind. Breathe in from a vast ocean of energy. There is energy in the form of oxygen suspended in the vast space around us. Our tiny nostrils are breathing from the same source as are the tiny nostrils of all other creatures. Our tiny lungs are opening and closing and receiving life energy as are so many other creatures…"

I continued this hatha series for a year. The TM movement had taught us a few postures, but no practice had enlivened this vitality.

After his visit to our home in the fall of 1983, Guruji returned to the London ashram on his way back to India. He had stayed with us for a month and lectured from our living room. He had made me responsible for bringing people to see him. And they did come, friends bringing friends, but many did not return. I imagined it was because of his rudimentary English. We were told that in Hindi he spoke the equivalent of Shakespearean English—a classical style full of allusion and double meaning. Our Guru struggled in English. He had come from a village and had not been schooled in the British system.

When our Guru determined to come to England and America, he memorized the dictionary. His first English lectures had the sentence structure of Hindi, so his devotees in England sent him to college for a course in grammar.

The philosophy was succinct and inspiring. There was no doubt as to his mastery of the material. But most people in our semi-rural county in Ohio had no background in Indian philosophy, and the rewards of listening to him did not reach them.

I experienced a deep sense of gratitude opening inside as my inner life began to expand. Lying in bed thinking of this and visualizing him in London, I began to feel very still. A light opened between my eyes like a flashlight. I felt a beam directed onto my forehead that penetrated inside the skull. Oddly, it was not so much a sense of light coming into the body, as it was the body understanding that it was akin to light. And it was not my body. It was a body, filled with an all-encompassing quiet. A simple thought entered my mind. "Teach yoga."

The next week, I found a Methodist Church in Kent that would rent space. I put up flyers for hatha yoga, and started with four people. Simple postures, breathing, and some readings from the *Bhagavad Gita*. I had found a way to teach and build interest in yoga as I waited for him to return.

In this first series, I included readings from the *Bhagavad Gita* before we started breathing and moving. At the end of the series my friend who had a PhD in literary criticism told me my thinking was not ordered. It was random. She advised that I rehearse what I had to say by speaking it out loud.

I decided I was overstretching myself, and my students, by including the *Gita*, so for the next series I held in my living room I set the *Gita* aside. I chose a day and time when the boys were in school and invited mostly Kent State students. One was divorced with two children, and finishing a degree in nutrition. My routine for preparing to teach was to contemplate the class as I sat to meditate in the morning. I would turn my thoughts inward, a familiar sensation of peacefulness and focus—attentive relaxation—and I would begin to hear a clear stream of philosophical reasoning.

"*Dharma*, what is *dharma*?"

I would answer myself, "*Dharma* is action that uplifts life."

"And?"

"...Makes it possible for us to lead a life that serves others. If we feel contentment within ourselves we can add to the upliftment of others...and if we are always seeking to fill ourselves by the events and circumstances we find ourselves in, we will be too needy to serve.

That is why we meditate, first thing in the day, and any time we feel overwhelmed by a sense of lack or loss..."

And so I continued in my head. Eventually the string of ideas would cease. I would peep my eyes open, pick up a pen and jot the outline of thought down on a pad I kept by me. This kind of lengthy entry to my meditation once a week became a constant. Resuming meditation, I went deeply into silence. Bill and I learned from our study of Patanjali's *Yoga Sutras* with Kanta Didi that the first stage of *samadhi* is *samadhi* with reason. Finally, I was able to quiet the mind by thinking more deeply and having my thoughts take me to where I was satiated and silent. That became the topic of another short discourse that I shared with my students.

"If it bothers you that you think too much, you are with the right people. Think more, until your thoughts reach a point of resolution. That is the purpose of philosophy."

At the end of six months, the woman with children told me that my short talks guided her life with her children. And the only pose she did at home was to lie on her back after school and go inward until the stress of the day subsided and her thoughts suspended. She felt filled and content enough to be the mother she needed to be.

None of my students were interested in studying with the swami, sometimes they visited with Didi. But I was growing as a teacher in my own right. Mostly what I felt was not pride that I was becoming a good teacher, but a profound gratitude that I had a complete cessation of my own inner fretting while I taught. I just as effortlessly regressed into the fear of moving ahead as a teacher when the inner chaffing and sense of shame and doubt returned. When I was agitated I did not think I could ever detach again. But when I did, doubt vanished, and I went ahead with inspiration.

Seated next to my Guru on the floor, I told him I would be nothing without him. I could not have created this inner state of freedom on my own. He patted me on the back. The flood of bliss that came through my body was a marvel.

There is a verse in the *Bhagavad Gita* that had this feel to it:

And by the wisdom sacrifice, others, sacrificing, worship Me as the one and as the manifold, variously manifested, facing in all directions.   *Gita 9/15*

In all directions, in all events, in all beings, the seer is seeing. The imagery of the *Gita* evoked a feeling of the knowledge. I was maturing through my study. It became possible to read one verse a day and find the same depth I had found in years of reading many verses. A single verse resonated in me as though it were a stone dropped into a deep well. I would feel the verse hit bottom and know that my depth had been plumbed.

This is what I wanted to share.

15

The moon is constant.
Deng Ming-Dao

Guruji instructed us to sit in meditation, visualizing the globe of the earth in space, and feeling the sun nourish us. From the beginning, he encouraged us to find a practice that included the world.

During the winter Didiji stayed with us, she worked transcribing Guruji's English lectures from tapes, a tedious process. The lectures were given in England in 1980, before his first journey to Cleveland. She wrote each word in longhand and then rewrote the sentences in the margin. After a few tries she would again write out the whole lecture in longhand. Much of the transcribing she did at night while we slept. In the morning, after her practice and breakfast, she would ask me to check her sentence structure.

She called the book *Towards Divinity*. The series of lectures were about how the Hindu faith is monotheistic but with many faces. Three main aspects of God are power, love, and knowledge. Mother Goddess is the power of divinity to manifest. Love is how life is maintained. Rama and Krishna are vibrations of this love. Knowledge has the power to transform. Shiva is the deity of transformation through knowledge, but also of destruction and asceticism. This reading did much to dispel my ignorance of Hinduism. She explained that the Brahmrishi Mission had a press called Divine Radiance, which had published numerous books in Hindi based on his lectures—only a few in English. She had studied for her master's degree in Sanskrit in English medium. English medium means that the classes were taught in English rather than Hindi or any other dialect of India. She was more qualified than others within the mission to write in English. In the 19th Century, the Sanskrit *Vedas* were translated by German scholars. Many of those texts were subsequently translated into English. I found her written English difficult to understand. She favored long sentences as a way of conveying subtlety, but I thought they obscured the meaning.

Helping her made me regret that I had not finished my college degree. I felt uncertain about a major, but I had decided to have children rather than commit to a major. I asked Didi about college.

"Should I go back to school, Didiji?"

"Why not?"

That felt like a positive response. "I could never decide on a major."

"What would you like to study? History?"

"I trained in art. What about art?"

Didiji wrinkled her nose. "Art is just taste."

I was fascinated by her response. If I accepted her premise, it would turn all my East Coast training on its head. Appearance is merely taste. Certainly, living in a dusty, partially re-modeled cottage during a long winter, confined with plastic toys and diapers, was challenging my aesthetics. I felt a sense of loss. I had been trained to see the world from an aesthetic point of view. I could see how my training tooled my vision to look externally.

History was also embedded in my past. My father taught history. My maternal grandfather was an historian and Boston Unitarian and must have associated with the Ramakrishna Order that sent the famous emissary Swami Vivekananda to Boston in 1893 to teach Vedanta Philosophy and the practices of meditation. After my grandfather's death, I found a copy of Radhakrishnan's *The Principal Upanishads*, a Muirhead publication, in his library and asked my grandmother if I could keep it. It was published in the year of my birth, 1953, and it is still my Upanishad reader.

The Vedantic teaching of philosophy and meditation arrived in the States long before the practices of hatha yoga. The Vedanta Society was founded in Boston and began publishing English translations and commentaries on basic texts from India. R.W. Emerson's father was a Unitarian minister, and in the late 1880s his writing and that of Walt Whitman spread the essential philosophy of the Self of the *Bhagavad Gita*. This was my mother's Boston. My father's family was of Quaker Philadelphia. On both sides, there was an abiding interest in cultivating our humanity by reflecting on universal principles.

"Then what should I study?"

"History is good. Guruji likes history. He has a profound historical sense."

I agreed. Guruji placed his teaching in an historical context and loved to talk about Greece and India and the exchange of ideas. He spoke of Socrates as if he were a brother or perhaps himself in another lifetime. But none of that compelled me. I needed to find what I liked. I had left MIU in Iowa just before choosing a major. Psychology would have been my choice, but I was hesitant to commit to what was a relatively new field.

"You know," Didi continued. "All of the didis in India have master's degrees and PhD's, sometimes double master's."

"In what?"

"Sanskrit. Brahmrita has hers in Political Science because Guruji wanted her to be a politi-shian." Her Sanskrit training brought out a precise pronunciation of vowels. "But I was the one who encouraged them to get their degrees."

I began to get a sense of her position within the Brahmrishi mission.

I was interested in transcribing lectures from tapes to written form for the magazine in India. Didiji touched my hand when I told her this. She was happy, but by her gentle, insistent touch, she made me look at her.

"Don't change anything. No words—nothing."

"I won't." Seemed best to agree with her, but I doubted this were possible. She and I had focused for hours shifting the Hindi sensibility of grammar toward our English idiom.

"What he says is special in its own way, and it is easy to change the meaning. So be careful."

The first lecture I transcribed, we named "the Sermon on the Mount," taken from lectures in Hudson, Ohio. The verses of the sermon became yoga philosophy. "Knock, and it shall be opened" was the inner practice of meditation. During this series, Guruji emphasized light, life and love, or what he explained as head, heart and hands. The article was printed in the Divine Radiance magazine, which circulated to a mostly Indian audience. Not all Indians speak Hindi; they may read and speak Gujarati, not Hindi, and English is their second language.

It took me a long time to transcribe and edit. In 1984, we had an early IBM computer with MS-DOS software. I liked transcribing, but lacked stamina. I could write one paragraph and then an edginess and impatience with language would repel me.

Something was stirring in me as I used his language—it was not mine. I loved the philosophy but wanted to express more of myself. I was thinking of William James' idea of the perennial philosophy, the inner search for wholeness that expresses in many cultures. In the Vedic tradition, this human inner demand for wholeness that drives all of us, both with and without a religious orientation is called *sanatan dharma*.

"There is no such thing as a convent in India," Didi continued our conversation.

"Women have not had much education. I suggested to Acharya Shri..." she used a title for our teacher that meant "glorious and sublime teacher ..."that he model his idea for his disciples after the Cattau-lics."

There is no "th" sound in the Sanskrit alphabet. "Th" comes out as a "t" with extra breath.

"The girls have all studied hard," she said. "We rode bicycles to school."

She laughed, leaned forward and touched my arm. I smiled, trying to visualize Didi in a sari on a bike with her books. It must have been a small bike.

"Many of them run schools now. We are a teaching and preaching order of nuns. Didi means 'sister.' It was my idea to call the women "didis" after the Catholic sisters."

"I was the eldest of all the didis, and I knew Sanskrit when I met Acharya Shri. He was preaching and going from city to city. Whenever he came to Ludhiana, we would run to see him. A number of us didis came from my city, Ludhiana. Manisha was especially close to me. She went to see him because I went. But when he left town, we had no idea of how to reach him or talk with him. I asked him to write us letters. But he did not. It was only later that I found out that he could not read or write, that he was quoting from memory all the *Shastras* and *Upanishads*—so high a guru he is. Such a great guru you have. It all came from his realization. After some time he learned to read and write so he could write us letters. His handwriting was uncertain, since he had not used a pen in childhood. He mostly dictates his letters. But he has since studied all the holy books and memorized a great many texts.

"You know it was not easy for us didis. He was a tall young man, and used to be a wrestler before his Guru came to him and hit him on the forehead and raised his *shakti*. He was awakened to so many past lives. His Guru, Chandramauli, lives in his subtle body. He has not taken human form for…we don't know how long. Not for centuries. Chandramauli, which means 'beautiful like the moon,' teaches from his subtle body or, if he needs a body, he borrows one. He borrowed a beggar's body to give initiation to our Guru as he was walking down a street. At the time of his initiation, Swami Bawra was a young wrestler, gaining his strength from the worship of Hanuman, the monkey god, the servant of Lord Rama who keeps Rama and his consort Sita in his heart.

"After initiation, he was wildly passionate about finding this elusive guru. He gradually followed the path of a renunciant. It was during this period our Guru received the nickname of Bawra, 'madman.' The only problem was that he had a wife. So he went home to give her children and then left with his older brother's blessing to follow his *dharma*, his chosen path. His brother only told him to be successful in his new life. He would care for his family as his own."

I could not imagine leaving my family. Didiji expressed this fact as if it were the most natural behavior. In India, with extended family, maybe it was.

"Off our Guru went to do higher practices and to wander India for twelve years, studying, fasting, praying and living on alms. He went from village to village wearing only a loincloth and wooden slippers, chanting *Ramayana* as he entered the villages, while playing on a double-headed drum. People gathered by the thousands to listen to him, such a glorious figure was he. He was just a few years older than most of us. Though I am the elder, I am not much older than the other girls. And you can be sure that our parents did not approve of our interest in this young guru who had no ashram, no respectable place for us to visit.

"We had to resist them. I fasted for many days in my room, eating only spinach and water. My mother cried outside my door."

Didiji had told me about fasting on spinach and that was why she now had trouble with her digestion.

"But all that finally changed and we created our big center at Virat Nagar in India in 1974. We had begged our Guru to stop wandering and create a place.

"There was no bridge on the new land. It was jungle and we had miles to travel into town by bicycle, crossing a river with no bridge. The bridge was built ten years later. This was our first ashram. Most of the Didis continued with their education and gained Masters and PhD's."

She paused and looked at me.

The impact of having a guru, who, despite being illiterate, had learned all the scriptures, was enormous.

When I saw Guruji the next summer I mentioned my plan of completing my Bachelor's degree in psychology and then begin master's in counseling.

"Some people will care if you have a degree, some will not," he said. "The main impact you have is your divine radiance. Do your practice."

My daily practice grew.

Every day, I read the *Ramayana* in Hindi and a companion of Tulsidas's *Ramayana* in English. In one refrain for the glory of Ram, the deities rain down flowers, covering the path where he walked in the forest. I returned to college when Paul was in grade school and Matt was in preschool. I began research papers, scouring through the narrow catalogue drawers for periodicals in psychological journals and books, and then took the elevator up to find them. I had two hours to find the material, use the copy machine on what could not be checked out, and return to pick up Matthew with his packed lunch: a cheese sandwich, juice box and fruit, which he ate in the car with much pleasure and appreciation.

It was a challenge to dedicate myself to my children, my meditation and then to my college studies in psychology. Through practice and study, I was energized; I sometimes felt as I went through my mundane errands that the gods should rain down rose petals on the parking lots, as they did the paths of Ayodya—pink on black asphalt.

By this time in the mid-1980's the research of Jon Kabat-Zinn had been published. He had gathered information from 900 subjects regarding the efficacy of meditation and a few basic yoga postures in the treatment of chronic pain, measured with simple self-reports of quality of life. I felt encouraged to continue studying.

Our teacher told us that practice is best done when our lives are stable and not fluctuating. Within the security of stability, one can learn to dissolve the grip of the ego. My Guru's job was to dissolve the grip of my ego, but it was my job to find a stable identity. I had a strong historical sense that I was part of a drift of the yogic knowledge to the United States. Finding Bill was an intrinsic part of participating in the migration of knowledge. My family background played a part.

After learning the Sanskrit alphabet, I read *Gita* verses after every meditation with a minimal comprehension of the terms, making a contest with myself over the amount I read. I slowed myself by trying to sparse out the meaning from the transliteration written below. One chapter a day took a fair amount of time to read in Sanskrit and English. I refused to omit the Sanskrit. The thrill of the language inspired me as much as the meaning. Sometimes the *Gita* was all I read each week. Occasionally I read a weekly news magazine. I felt the verses work in me as though they were distilling my essence through philosophy. I felt myself in each verse—a resonance.

One evening a week, I drove nine miles to Hudson to attend a hatha yoga class in the Shivananda style. I was learning more about the poses and sequencing, and the intense hatha amplified my inner expansion. Returning home, I would continue to meditate for an hour, until I was sleepy. During the day, if the house was empty, the boys at school or out with Bill, I would feel complete in the silence, simply lying in the sunlight or watching the light play off the lake onto the living room walls.

Sometimes in meditations when my burdens would lift, I felt weightless and free. I compared this feeling of simply "being" to Descartes' maxim that had upset me in high school. He placed the experience of being as secondary to thinking. I was disturbed, assuming his statement encouraged excessive thinking, rather than quiet. It felt strange to be disturbed by *cogito ergo sum*, "I think, therefore I am." No one else cared; his maxim was accepted as truth. In meditation I felt my "am-ness." I thought Descartes' statement should have been, "I am, therefore I think."

But the weightlessness was also a problem that I complained about to Didiji.

"I feel like meditation creates a vacuum; I need to eat to become heavy. I can't believe how empty I feel."

As the grip of unease lessened, I felt as if I had been washed and hung out like a piece of their worn cotton clothing.

"Yes, this happens," Didiji said.

She did not mind feeling weightless.

I was striving to find a way to stabilize my mind and emotions. When Guruji was in town, I felt in every moment as if hovering above my life, all pieces just below, entanglements suspended.

I did not speak so freely to Guruji. I let his observations come to me when he was ready. While sharing a short moment on the deck of our house by the lake, just big enough for two chairs, he leaned in and spoke carefully to me.

"You do not live here in this house by the lake."

I raised my brow in question. Clearly, he saw how often I felt confined by the little house by the lake.

"You live on the whole earth."

Our conversation was over. I felt the impact of his words. And when I stood by while Matt swung on the A-frame swing set with its rusting metal poles, I could feel it. I could feel the expansion around our house and know that our teacher was a world teacher, and I was standing on the globe blanketed by an atmosphere suffused with oxygen creating our blue sky.

He continued later when we sat with him in the evening after the guests had left:

"The *atman* is the part of us that is eternally free, the real self, not bound by circumstances, birth, education, or achievement. Our self is bound by the needs and desires of the individual *jiva* or soul."

He held out his arm across our living room.

"Go beyond this. I teach *brahma* yoga, union with the vast, infinite source. The higher self, the *atman*, is a ray of one sun, one expression of *Brahman*. The soul, *purusha*, is one cell in the body of a larger *virat purusha* or world soul. *Brahman*, is beyond even that—an existence beyond light itself."

Virat purusha, the great body of light and consciousness, has the shape of a human form. I visualize it as a silhouette of a primitive man on the wall of a cave, painted there by the hand of some open soul who received a vision of the original *virat purusha,* the light body of which we are all a tiny part. The greeting of our Guru's mission was *"Jai Virat,"* "All glory to the soul of the world."

My essential demand for wholeness was prompting me to seek a path that might inspire me to skip over the smaller needs of my *jiva*, my little self. But I was edging closer to understanding that I also needed my smaller container.

I would take myself to bed during the day when I felt ungrounded and rest curled on my side with a burgundy-colored wool blanket that had belonged to my grandmother. I pulled it over my body and up over my head. I would leave the children to play on their own, while I unraveled within myself and satisfied some fundamental need for security.

The simplicity of being still was helping something small, grow bigger.

16

We live in a vast ocean of energy and consciousness.
Swami Bawra

I needed sky—the real blue one. I needed water. Bill and I kept a small sailfish my father had given me when I was fourteen. I had managed to convince my brother David to haul it from Philadelphia to our brother Chris' wedding outside of Boston. Bill and I drove it home.

Tethering the boat to the top of our Datsun F10 was a test of sailing: nautical knots tied while calculating the simple physics of resisting wind pulling up the nose of the craft. I restrained the bow under the front bumper. Bolin, half hitch, hand over hand, through and under-hand—pull tight, but able to unloosen. That is how Dad taught me. Knots need to release effectively. If they are secured and cannot release, it could mean your life.

Sailing on our forty-acre lake in Ohio was a vital relief. Bill did not sail. So when the boys were okay, I hauled keel, tiller, mast and boom wrapped with sail and rope down from our house to the lake, slid the boat in and outfitted it. Quickly, I'd be off pulled by gusts, listening to the play of water on the hull, hiking out to the wind-ward side to assist the small keel, and then capsizing anyway. Capsizing was part of the joy, a full plunge, then lean heavily on the keel, then the gunnel, and then slide the belly on board. With rope and tiller in hand I'd be off again to dry the sail in the wind before landing and wrapping it around the mast for storage.

Water is part of living in our area. Brady Lake lying just east of Kent is one of many small lakes and reservoirs in the Kent and Ravenna area of Portage County. Creeks flow into the Cuyahoga River that runs through the center of Kent dividing east and west. The Cuyahoga River means "crooked river" and if you fly into Cleveland, you can see numerous

96

switchbacks and bridges where the river seems to loathe reaching its destination in Lake Erie.

There is a dense cloud cover because of Lake Erie, called the "lake effect" that comes most every week, sometimes staying for the week. It resembles an up-lying lake—pure grey, pure moisture often with no precipitation.

Kent itself is in a low-lying, boggy area. Water wells that serve the city are sunk in a spongy wetland that includes Brady Lake, a kind of depression pressed into the wetlands. Underground springs replenish the lake. The water supply for all of Portage County is an underground aquifer that refills from the seepage and filtration of green areas, farmland and parks. Bogs are replete with groundcover and ancient pines found in Northern Canada, left by receding glaciers. The specimens of trees and groundcover are also found in Maine, where I spent my summers as a child. Local people are proud of this natural heritage. I was grateful for it, except when the same boggy ground seeped into basements spreading mildew smells in older homes and buildings.

On the eight acres of land where I grew up outside Philadelphia, the weather could be humid and hot in the summer like a southern climate. But we also had droughts that would dry up the water supplied by our springhouse. For three summers in a row in the 1960's, forest fires burned up the dried vines of tall trees at the edges of our fields, turning them into torches. An infrequently used well covered with an iron grid, accessible by bucket and rope, was in the utility room just outside our kitchen. When we had droughts, Dad would remind us that we could haul buckets of water from the well in any emergency. In winter when we were without electric, or in summer during a drought, the well was there.

After the droughts my parents had a deep artesian well dug in a field above our white stone house. Before then the water was pumped from a springhouse downhill from our home, near a streambed valley at the end of our long driveway. It was a small, stone house built into the side of a hill, also whitewashed with a roof of wood shingles. It sat in the shade of an old beech tree. The shady dampness curled the rough-cut shingles, and a green moss grew thick on the north side of the roof. The branches of the beech reached over the hillside and the valley, and, on the bank of the hill, exposed roots thickened and tangled into a wall of ladders. My brothers and I played along the stream and pond, and in the fields and woods surrounding our place, but rarely went into the springhouse. Once a season, we would race each other to the place where the key hung on a nail under the uphill eave. The first one there would reach below the musty eave into a fistful of spiders' webs and mulching leaves to find the key waiting like a distant memory.

Once the stiff padlock opened, we rushed through the short wooden door and descended steep, stone steps to a ledge. It was cool in the springhouse. There was an orange hue to the stillness—a rusty cast of light from the stone lit by one high window and from the sand under the water. The water was quiet. The dry stone bank was wide enough for the three of us to lie next to each other on our bellies to gaze in the water. The lightest touch spread clear arcs of ripples. At the bottom was the silent world of crayfish, their sideways movement leaving the surface undisturbed.

From the rim of the square pool we watched. In the quiet, time opened like an eggshell revealing its soft contents.

Pulling up our sleeves, we would plunge our forearms straight down and find the pool deep and cold. Water dampened the edge of my sleeve. Cold spring water seeped from underground; the springhouse pool had served as a cooling shed for milk.

When I lost my home on Saw Mill Road, I lost a sense of place. In Northeast Ohio, I did not like the cloud cover, but I loved the plentiful rainfall and the many small lakes and ponds. I feared drought. I swam in the ponds, lakes and quarries whenever possible, in sunny and cloudy weather. I was content swimming on my back gazing at the underbellies of dark clouds. Water alleviated the inner drought that would come over me—a sense of deprivation.

Living by Brady Lake, I swam across to the far shore and back.

Brady Lake was a residential lake with a tea-house across the way. The original community of 150 acres was developed in 1890 as Brady Lake Electric Park. It sported a roller coaster, carousels, a midway, a pony track, a dancehall and beachfront. A steamboat and rowboats crowded the lake, as the Interurban rail brought thousands to play in the summer months. By 1902, the Spiritualists had claimed the setting for their summer reunions.

Our home was across the street from the remaining park, where the cement carousel stand still stood. A lunch program for Brady Lake children was served in the shadow of the whitewashed and rotting walls of the midway. The owner kept a wide beach open, and for a small fee I took the boys to play in the sand and shallow water.

But in early mornings and in the purple and dark blue skies of evening, I swam alone, turning my mind on the shape of water, reflections, the occasional flight of a seagull or songbird, silver movement and the murmurs of water—the texture of my wide reprieve of time.

I had learned the Sanskrit letters and pronunciation and they were similar enough to Hindi that I was attempting to learn Hindi. I would take the book, audiotape and player to the grass by the lake, and while the boys played, repeated the same chapter many times. My focus continually wandered.

How did my Guru memorize the English dictionary when he did not speak English? It was no small task to memorize a dictionary to prepare for London.

There were other details too. Before our Guru made his first visit to England in 1972, his disciples insisted that he cover his loincloth. So he started to wear a rectangle of cloth that he tucked into itself and which served as a skirt. In India, less clothing on the men indicates asceticism. Here it would have been distracting. Because of the cold and damp weather, a disciple also cut two squares of cloth and sewed them together on three sides, leaving holes for the head and arms. A simple shirt so Guruji would not go bare-chested under his shawl.

Guruji had tolerated Himalayan cold in just a loincloth and sandals, but now he was older and traveling. By the time our Guru came to us in America, he was more acculturated than I had first understood.

There was something about living near him that made me increasingly feel that water was water, food was food and breathing was breathing. The essentials of living were highlighted, appreciated and created a kind of satiation that quelled restlessness. His restlessness never appeared. His connection with every moment was a seamless immersion in the moment: an acute awareness coupled with the simplicity of the events. Even waiting was not empty; it was replete with the present moment.

In the beginning, as he was often without Kanta Didi, I did my best to cook vegetables with Indian spices, as I had been taught. Ginger first, then turmeric, cumin, salt and pepper, and then a mix of all kinds of cut vegetables. I made *dal*, the bean soups, rice and *chapatis*, the round flat bread in the way that Kanta Didi had carefully instructed me. But during one visit, before we had found a permanent ashram for him, and while the children were still small, we placed Guruji in a house among a community of aspiring meditators in Hudson, Ohio just north of us. The house belonged to a friend who was out of town and had offered his place. It was a twenty minute drive, just far enough away to increase the challenge of caring for both my Guru and my children.

As I pondered how I would manage, Guruji cheerfully announced that he would fast on bananas and milk. I had no idea how much he was adjusting to my needs. An Indian woman would have cooked for him no matter how inconvenient.

He was at ease in his solitary life in this house. When I came by in the late morning, he would have completed a long session of *pranayama* and meditation, following the usual series of cleansing exercises that soaked the bathroom floors with water.

If I came by when he was bathing, his strings of beads would be on the bed. The beads used for repetition of mantra, called *japa*, were kept pure, and were never taken in the washroom. The idea was that they held a kind of charge from the mantra, which was caught in them, vibrating. He emerged fresh from a moist shower as if he had been bathing in the rivers of India, the Narmada, Yamuna or the Ganges that are worshipped as the Mother. He would then sit straight on his cotton quilt bed on the floor where he practiced long meditation in unwavering *samadhi*, and he would carefully pull the cleaned, square, orange cloth over his head. The shape of the cloth left small eaves above his shoulders.

From a clear glass bottle, he would tip a spot of almond oil into the cupped palm of one hand, rub it with the other hand to warm the oil, and then smooth his beard. One hand pulled down, and then the other, over and over until the two sides of the beard joined like a confluence of two rivers. He was quiet through all this.

At the end of his ritual he lifted into place the beads of crystal and *rudraksha* around his neck, all together, like a child putting on a coat before going out to play.

His energy, like his voice, was magnificently strong. He would sit smiling on the edge of his bed after practice and lean forward on his hands like a child to see what was on his breakfast platter—banana and milk, as usual. When I came, I added almonds, walnuts and raisins to his meal. When I could not make it in time, he served himself. No one else came to help.

Swamis generally do not have this kind of independence. It is disrespectful. They are fed by others, or in his case, he liked to feed others. They are not alone.

He made himself content. I was innocent.

One morning he said to me, "You know what fasting does for you?"

I shook my head "no."

"When you fast, you slow. When you slow, you observe. You can find the observer."

He smiled. His pleasure was obvious.

I had been encouraged by Didiji to follow the mission ideal of fasting on Tuesdays, which is the day of Mother Goddess. A diet of fruit, milk, and vegetables without salt created a softer condition in my nervous system. There was no energy for anxiety. When I fasted, I sometimes felt tired and had to push my body through chores, but my meditations were deep and soaring.

Guruji would eat each bite of his food slowly, and wash down fruit and nuts with long swallows of milk until the tumbler was empty. He would make an almost imperceptible grunt at the end, and then swipe his moustache clean, lifting it off his lips, side to side, before pushing the tray away. If Didi were there, she would take the dish to the kitchen and share the remainder of his food with whoever was around. Since I had no habit of this, he left nothing for me. She would not eat until he had finished. She told me the remains of his food were *prasadam*, a special gift. In the *Gita*, Lord Krishna says that to eat the remnants of sacrifice is not a sin. I only gradually learned that he carefully refrained from eating all his food so that his Didis could practice restraint until he had eaten. Service to the teacher was also a special gift for practice. By selflessly serving, we elevate ourselves above our personal needs.

After breakfast, he would study, read the paper, or speak in Hindi on the phone. Every movement was methodical and peaceful.

As long as he was in town, I felt calmed. When he left, it was not easy for me to settle back into my life. I needed to immerse myself in water, sailing and swimming faithfully to feel peaceful.

17

Its water feels itself neither wet nor dry
and its waves to themselves are neither singular nor plural
They splash deaf to their own name
on pebbles neither large nor small
Szymborska

A tall black man, glistening with drops of water that reflected the bright sky, walked toward us over the crest of the arching sand. He wore a cloth folded around his middle. His hand held a spear. When he was close, he was haloed by sunlight. David, Chris and I must have been squinting, looking worried, because he smiled.

"I am Mara."

He pointed at his chest with his free hand. "I am Mara." Then he held his hand up to us, indicating for us to wait. My feet were immovable. Once he left, my little body was like patient grass.

"Mara was from Antigua," I mused.

Here I am listening to my Guru—the swami I am coming to gradually trust as my Guru—and these vague memories of my earlier life outside of Ohio started to bob to the surface.

When I was three years old, my family took a trip to the Caribbean. I played in the shallow water with my older brothers, each of us with a mask and snorkel. The masks leaked and fogged. The sky was blue over our backs. The water was clear blue, and my parents swam not far off in deeper water. With my head under, the sound of my own ears blended with the lazy water of the lagoons.

We stayed near the beach. Naturally, my brothers and I pleaded with our parents to take us to the sea in the early morning, but they were not ready to leave the house. My mother went out to the edge of the dried grass that served as a lawn and pointed to a path, saying, "You will remember the way. Don't worry." So there we were standing where dry grasses met bald bluffs of sand.

Mara returned. He was smiling. He flung something from his spear near our feet. A wide fish danced, rainbow colors shimmering. I said to myself, "Mara, Mara, Mara." I loved his name. It sounded like the ocean. In French, sea is "*la mer.*" In Spanish, "*del mar.*" I did not know then that Mara was also the name of the goddess of death, and associated with *kama* or sensual desire.

Now I am listening to my Guru say, "So he gave him the sound of "Mara." Repeated, it became, "Mara-mara-maram--arama-*Ram.*" A robber and murderer wanted the *Ram* mantra to help him become free of his sins. He pleaded with his guru and received a mantra backwards.

"Mara" is the sound I used as a child. It was also the name of a childhood friend. When I was eight years old, the two of us camped in a tent in her back yard. Then Mara's family moved out of the area, but their house was on a bend in the road we took to the city. So as we slowed, I would repeat her name over and over in my mind. In my mind I returned to the spreading tree above the tent in her yard and felt a sense of completion mixed with longing.

The story of Rama and Sita is a story of longing for divinity. Sita is stolen from Rama by a demon named Ravana. Most of the text is devoted to his search for her. Valmiki was aware that he was writing an allegory of our soul's feeling of separation from divinity and the long journey and battle for wholeness.

So I had no problem with mantra, ever. Lots of people do.

I had taught TM at Kent State University and at Northeast Ohio College of Medicine when pregnant with Matt. Part of our TM training was to reach out to the community. After the introductory lectures, we individually taught them to use mantra. We chanted the *puja* and turned to the person witnessing the long chant and offered them a mantra as if inspired by their presence. I had no objection to the ritual. We charged a fee of thirty-five dollars in those days. It felt like service.

A Christian group of Northeast Ohio did not agree and members of their denomination, dressed in suits—warring with my own conservative skirt and stockings—passed out pamphlets on the evils of meditation outside the room where I was teaching. They thought that the idleness of meditation was the devil's playground and, without prayer, a person was prey to the forces of darkness.

My experience of mantra was not this. I felt elevated and reassured by the vibrations. My teacher's voice in Hindi was powerful. When he chanted verses in Sanskrit, the thrill of an even deeper peace would ripple through me, alleviating my struggle with myself.

Sage Valmiki, the first to give the epic tale of Rama and Sita in the *Ramayana*, received his mantra backwards as "Mara." Many times in his early lectures, our Guru emphasized that the transformative power of this philosophy was available to all, regardless of how they may have lived. If we can understand deeply that our connection with divinity is direct, full, and immediate, then we can transform our lives quickly. I wanted transformation.

Valmiki's awakening occurred when one day he attempted to rob a saint. The saint had no fear of him and remained calm. His behavior made Valmiki pause.

"Why do you have to hurt others and take their goods?" the saint asked.

"To support my family," Valmiki replied.

"They do not share in your sin. You may think you are doing some good through your actions. But ask your family. They enjoy the benefit and you take all the sin."

Valmiki let the saint go past, and then ran home to his family. He asked them one by one if they felt responsible for his actions.

"No," they all replied, "How you earn money or get food is not our concern. What you do is entirely yours."

Valmiki realized then that if he did not change his ways, he would suffer more than his victims. He had been rationalizing his actions as a way of taking care of his family. Now, having awakened to his self-delusion, he wanted a spiritual practice, and he ran back to where he had seen the saint. It was a few days before he saw the saint coming down the road. He ran to him eagerly and prostrated,

"Give me a mantra, oh my master, I understand now that I have been deluded."

The saint looked down at the changed man on the ground. He thought carefully. "How can I, my son? Your sins are heinous and would defile even the name of God."

Valmiki did not move from the ground and held tightly to the saint's feet.

After some time, the saint spoke. "All right, I can give you the name backwards, and as you say it, it will reverse itself and you will be singing the holy name." So he gave him the sound of "Mara."

When our Guru was away, my mind was more fickle in meditation. In the spring of 1983, on his second stay with us, as I was driving him home from a lecture at a nearby university, I ignored my insecurities and boldly asked him if he could help me with my mantra. I had practiced Transcendental Meditation with a *bij* or "seed" mantra for nine years. I felt I could use more help.

"I am not happy with my mantra," I said.

"I completed your Transcendental Meditation mantra, yes?" He had added an *Om* at the beginning and *namah*, "I bow down," at the end to create a more powerful feeling of supplication and surrender. In the TM organization, these syllables were added if you paid more money. Bill and I were convinced of the folly of the organization we had left, though I was still grateful for the years it had helped me.

"Yes, but I don't like it."

"You also have the mantra with breath?"

There are many kinds of mantras. The sound repeated with the breath is universal, because we all breathe. It is powerful because our soul is linked to life through the breath.

"Yes, that is okay, but I want something more."

He looked sideways at me. He seemed smaller, almost vulnerable.

"I want a sound that inspires my devotion. I want to feel completely absorbed in it when I meditate alone. I want a sound that will guide me."

I loved the sounds of Sanskrit and Hindi. In March of 1982, the first week we met our Guru, we went to a different house every evening for the chanting of the *Ramayana* by Tulsidas, a 15th Century saint who had rewritten the ancient story of Lord Rama and Sita into poetry. In the Hindu calendar there is a nine-day celebration of the *Ramayana* every spring and fall. Meeting our teacher during this festival meant that we heard far less English than Hindi. The chanting was in classical Hindi, and the refrains were of the name of Rama. The lectures were in Hindi. So after the chanting, we would continue to sit and feel the vibration of his voice as he spoke to the gathering, enhanced now and again by his singing a verse in the middle of his talk.

A year later, driving up a tree-lined street near our home, I glanced at him. He had tears in his eyes. Lacking his usual projection of confidence, he said quietly, "You want the mantra through which I realized my Lord."

Without knowing what I was agreeing to, I acquired a one-syllable mantra, the simple name of *Ram*. He spoke it aloud to me the next morning before I had eaten breakfast. He called me to sit with him, pronounced the sound and told me to repeat it inwardly with each breath—one mantra with one inhalation, one mantra with one exhalation. I later came to understand that because it was a guru-mantra, I would be helped by the power of his realization and devotion. And his actual speech carried the power. His voice carried the vibration of his realization.

Years later I told my Guru the story of how I heard the name Mara as a child. We were in a car in London. One of his disciples was in the front seat with him.

She looked back at me and asked, "So what did you do that you received the mantra backwards?"

I was familiar with the moralism of the Hindu culture—they believe being born in the West is an inferior birth, born to fulfill desires that are impediments to the path.

"I received the mantra in the West." I replied. "The West is backwards from the East in many ways, so?"

My answer was clever. I thought about her remark later when I was alone. I knew the innocence of a child never warrants shame. I had received and felt the power of this sound, even if backwards, in a culture that did not recognize mantra. I felt proud of myself for having received any mantra at all. I had started a daily practice of mantra meditation as if it were a natural part of life. It was dawning on me that without the prompting of my fear, I might not have been so dedicated. I might not have sustained meditation since 1973, when the word itself was foreign to our culture. Somehow the vibration of the sound had made its way to me. Somehow I knew. That knowing is what continues to awaken. A knowing that helps us to feel a sense of self that is beyond time, beyond culture, beyond circumstances. I had felt this through the vibration of sound. The knowledge of mantra belonged to the tradition. It was part of me.

What I wanted to tell her was: "How could anyone possibly find a mantra in the U.S. in the 1950's? This was 1956!"

18

I laugh when I hear that the fish in the water is thirsty.
Kabir

Bill's flight home from a five-week trip to India was late. Bill's trainings for his job with the Internal Revenue Service took him out of town for three to six weeks at a time, a few times a year. In 1984, he went to India to travel with Guruji. I was learning how to be on my own.

I found easy routines with the children. Paul was in pre-school. Matt was home with me. Mealtime was less formal. We read lots of books at night. I played guitar after they went to sleep. Because Bill was with our Guru, there was also a special feeling inside—a shift I had yet to understand. I played music with a feeling of comfort. Occasionally Bill's threat of abandoning me for the Himalayas would surface in my thoughts. But I understood better now.

Bill finally arrived long after the children were asleep. It felt good to be with him but strange. Almost before speaking, he placed his suitcase in the middle of the living room floor and knelt next to it. He unzipped it, and lifted the top. The sweet smells of earth, dry dung, and incense floated out like a cloud. Already I liked India. Bill dug his hands under layers of cloth and pulled out a small bag of sugar candies.

"They come from the Sita Ram temple, at the ashram," he explained.

I pressed the sugar beads against each other through their plastic wrap. The wrap felt different than ours, a little brown with dust.

"The priest dips his fingertips in a bowl of them and places a few in your open palms. It's their *prasad.*"

This was new. Bill and I had thought *prasad* was large, like fruit. Here it was small and discrete, more an idea of sweetness than something to eat. Then he drew out two shawls, one for me and one for him. "For meditation."

The wool was fine. It invited my fingers to play and yield the smooth surface out of its ironed and packed shape. He brought out light cotton suits for the boys in a linen color, small sizes that I could see the boys wearing. Then in Bill's hands were shiny silver packets of incense and a funny picture, gaudy, the outer glass painted with a curtain so you had to peep in to see a shrouded figure.

"It's a picture of Mother Goddess—a temple picture. The mother's face is covered to protect you from the power of her glance. She's from Vindhychal."

Bill told me more about the powerful internal feeling he had at the Ashtabhuja Temple in Vindhychal, Uttar Pradesh. The temple is on a low hillock beside the Vindhya mountain, a site sacred to Mother Goddess. As a young man, our Guru had isolated himself in a room near there for fasting and long meditations. Upon coming out of the room, he gave a lecture while leaning on a pillar for strength. He quoted extensively from many scriptures, never having read them. He was illiterate at the time. The explanation was that from his meditation, the memory of his past lives returned. He had been a guru twenty-eight times before. While I stared at the picture of Mother Goddess, Bill also told me about meeting Bhaiji, our Guru's brother. Bill and Bhaiji communicated with gesture and intonation, and after a few days, a few shared words. Bill did not say much about him. He went on to tell me about a few of the didis, but I felt something as he talked about Bhaiji. A connection with my own self that happens when I least expect it—a settling into place that appears to have always been there.

Bhaiji had raised Guruji's children. Our Guru took *sannyas*, the life of a mendicant, at a young age, after he had already fulfilled his arranged marriage and had two children. He could only leave them to devote his life to spiritual practice and teaching because his family would help. It is not uncommon for families to share in the task of raising children. Guruji left his brother Bhaiji in charge. It would have been a disgrace to leave a single mother with children. But to become a spiritual teacher, my Guru could leave her with the protection of his brother.

There are two honorable courses in life. The one most of us follow is called the householder life, where we devote our energy to the tasks of raising children, earning a living, and keeping up with the demands of a home. The other is a life devoted to the spiritual, called *sannyas*, the life of a mendicant. A *sannyasi's* family is the world. All families are theirs. Often they wander and beg for their meals as part of their practice, belonging to none and to all. Guruji lived in this way for twelve years. He explained the discipline of choosing only two houses at which to beg for a meal. Each day you knock on the door, say a few humble words of greeting while holding out a wooden bowl. He was told to only receive one *chapati* from each house. All mothers knew what to do. They cooked extra food for just this service. Then you eat whatever you have, and that is sufficient. He also studied scriptures and did many higher practices of meditation, but that was how he ate. He lived in the lap of a large family.

Bhaiji raised the children as his own, and Guruji's son, Rajdev, did not know who his real father was until he was an adult. Bhaiji raised Rajdev's children too, when Rajdev went to England to serve as a *pundit* in a temple established by the Brahmrishi Mission. Bhaiji lived the spirit of sacrifice as it is understood in the tradition of the *Vedas* and in *karma* yoga. Sacrifice is not what we give up to achieve. Sacrifice is what we offer into the flow of life in the spirit of transformation.

Bhaiji sacrificed his life for his family. He offered his time and energy to care for others in the spirit of service. He saw this as his duty and practice. This tradition makes a distinction between living to fulfill our wants and desires, and living in a spirit of service. As our teacher told us many times, "Through sacrifice we transform our humanity into divinity. Then we can live in heaven while on earth, while in our human bodies."

Bill and I talked little that night. I felt his words about this new friend and kept putting the shawls and the small boys' outfits up to my nose to smell what is deeply India—a place I would someday visit. He went to sleep. It was late, maybe two in the morning. I went to play my classical guitar.

I had isolated myself when Bill was gone, still not knowing many people in the area, and taught myself classical guitar at night. One person who visited with Didiji in our house had brought a guitar and chanted the refrain of a *Ram* chant with great ecstasy and enthusiasm. He ended up jumping up and down as he played. I took a hint and purchased a guitar, but I had been so thoroughly trained in classical music that a classical guitar was my choice. I bought a primer to teach myself and set to work. Through Matt's pre-school, I had met a few friends who also loved music. I had written lyrics for one to compose a song and the other to sing it. Alone, I composed a song with a complex accompaniment about the feeling of comfort and trust that comes with meditation. I wanted to feel devotion, but I had no clear feeling about God—just an inward state that was growing.

Bill came out after a few minutes, looking frustrated with me.

"What are you doing?"

"What I did to make myself okay when you were gone."

"Put the guitar down and come to bed!"

His unsympathetic response mingled in a confused way with my agreement with him. It was odd that I went back to my guitar. I could barely feel that I was angry with him for being gone so long. But acting in a way that would get him angry was not a good idea.

I did not understand how I provoked him. In time, he would help me see through my behavior, but for years I could barely glimpse the reality of how I behaved in a cold and removed way.

The next day I said to him, "Bill I had that oddest feeling when you were away—that you had done this before. You left our family to become a monk."

"Yes, I had the same feeling."

I did not expect him to agree. My mood lifted. He felt like a true partner then. Truly home. The distance between us dissolved. The feeling of being married, our history with the children, our commitment all fell back into place.

"And maybe that's why I started our life together so scared—scared that you would leave again, the way my dad left."

Bill nodded.

My parents did not have the burden of my emotions. Bill did.

In spite of my resentments, I trusted Bill's feeling that a change would be good for all of us. Since he had gone to India in the winter, he wanted to share with me some immersion with our Guru, away from our responsibilities. So he arranged for the two of us to go to the England Ashram in March of 1985, where Guruji was staying. The ashram was a small house in Southhall, just outside of London. We left Paul and Matt with Bill's mother for ten days. Bill's mom had been widowed when Matt was six months old. She was a canner and a baker, the Italian and Romanian side of Bill, the gentler half of his parents. Our boys were ages seven and four. Being with my children was the simplest way I connected with life. I knew that letting go of them for a while would be good for me and them. Bill had convinced me that I could trust they would be fine.

It was cold in early spring, and we were touring London by taking the subway in by day and returning to Southhall at night. The ashram was tucked into a Hindu neighborhood. The signs over the stores, banks, and snack shops were all in Hindi. We bought *samosas* and *burfi* from the corner store on our return to see Guruji. His room was upstairs. He was sitting where we had left him earlier in the day.

Guruji dangled a set of *mala* in front of Bill and me and asked whose it was.

I looked closely. "Mine." I felt sheepish.

"You left these in the washroom. Be careful."

I felt completely transparent. I had been feeling critical of Bill and was trying to hide it, and yet I was the one who was messing up. It may seem like a small thing, but I was being criticized for lack of purity. The beads are not supposed to be in the washroom. Guruji's gesture and admonishment made me see clearly how I had been caught for some time in judging Bill for almost everything and ignoring my own behavior.

I took the beads and sat quietly. Guruji had nothing more to say.

Guruji had found my beads in the washroom in the back yard that had wooden doors and walls and made me feel like we were camping in the city. At night we slept upstairs in a room adjacent to his. The Didis slept in the same room with him. His wooden bed was elevated about a foot off the floor. They slept on cotton mats on the floor. I could not sleep well in our room. I felt as if a light beyond the wall was watching me, penetrating into our room. He closed the distance I normally kept between myself and others. I knew it was his expanded consciousness, but I was afraid of being transparent. His ability to see through me was uncanny and liberating. I could feel some separation from my patterns of thought, but I did not know how to prevent the habits from returning.

During the day we went to the Tower of London and saw the vast display of the British Empire's ingenious weaponry. At night we visited a Hindu temple where an idol of Lord Rama and his consort, Sita, were washed and dressed in new cloth. The congregation sat on the floor and chatted throughout and then continued with evening prayers. The women had tugged gently on my pant leg, inviting me to sit close to them on the floor. It was crowded, and it was their way of welcoming me. The men sat on the other side of the aisle.

In the evening we returned to Southhall, passing the line of shops, and took our evening meal late. Guruji calmly watched us eat.

111

"Guruji, the contrast today between the brutality of the British and the gentle people at the temple made me very emotional," I said boldly.

He looked at me with no change in expression, as if he were questioning why I let myself become so emotional over such a thing as human nature. He left me on my own to puzzle out my feelings.

I was coming to understand why I became upset, and it had to do with what I felt in the Indian culture. An intimacy with being simply human was embedded in how they touched and spoke together. Before beginning a disciplined practice of ascending towards divinity, the culture itself held open a lap of acceptance. Shame and domination may exist in Indian culture, but the warmth I felt in the Hindu temple was not what I felt from the women of my childhood. My own mother had left me to balance on the edge of her bed filled with my nightmares, rather than hold me close. I was beginning to find clues, and uncover what I was missing: human touch and simple containment. This culture already had these in place before beginning an inner practice.

I felt that kind of containment with Kanta Didi, a woman who would sit with me and listen to my concerns about meditation.

"Didiji, I can become quiet, but I feel a disturbance because of my past. My parent's divorce created a difficult time for me."

She put her hand on mine.

"What is past is past," she replied.

"But it is not always past in me."

"We can move beyond any circumstances. And you must know, in India, a divorce in the family is considered shameful. We don't talk about these things. In time you will be okay."

Living with Bill and me for months had given Didiji a chance to observe our differences. She said, "Bill is like a cantaloupe and you are like an orange."

I was completely lost. "Didi you have to say what you mean."

"A cantaloupe has ridges on the outside, and is smooth on the inside. An orange is smooth on the outside and has ridges inside."

With these two fruits, she handed me a way to see who Bill was. I thought I was nicer than him. She was telling me that I was not so great inside myself, though I appeared to be conciliatory and kind. I had Bill carrying my darkness like some beast of burden, while she saw his goodness. She expressed her perception calmly, handing me the image to digest on my own. She liked me, but she knew of my distress. When I sat up with her late one night I had cried with incomprehension, while Bill was sleeping. He did not understand how my reading of the *Ramayana* and staying up late with Kanta Didi were helping me. He challenged me. I felt hurt and diminished.

Bill's relationship with Kanta Didi was quite different than mine. She was my teacher in so many ways. Bill was comfortable arguing any point with her. Not many had his logical skills and self-assurance. While scheduling her airline tickets, he ran into her resistance to traveling east on Tuesdays. We never understood why. But it was one of her traveling maxims. We had to yield. She had quick calculations of numerology regarding dates and addresses, that prompted conclusions of auspiciousness or its lack. She would not yield to his logic.

My difficulties with Bill's personality felt similar to my reaction to England. Harshness that I could see outside of me bothered me. I could see that it was part of my culture, but I could not see how it was part of myself.

After this trip to England, Kanta Didi wrote to our Guru of my difficulties with emotion and my sense of overwhelming confusion. I could feel perfectly stable in his presence, and then separation from him would prompt a period of confusion as I was thrown back on my own unmoored sense of self. His reply by letter:

Dear Bill and Margot, blessings with sweet love,

I believe that my letter will find you all happy and healthy. Some days ago Didi Krishna Kanta sent your letter. I received and noted the contents. My dear! Our present is the result of past and root of future. Past is past but that has left some impressions on our mind. Our present activities are influenced by those impressions, but it happens on the natural ground. In other words, impressions of past deeds and their influence work only up to our mental consciousness, not beyond that.

In fact, mind is not our real self; that is part of our subtle body, in other words, mind is only an instrument. As I told you many times, director of our all activities should be our wisdom; that is the abode of knowledge. When you will be aware about the greatness of wisdom, automatically your mind will be under control.

The path of divinity and spiritual practice is the work of wisdom and not of the mind, so you must be bold, watch and analyze your mental activities and whatever is un-desirable or against your will that must be controlled. Be aware that inherent impressions work only in the mental level and not beyond that. When you will analyze your every level of consciousness and its activities you will understand that your spiritual desire is not the effect of nature but spirit.

I would like to suggest you another very important thing that spiritual practice is not related with time, place and circumstances; that is the work of higher intelligence because bondage and release of impressions of karma is related with ego, or small "I." When you will be aware about your real position in the light of your higher intelligence, you will realize that you are already free from all kinds of pairs of opposites.

Try to concentrate and centralize yourself into brahmachakra and see unity in diversity and try to peep inside and you will see an ocean of energy and consciousness behind your little "I." Realizing oneness in all is the purpose of spiritual practice. My dear! Relations between guru and disciple is divine; that is related with higher consciousness and is beyond diversity. I know that guru's physical presence has great importance too, but my dear! You know how it can be possible forever. I am always with you in my higher conscious level because there is neither distance nor separation. Convey my heartiest love to my dear Paul and Matthew.

My heartiest blessings and love is with you always. Yours own, Bawra.

I would not understand this letter for many years. I was trying to resolve a fundamental insecurity and close the distance I felt between myself and others.

19

In your presence I don't want what I thought I wanted.
Rumi

I lost my wedding band in the soil of the garden outside our house. I was weeding among the tomatoes and beans. It was gone. Bill bought me another one. I doubted our marriage. Losing the band made me feel my ambivalence.

I went to a therapist who asked me what I wanted. I said I did not know—I tried to live according to what I should do, not what I wanted. She correctly saw that I was placing pressure on myself to conform to perhaps an impossible ideal. I was forcing myself into a box. Then she also made the obvious suggestion that I leave Bill if our differences were making me unhappy. I did not think I should leave Bill, or disrupt our lives with the boys. I knew Bill was not an ordinary person. I knew Bill was unusual. And I knew that I was suffering from a lack of a healthy core sense of self.

While playing in the yard in the spring, Paul found the first wedding band. Then I wore both, which did little to resolve my feelings.

Paul was unusual. At eight months old, he had sat up cross-legged in bed with his eyes closed. I used to put him down again. I'd look over and he'd be sitting again. I'd lay him down. I did not think much of it until our Guru instructed us to sit in meditation in the night when we surfaced from sleep. Meditate in the night when it is quiet. Was my baby doing that?

When Bill went to India in 1984, and I was alone with the boys for six weeks, I lost my car keys. Paul was in kindergarten; he had just turned six and Matt was three. I used to have them help find my car keys by offering them a quarter. They had earned a bit of change, but this was different. I asked Paul to go sit in meditation to look for them.

115

"Just close your eyes and see what you see," I suggested in calm voice, though I felt none.

Paul went back into the big master bedroom and sat where he could face the lake. A minute later he walked down the narrow hallway to the front of the house.

"Look in the toy box in the hall," he said.

He pointed down at a cardboard box for toys that we had set in a corner of a hallway that jogged to one side.

I went, looked, dug down and retrieved the key ring.

"How did you do that?"

I was amazed.

"I sat and closed my eyes and saw a dotted line where the keys fell from your hand into this toy box."

Simple for him. And a kind of awareness that was simple for his father.

Being alone with myself without anxiety in whatever manner possible, even for a short time, was good. I was developing skills, finding some friends through yoga and the children's schools, but I remained easily rocked by any change in routine. If we visited Bill's mother, who lived less than an hour away, I would come home unsettled. The visits were fine, but I was agitated with fear when we stepped back in the house, fear of loss, fear that my life would fall apart and dissolve. I reassured myself by stepping in the kitchen, looking inside the fridge to gaze at the milk and the mustard in the glow of the appliance bulb. Some things were steady. I'd call a friend, schedule a walk. I needed to de-sensitize myself to my fear of loss.

The hardest symptom for me to admit to myself was my separation anxiety when Bill went to the office. A toxic anger at being left alone or with our children when they were younger would predictably build in me. I did not want to feel this with my children. I contained the anxiety. I would play yet another round of the Ewok board game with Matt, placing cardboard faces of fantasy figures on pie shapes of destinations, while waiting for Paul to come home. I rallied a great love and patience for them. But I was almost never free of a nagging tension behind my patience, as though I had left something burning and it was impossible to remove its bitter smell. When Bill came home, I would unknowingly provoke him. The strain of being a good mother would overwhelm me. I knew Bill was doing his best as a parent and my partner. But there was no reward.

"Margot, don't push on me so hard," Bill said, trying to appeal to me.

"Am I pushing on you?"

"Yes, you are trying to recreate your own feeling of loss. Don't make it the loss of me."

I knew he was correct. But I could not find resolution.

The problem was that as I was becoming more responsible, there were still moments when I could not function at all. I had no language, I was catatonic; I was useless, unable to cope. I became a helpless creature with no abilities, which was not true; I had many skills—but they could be lost in an instant. I found myself in a kind of free fall with no ability to hold on.

"Bill, you need to change."

I was keeping him awake again.

"If you changed, I would feel better."

"It's not me, Margot. You know those moments when you feel better, I have not changed. I remain the same person."

His logic was good, but it did not help me.

"I am certain, though, that if you changed more I could change." I was unrelenting. We both wanted change.

Adulthood did not come naturally. I pieced the problem together only slowly. Why I felt such separation anxiety and a need to be rescued was a puzzle.

I pressed my mother for facts. She reluctantly told me that raising children with my father did not go well and she did not want more children. Since she was Catholic, they had a problem. But there we were three of us under the age of three, all in diapers. She told me that when I was six weeks old the doorbell rang on the house at Beacon Hill in Boston and she broke out in a cold sweat—a panic. I realized that was my bond, how I knew my mother—walled-off panic. She also hired caregivers to help her. A woman named Emily came to help when I was six weeks old. A woman named Frieda potty-trained all three of us simultaneously. I wondered if something had happened that my mother knew nothing about.

One night after meditating late, I went to rest with a flood of *prana* coursing through my limbs, opening a steady core of light. Bill turned to me almost in his sleep and touched me. I did not want the grounding effect of touch; I was floating, not feeling the boundaries of my body. But I lay still and watched what happened as he touched me. Without speaking, I knew. The moment itself was a confirmation of our partnering and our Guru. Bill had wanted to find this part of me, the place he knew in himself and wanted to share with me. He had been patiently waiting. This was love.

A few years later we went as a family to a beach on Lake Huron where the waves were high. The boys went off playing with a ball. Bill was face down on a towel in the warm sand. He had been reading and then settled into sleep. I had been reading too, but decided to take a dip. Edgy as usual, I had a habit of pushing the newer wedding band on and off the knuckle with my thumb. I walked into the pull of the surf and quickly jumped out to the deeper waves. Diving under, coming back up, then wiping the hair from my eyes, I noticed the ring was gone. I turned back to Bill. Walking in the sand is slow, and between the wind and my disappointment, I did not want to yell out to him. What could he do?

I stood dripping next to him. "I lost a wedding band, again."

Bill turned slowly over. "Oh," he murmured. "Where were you?"

I pointed. He got up, tipsy with the heat and his drowsy state, and walked at a diagonal across the sand to where I had been. He swept his hand through the surf, looked in his hand, and walked back.

"Here." He lay back down to rest.

I looked at the ring and wanted to talk. Bill was already lying on his blanket in the hot sun, almost back asleep. I sat watching him.

Who was this guy? Nobody does this. I wished I felt closer to him. I knew it was good to stay with him.

20

How much difference between yes and no?
Lao Tzu

Years before, soon after we met Guruji, when he was lecturing on philosophy at Evelyn's house in Medina, he paused within a philosophical discourse, put his legal pad of notes aside, and began to speak about cows and why they are sacred. He leaned back, crossed his arms, beaming.

Matt had just toddled around a corner and came up alongside me to nurse. Sitting on the floor facing our teacher was a growing group of Americans, including a number of Indian families. The Indian women were dressed in traditional colorful saris, the men in long cotton tops. This lecture took place at Evelyn and Frank's house in Medina, soon after we met our teacher.

"The cow is sacred because she makes more milk than her calf can drink," Guruji said.

Matt was lying across my lap. I had unbuttoned the middle of my dress that I made for just this purpose; I would not have to un-tuck my shirt and expose my belly. I learned later that Indian women expose their bellies under their shirts and saris but their ankles remain covered. My dress served opposite purposes, hidden belly and exposed ankles.

"That generosity, taking care of more than one's own, makes the cow a deity. Cow's milk comes from devotion."

I began to relax as Matt settled down.

"Mother's milk is also essential for a child. I myself was fed mother's milk for five years. When my mother died, my grandmother fed me her breast milk."

I stared up at him. I had never heard of such a thing.

"And in my higher practices, I went for years eating just two bananas and two quarts of milk, twice daily. That is all."

Smiling, he swung his hand out, held it steady and then set it back in his lap. "My pure diet made it possible for me to perform miracles, and I became popular for my special feats. I did not yet know that miracles were nothing and knowledge is everything. One day a saint challenged me. He said, 'Do you want to be known as milk-*baba*?' That means a kind of special milk-saint. My attachment to milk would make a fool of me."

A kind of inner luminescence lit his face. He explained how he returned to a normal diet of cooked vegetables, *dal*, and *chapati*. By his feet, a bowl of fresh Brazil nuts and bunches of bananas were waiting to be distributed. When he finished speaking, people would line up for *prasadam*. Food was important. Feeding others was important. The image of the sacred cow and the divine mother were woven into his theme of selfless service as a sign of divine life. He was inspiring us to serve others; serving merely one's own family was considered selfish—no better than animals caring for their own brood.

Early on, our Guru emphasized that with practice we change our humanity into divinity. The signs of divine life are doubtless knowledge, lustless love, and desireless service. Serving divinity is *karma* yoga, the yoga of action, serving all beings and not caring for personal gain. Guruji used to say: "We pray to God, God gives us what we need." This was similar to Christ's teaching that we should be as innocent as the lilies of the field.

After the lecture, when we were through eating our *prasadam*, Bill said to me, "Swamiji digressed from his topic for you. Some people seemed upset by your nursing Matt during the lecture."

"Are you sure?" I was puzzled. It had not occurred to me that people who sat on the floor would mind.

In our first few years together, Guruji stayed at Frank and Evelyn's house, when not at our house east of Akron. Theirs was a white Victorian with gingerbread trim. Tall ceilings and a long bay window made a regal frame for the couch they had set for him in the large parlor. After Guruji left town we would visit them. We watched Star War videos in their parlor on a large console TV, each of us with our own bowl of buttered popcorn that Frank served up. Evelyn weaved ribbons in her daughter's hair during the full-length feature.

Our house by the lake was smaller. We had removed inner walls to create a great room where we fed people on the floor on vinyl tablecloths and then cleared the same space for the lectures.

Our Guru taught us during the summer. He returned to London and then India before the cold of winter. Three years after the first attempt at maintaining the ashram where Didi had briefly stayed, he told us again that he wanted us to continue the effort of finding an ashram. He was encouraging us to perform selfless service. The next winter, the house adjacent to ours was put up for sheriff's sale. We bought it in March. We wanted to surprise our teacher with a new place and this would be possible. Since our home was forty feet away, we could work while the boys played comfortably nearby. And work we did.

The previous owner, a nice enough guy, had not done well by the house. He had torn off the peak of the roof and added a north-face clerestory that spanned the length of the house. Under the higher roof he added a solarium the size of a small gym. The supporting walls had been removed. With strong winds off the lake, the house shifted like an empty cardboard box. Before tearing off the solarium, Bill rented a jackhammer and tunneled a three-foot trench down the middle of its concrete floor to pour a concrete footer for a new base, narrowing the house. After we tore the roof off the solarium, we watched a spring snow blanket the inside floor and the peaks of the free standing windows with four inches of heavy white snow. We took a break while the snow melted, then removed the windows to sell them, leaving half of the house exposed like a dollhouse.

Then Bill started in the basement, adding steel beams, removing termite-infested wood, and rebuilding the walls one by one, all the while listening to the chanting of mantras on a dusty tape player. I worked alongside him, putting up cedar facing on the beams of the living room, holding my hands over my head longer than I thought possible, as he hammered and punched in long finish nails. Moments of sweet bliss accompanied the energy applied to the intense labor. We had acquired other chanting tapes, and I chanted along with them—the same chants over and over—bringing the boombox into every room. Lying down to sleep, I would hear the slow melody of *Keshava Madhava Govinda*, a chant to Krishna, and often drifted into an expansion of awareness that sent my consciousness over the back yard where the neighbor's mastiff lay asleep, and above the low roofs of the lake cottages that stood along the hill north of our bedroom.

If a passing raccoon set a dog barking, the others around the lake would open a trail of sound defining the shape of the lake like stars define a constellation. My mind would open with the sound, but then anger came quickly. I would jump out of bed, pull open the window and yell at the neighbor's dog to shut it up—a futile "hush."

Often Bill asked me to do some intense labor, usually at the last moment before he set out to the office. Anger would rise in me. I had little choice but to comply. Once the heating and cooling men came and needed to install tin ductwork in a crawl space that Bill had forgotten to dig out, and he handed me a shovel just as they arrived. "Like hell you want me to do this!" I yelled at him, barking and cussing. I was in my menses and digging like that would cause hemorrhaging, increasing the days of my flow. I refrained from giving that information to the workmen.

"You want me to work like a man, I'm gonna cuss like a man." I yelled.

That quelled my resentment for the time being.

"Be reasonable, Margot." Bill said.

I held my shovel in the air, threatening him to speak again. He was quiet, and I was quiet because I had finished. Then I dug out the crawl space. Fortunately, there was no floor yet. I could take the wheelbarrow in and fill it, heave it up across a plywood ramp, and out the back while the heating guys hammered in the basement. My resentment quotient built back up as I scraped the space to a level two feet, six inches deep by ten feet wide. I had a drive that made this kind of task possible. I could not have agreed, and Bill would not have asked, if the energy were not there to burn. The task was hard on my body, but my emotions had a place to work themselves out.

For me to feel that much anger and resentment was bittersweet. I was feeling; I was feeling strongly. I was pushing Bill away. I could justify my actions. It was empowering. But I did not know it was only the beginning. If I could have had self-awareness then, I would have understood that the heat was being turned up. I was gaining expansive experiences. Life was providing the next stage, testing my equanimity. I was not even-tempered; I was also unable to set boundaries on how I would serve. I felt a kind of helplessness, as if the story of my life was not mine: it was about others.

Guruji had told us that the philosophy he was teaching us was "idealistic realism" or "realistic idealism." If that were the case, living with Bill made reality a close companion.

When Guruji came in the summer, he entered the house, looked up at the cathedral ceiling and told us to move our family to this house.

He felt the setting was not right for an ashram. He wanted the ashram to be on a main street with more parking. Bill defended our choice by saying it would be easy to take care of the ashram if it were near to us, but the matter was not open for discussion. What was strange is that I accepted this with complete equanimity. After all we had done thinking the house was for our teacher, it became ours.

21

And so the tongue fell out of the mouth of the world for days.
Hafiz

Guruji left the area before we finished renovating our new home. I was happy to have a new home.

Kanta Didi acknowledged our efforts to create an ashram. She phoned us from India and suggested a fire ceremony. The Didi from the Canadian mission would help us. We knew her.

Jyoti Didi came down from Canada to preside over our house-warming. A disciple drove her from Ontario to Ohio. She did not stay long, just a few days. I had heard her lead the prayers in Canada; her voice was strong. Soon after she arrived, I sat her down at my kitchen table with a tape player and asked her to record chants so I could learn them. She was happy to help me. She was also a good cook and offered to show me how to cook with yogurt, but I was less interested in cooking.

This was our first experience of a *hoven*. We invited friends. By the time she started, the house was filled. Parking on our hill was a problem, but the guests managed to find a place for their cars, and then for themselves, sitting or standing to witness the ceremony in the middle of our new living room.

Jyoti Didi brought shopping bags of supplies from Canada for the *puja* and *hoven*. She had asked me to buy flowers, chrysanthemums, and to have sheets and a roll of tin foil. We spread the sheets over the living room carpet where people would sit. Then we spread a square of tin foil over a board as a base for the ceremony. When we were all settled, Jyotiji began a *puja*. She lit a cotton ball that had been twisted into the shape of a Hersey's kiss, leaving a tall thread of wick at the top. The cotton ball was soaked in a brass dish of *ghee* that fed the small flame. She chanted invocations in Sanskrit, turning the pages of a little cloth-bound book

124

while signaling us to sprinkle water, rice or flowers petals over the flame. Using the red paste that swamis trace in a line up the centers of their foreheads, with her little finger she traced a reverse swastika in the base of the plate. I glanced up at her with a questioning look.

"That represents the earth," she said.

Since it was our home, Bill and I sat right by her to participate and receive the most blessings. We crossed our legs tightly and sat in close so we could lean in over the steel plate. She waved her hand for us to sprinkle water with a spoon, or rice and flower petals from our fingertips. Among the guests, rice passed hand to hand until each held a small bit warming in their palms. Long stalks of mums were also passed, each person tearing a few petals from the flower heads. When Didi indicated, the rice was tossed onto the plate with the flame, as if after a wedding. At the close, everyone pressed in to sprinkle flower petals on the plate. Many missed. Petals sprayed over the sheets.

For the *hoven*, Jyoti Didi held a match to another cotton wick soaked with ghee and set it under a few twigs in a square metal box. The box was made for *hoven*, and it was elevated on short metal legs. She fed the small blaze with larger sticks and motioned to us to feed *ghee* from spoons into the fire, which caused it to flare upward, silently. Then from our fingertips we tossed rice and a sticky mixture of herbs called *samagri*, which made the flame hiss. After more flower petals and *ghee*, smoke thickened as Didi rapidly chanted mantra from the same small, worn book.

After half an hour, she closed her book, tucked it back in her bag.

"Now sit properly," she said.

Everyone sat as well as they could in meditation against walls and on small pillows, squinting in the acrid, fragrant smoke. Didi then began to lead one hundred and eight recitations of the *gayatri mantra*.

Om bhur bhuvah svahah, tat savitur varenyam.

Bhargo devasya dhimahih, dhiyo yo nah prachodayat.

We imitated her sounds. I began to shake as an intense energy rose inside my body and up through the top of my head. This was an experience of chanting I had not felt before. The recitation took close to an hour. Then she translated in English,

"Om, earth, space, and galaxies, may the splendor of the light of the universe illumine our intellects that we may always live near the inspiration of the divine."

As I served my guests fruit, *halva* and tea after the ceremony, I was jumpy with energy, almost unable to focus. I heard someone say behind me,

"She must be anxious."

Another replied, "No, that is the *kundalini*."

I did not use that word to describe my experiences, but I understood what they meant. I was feeling powerful energy in my body. In my case the energy was making me move quickly.

It was easy to stay silent. The energy inside my body pre-occupied my attention. At the sink, I leaped side to side finding cups to wash.

An Indian couple handed me a gift, a vase of red plastic roses that we plugged into an electric outlet beneath a tall picture window. I paused a moment, grounding myself by admiring the base molding I had carefully painted, and then admired the glow from tiny white Christmas lights in each red flower that softened them to pink. I thanked the Indian couple. I could see their sincerity.

"You can keep light and flowers by your Lord on your altar," the man gently offered.

I was beginning to understand that I was charged with a different kind of energy. I could use it to attend to others or just be within myself and enjoy the power. It had nothing to do with any altar or anything. The energy was distinctly universal—just energy—though it seemed to have been sparked by the mantras and the *hoven*.

Before everyone left, a woman with striking blonde hair came up to me. She introduced herself and then asked if there had ever been a fire in this house.

"The roof rafters and plywood in the attic are charred," I said.

I pointed up to the small door we had set into the loft attic of the cathedral ceiling area. There was no apparent way up, as we planned to bring in an extension ladder from outside.

She looked up and then back at me with large blue eyes.

"A young girl died in the fire."

"Oh?"

"Do you by chance experience much emotional distress?"

"Well…" I shrugged, thinking "yes."

"I saw her screaming during the ceremony, just a flash. You know I could come back and free your house. The girl is really upset. It could help you."

"Thank you. That is very kind." I could see her sincerity. She associated what she was feeling with another kind of fire, and related it to her psychic gift. I gave a small bow and backed away. Her offer for psychic relief was far too simple. My distress had been going on long before the move to the new home.

Then she turned to Bill and told him that he would come into his power after age fifty.

When everyone left Bill told me what she had said about him, but I had already dismissed her opinions. He wanted to retire early. His job was stressful. But none of this meant much to me at the time. He also overheard Didi speaking to her disciple from Canada.

"She said that a man had come up to her and wanted to shake her hand. What she said was, 'I could not touch him. I don't know what it was. We are not used to shaking hands, but maybe it was because he ate meat?'"

"I can't believe that," I said.

"She felt a strong aversion."

"Yeah, maybe even fear, but she observed it."

I breathed quietly to let my feelings dissipate, and thought further. It was apparent that Jyoti Didi's reaction was a way of framing her feelings according to her culture. She might have been shocked by how the man felt to her. It was easy for me to see her aversion and call it a problem. What about my own? I could see hers; mine were not clear to me.

In time, Bill and I have come to accept that we are all bound by culture. Our association with the fire ceremony felt powerful. But ultimately energy is energy. Consciousness is consciousness. Both express in a variety of cultures. Nothing we do places us truly within another culture. Meditation practice does not erase culture.

Later, Jyoti Didi and I shared a list of differences, marveling over our potential misunderstandings. One was that when we are sick and do not look well, in the States someone might gently ask if we are okay. By contrast, Guruji and the didis might tell us we looked weak, as if it were a sign of weakness. I would feel confused by their statement.

When we are in the world, the lens of our culture remains the one taught us by those who have cared for us. Our work is to see through our own lens more clearly and be responsible for who we are. I had much to learn.

22

We must drown away from heroism.
Rumi

The new house was a mixed blessing. It was a nicer home for our growing boys, now six and eight. They were athletes already. Paul was on an indoor soccer team for third graders and Matt joined the same team as a fullback. He was a short and skinny defender with knock-knees that I thought might break when he stopped a forceful kick. But he was fine. He liked it. In our new house, they could kick a miniature soccer ball around in the basement with their friends. But the task of finding an ashram remained.

Within six months Bill found a condemned house in Kent on a busy main street, a north-south artery that ran parallel to the river and the train. The Cuyahoga River had served as a major highway from the Great Lakes to the South before the advent of the railroad. A block north and across the street was the city cemetery, Standing Rock, named after a rock the size of a small home that rises out of the river bed. The rock was a signal spot, a landmark for the Native Iroquois and Shawnee for whom the river was transportation through these cloud-covered tree-infested hunting grounds of the Black Forest. Our county was called Portage after the portaging of canoes the eight miles between the Cuyahoga River and the Tuscarawas River. The Tuscarawas fed into the Muskingum, which joined the Ohio, which in turn broadened into the great Mississippi, thus connecting the Great Lakes to the Gulf of Mexico.

Kent was originally called Franklin Mills. It was settled in the 1790's along the rock bed of the Cuyahoga during the westward expansion. Along a bend in the river, the banks of rock ledge yield to a flat plain of mud, where grist mills, wool mills and tanneries started their commerce, and the people came and stayed. With the advent of the New York to

128

Chicago railway in the mid-1800's, the town became a whistle-stop with an opera house and a surfeit of bars and brothels on the East side. The West side sported churches, steeples, spires, and belfries—reminders of the hard-working and chaste life of success.

Our new ashram was on the West side of town. The high school was just a block north on the same side of the street as the ashram. Homes along this street are buffeted by the noise and soot of large trucks, school buses, and trains that run along the bank of the river running straight through town.

Once again with children needing me in the summer, I found myself removing the gutters of steep roofs, pulling the bent sinkers from two-by-fours so they could be re-used, making trips to the lumberyard. I was deeply exhausted by the filthy task of removing old plaster from ripped-out ceilings, clearing the basement of cast-off furnishings, old cardboard, and trash. I removed wallpaper with a steamer, and spent hours painting ceilings, walls, and base molding. Then, making life simpler, the boys returned to school, but my back was sore, my hands hurt, and my spirit lagged. I was, at the same time, in college for my master's degree in counseling. I attended classes, wrote papers, and had little time left to cook for my family.

Bill was working at his job with the IRS, returning home with building supplies and going straight to the old house. As the September date for the opening of the ashram approached, he again used vacation days. A British disciple came to live with us to fix plumbing and set drywall. Many evenings, I cooked for a volunteer crew. I surrendered to cooking and the fatigue of serving. I felt content for a while. But with graduate school, the additional demands on my time created more restlessness and turned up the heat on my practice. If the practice is to maintain equanimity in action, then I mastered that equanimity while cooking, and, naturally, teaching yoga and chanting. Other tasks did not bring the same satisfaction.

The boys were patient. When they were not at school, and we worked too intently to include them, we had to find diversions. On a Saturday, Bill sent them off to the Dairy Mart with a few dollars and a soccer ball at their feet. They returned within half an hour. I was discouraged, tired, and wanted them to be happy. I called down from the upper window of the second-story front room—the closest I could get to them. I had been roped around the waist to step out on a lower roof and pull off sagging gutters with a long metal crowbar. By chance, all our volunteers and Bill had a fear of heights. The dumpster was almost filled. I contented myself with a wave and a holler.

The date of the ashram opening arrived. People sat expectantly on the new carpet. Our Guru came out from the double doors of what was designated as his room. A few touched his feet as he passed among the seated bodies. He began his opening talk with a brief introduction and a meditation. After a round of ten Om's, he began to speak. In mid-lecture he became quiet; he tucked his head toward his chest. After a minute he resumed speaking but with none of his usual vigor. He rested after the lecture, then returned to our home with the entourage of didis from India and Canada. Late in the evening, Kanta Didi came out from where Swamiji was resting in Matt's room.

"He is not well. I don't think it is simply nausea. Can we take him to the hospital?"

Bill suggested we wait until morning.

At fifty-four years old, Guruji had a quiet heart attack that masqueraded as nausea for twenty-four hours. His heart muscle was permanently weakened from the delay in being treated. The didis stayed with him in the hospital. I was confused and upset, but needed to be with my children. We postponed visiting for a couple of days.

When Bill and I arrived at the hospital in Akron, Guruji had been out of his by-pass surgery for a day or two. He was lying back at a low angle on the bed with an oxygen tube in his nose, monitors on his fingers, and a small notepad and pen on the sheet by his side. The didis, dressed in their usual orange saris with matching sweaters and cloth shoulder bags, were finishing their morning *path*, the reading of long mantras that are like prayers. They looked tired and had sober faces that did not change expression when they saw us. They were ringed around his bed seated on chairs and perched on radiators, as natural in their grouping and in orange cloth as they had been in our home or at the Kent ashram. A few held small prayer books open while murmuring morning mantras.

Swamiji smiled at me. I began to cry.

"Don't cry." He said, gently waving a hand to caution me.

I remembered that he disliked strong emotion just like Bill, maybe like all men, but I rationalized his response by telling myself that since he had been a guru for twenty-eight lifetimes before this, he had forgotten what it was like to feel emotional. His feedback might not be useful. I settled myself; I breathed more deeply and let my emotion soften.

"I am writing poetry. I have had great visions," he continued. "See how higher practice of oneness is a great blessing in all times. Inspiration comes."

I felt confused. Was he comforting me? I looked in his eyes and ignored the others. He went on to speak with Bill. I felt the didis gaze at me and recalled how Kanta Didi phoned us when he first went into the hospital. She insisted that I sew a shirt for Swamiji while I waited to see him. She insisted several times that I wanted to do that, while I had insisted that I did not want to do that. I did not tell her that her request sounded illogical. He did not need new clothes as he would be wearing hospital gowns. Now I saw that she wanted me to bring something that displayed my dedication during our absence from the hospital. Our absence was because of our children and our fatigue. We knew our guru was well cared for.

Guruji returned to Canada and then India when he was well enough to travel.

23

Our bewilderment goes on and on.
Lao Tzu

When Guruji finally returned to India, Swami Yogananda, who was not much younger than our Guru, was sent to live and teach at the new American ashram. He was a handsome and insightful man, and engaging when he spoke. His English accent came from his early schooling in a British medium school in the hill stations of the Himalayas. Medium schools were set up for government workers in India in the 1800's. Decades of Indian children had been raised on British nursery rhymes.

"You spend so much time inside?" he asked.

"Yes, it is winter."

"This is not like India."

In India, he was used to roaming outdoors in all seasons. The ashram at Virat Nagar was cold in winter with temperatures dropping to forty degrees at night with no central heating. Walking out of doors was a way to warm up during the day in the mild heat of the winter sun. The Indian ashram was set on many acres of open fields. The ashram rooms were built along an open-air corridor, where chairs were placed and laundry hung on lines strung between thick adobe pillars. The living quarters were at one end of a large campus that includes temples, schools, cowsheds, and fields of crops.

At first, Yogananda stayed in our home, where we cooked for him. But soon, he moved to his post of duty, our new ashram, where he had to fend for himself with the help of a few renters. He had never before cooked or even heated his own milk. The second day he was there, Bill and I came by in the evening. A spray of purple splatter marked the new light blue carpet.

"Hi. What happened?" we asked.

"Oh, *Jai Virat*," the swami began. "How are you today?"

He walked up to the splatter and followed our gaze halfway across the room.

"Yes, you know, I was getting myself some grape *jooze* from the fridge. I shook the jar…" His voice went high. "And the lid was *looze*. Yes, you see. I am sorry."

We purchased a throw rug.

When we visited him with the children, the double living room became a soccer field. The swami, the two boys, and sometimes their friends would have a match off the walls. One goal was the double door at the back of the hall, the other: the low wooden platform that served as our Guru's seat and in his absence, an altar. The swami moved with short quick steps, wearing a long gown down to his ankles and a loose shawl over his shoulders. He giggled and yelled in a high voice.

Swami Yogananda was not happy. He loved children but did not like America.

"The molecules here are coarse," he said.

He held my hand and looked closely at me for my response. We sat in the front room at the ashram, set up with comfortable couches and tables donated by Frank and Evelyn. He was on the couch. I was on the floor, a traditional division of levels suitable for his swami rank and my householder status.

"Swamiji, what do you mean?"

I wanted to understand him. He was intriguing, with his long dark hair and beard.

"I can't explain any more than to say the air, the water, the food are all different, not so refined." He looked intently in my eyes.

"Okay, we use cleaning chemicals here to make our environment pure. You don't do that in India so much."

"That is right."

He liked that I agreed with him, but he wanted something more than my logic. More empathy—while I was just trying to make sense of him, a younger swami, handsome, articulate and new to America.

Then while teaching yoga, he kicked his legs as he had done in his early years of yoga and hurt himself. The pain in his groin was intense. It wore at his resolve to stay and teach. He asked for a peacock feather to help the healing.

This seemed like a test out of a fairy tale. If I could find a peacock feather, was the feather the cure or was the job of finding a feather a test of my good wishes? I shook my head and forgot he had asked. Let someone else try, I needed to take care of my family. This seemed like the most absurd request given all that we had done to build a house where he could stay. He had asked for an alarm clock with blue digital letters, too. He thought red letters were bad energy. I could help him with medicine, maybe. Ibuprophen might work. Peacock feather, no.

When I came to visit a few days later, he was holding a peacock feather in his hands. Someone helped.

While he was sick, I made an effort to visit the ashram more often on my way home from class, or while doing errands. He would hold my hands and look deeply into my blue eyes with his large brown ones.

"You know I must return to India to heal. I cannot stay here and heal."

But he could not travel until he was better. To more easily care for him, we brought him to our house over Christmas.

These were the short days of December and one early evening, in our darkened living room, Yogananda gave us a lecture on the meaning of Christmas. He lay across the couch on his side. Our boys lay on Bill and me as we rested against the side of the couch, facing the glow of the tree. A small ceramic nativity scene was on a low table, with a small, pale Mary, Joseph, shepherds, cow and sheep, and a little baby Jesus on a bed of straw, his tiny arms outstretched. As we sat quietly, this swami from India spoke in a low, melodious tone.

"Christmas is the time of the child. This sweet infant birth gave hope to a people who were suffering due to politics. And they wanted a solution that was in terms of the power of the world. But this sweet child did not give that kind of hope. He brought the message of hope that lay beyond the things of the world, in that profound connection of the self with the divine source of life."

As he went on I was filled with a warm feeling of connection and bliss, one that included my children, Bill, all of our efforts, and a sense of the larger moment that contained all time and no time. I sank back against our couch with both boys leaning on my shoulders and listening.

When Jyoti Didi heard the swami was ill, she invited herself back to our house from her ashram in Canada. First thing, she asked for yogurt and showed me how to cook a curry in my kitchen. I was inattentive and ungrateful. I was overwhelmed. Yogananda had taught me some yoga postures before he hurt himself, and insisted that I push my spine into a deep plow pose. I had felt resistance in my spine—most likely due to the stress of working on the ashram—but I went ahead to please him. He had the attitude that Americans were tired from hard work due to the restriction of their own selfishness. He wanted to take me beyond my limitations. I had wanted to please him, and now my back was seizing up. I was diagnosed with sciatica. Waiting on him and taking care of the boys became increasingly grim. I did not have the time to deal with my injury. I adjusted by moving differently, slowly, and set my mind on serving the needs of my guests and family. In trying to serve, I ignored my pain.

Jyoti Didi would go back to Yogananda's bedroom, Matt's new room that he had vacated yet again for a swami, and she would sit for hours. We heard little. We assumed that since they were both renunciants from India with the same guru, and dressed in orange, they would be sympathetic, but she would emerge, disgusted.

"He won't speak with me." She was sullen.

"Why not?"

"He is resisting. He knows I want him to stay in America. I am asking him to come to Canada to stay with me, while he heals. Then I can bring him back here. He doesn't want to stay."

Later in the kitchen she continued, "I am wasting my time here. And to think I had begun a good routine of practice in Canada that I interrupted by coming here."

This time I understood her. I empathized with her resentment, although it was vented on me. I saved myself trouble by keeping silent. Bill and I had not invited her. She may have been asked to visit us by Kanta Didi or Guruji to encourage the swami to stay and teach.

On Christmas day, the two swamis sat unspeaking in our living room while the children opened their presents. Didis are also swamis; they have the same life as the monks, one of dedication to divinity, rather than to their own families. The whole world is their family. Swami Yogananda lay on his side on the couch, propped up on one arm so he could see. Jyoti Didiji sat in a soft chair with her arms crossed. I was with the boys on the floor, getting up and down carefully to minimize the pain. My back carried my resentment but I did not feel it emotionally. I didn't complain; I kept working.

A few days later, when I came home from some errands, I heard thumping and squealing in the living room upstairs. I had left Yogananda with the boys. They did not hear me coming. As I reached the top stair, the swami, laughing, was swiping the ball with a sidekick. Seeing me, he collapsed on the couch.

That night in bed, I told Bill about Yogananda's ploy.

"He acts sick when we were around. Clearly he feels better."

We decided we were all right with his return to India.

Before he left, Frank and Evelyn visited with their children. They had helped with the initial tearing apart of the ashram before rebuilding. Mira also visited and brought a Ouiji board. Mira had been Mary, a student of mine who began coming to all of Guruji lectures. She gained a new name from him after only a short while. Mira was a mystical poet of medieval India. This Mira questioned the value of the Ouiji board, but the swami wanted to try it. He was interested in finding out about the child who had died in the ashram by running in the street.

"One problem with your little ashram in Kent," he had told us the day after Jyoti Didi returned to Canada, "is the ghost of a child living in the house. I had a vision of him running into the street and getting run over by a car."

Frank and Evelyn's oldest son Elliot was excited. He had torn out the old windows; Bill and I fit the new vinyl ones.

"Remember how the windows broke in our hands? The windows cracked when there was no stress on them!" Elliot exclaimed.

I wanted to be excited, but I did not care to believe anything. Windows break. People die. Ghosts may stick around. Remodeling was just hard work.

I hung back as they read the board. Seemed I was the only one who did not care. The endless labor and disruptions to my family life were changing me. I felt more grounded in practice, more mature as a mother, more sure of my perceptions, less needy of the company of others. My spiritual path was clearly defined by work and practice, and not the paranormal.

In spite of that, just to check on Yogananda's vision, the next time we were in Kent, Bill and I rang the doorbell of the house neighboring the ashram and spoke with the owner. She confirmed the death of the child who ran in to the street. Our response to the swami's vision had been to see if there was truth in it.

When Kanta Didi returned she began daily fire ceremonies, multiple *hovens* that darkened the corners of the room with carbon smoke. Our Guru had become sick at the ashram. She had heard the rumor about the child, and she knew about the problem of Yogananda's illness. She performed her daily fire ceremony with small twigs and branches from the yard, and consoled us that all the problems were merely the clearing of obstacles. The Brahmrishi mission had many centers, including the one in Canada. Starting an important project could raise obstacles like dust on the track of a fast train.

After Yogananda returned to India, rumors came back to us that someone's "ego" was creating problems in Kent. Guruji had to clear that ego, thus, he had had a heart attack. Apparently, Bill and I lacked purity of heart.

Here was the frustrating quandary of the Hindu culture: How to cleanse a heart of all self-interest before performing tasks that are intended to remove self-interest? And when you look around, you see that you are doing the drudgery! The double bind was reawakening the core of my personal shame and distress. I was never good enough. The standards were too high, and I was supposed to carry shame. Feeling discouraged felt like weakness. I had worked too hard to carry shame.

My sense of self was growing, so the shame was less powerful. Bill and I questioned our dedication to the mission, and if we were gaining enough, given our sacrifices. We knew that service brings growth. I had many experiences of consciousness expanding beyond my normal sphere of awareness after community hatha yoga classes. This was important to me.

While lying in deep relaxation, my awareness would open first to the ceiling, and then above the roofline and the trees surrounding the building, and then into the undefined darkness of the sky. I attributed these moments of expansion to my Guru's blessing—not to myself. The others in the class had no guru. After yoga sessions, they could talk immediately. I could not speak. I could move, roll up my blanket, and quietly find my shoes. But I would linger in silence and listen, talking only after a while as I prepared to drive home.

Now I had sciatica and could not attend the hatha classes.

Now we found ourselves in a fight with our Guru.

Guruji sent a letter to Kanta Didi asking her to sell the ashram. The mission owned the house, so she could initiate the sale, but our signatures would be needed on the documents. She called us. Because we heard the news second-hand and over the phone, we naturally felt hurt. Bill was angry, while I was discouraged. He spoke loudly over the phone, and she assured him she would not sell the house. Our feeling of betrayal stayed with us.

I was discouraged but also determined that our efforts not be wasted; I was not ready to sell the house. I often felt conflicted with myself—any drama outside of me only made my inner conflict worse. I needed to reside in a peaceful place in myself—that was, after all, the reason why I had begun meditation practice years before. My seeking kept bringing forth non-ordinary experiences. I craved ordinary peace and quiet.

Within all our work, it felt as if rules were being made up as we went along, and the rules were not in our favor.

I had a key to the ashram and returned there one day in late winter when it was deserted and quiet. Kanta Didi had returned to India. Two renters lived in upstairs rooms; they were out of the house. Bill was in Akron; Paul and Matt at school. I went to the front room on the second floor where the swami had stayed. It had been decorated according to our budget: new paint on old plastered walls, plain curtains, and a fading shag rug that had not been replaced. In the corner stood a makeshift altar—the peacock feather stuck behind a picture of Krishna. The altar was set on cardboard boxes covered with red cloth, next to a window that overlooked the lawn where the boys had waited while we worked, and the street where the child had run.

I sat cross-legged in front of the altar and began reciting the *gayatri mantra*, the mantra we had chanted with Jyoti Didi from Canada during the opening ceremony for our house. I recalled the intensity I felt while repeating the sounds and the lingering energy in my body after the *hoven*. At that moment, deciding to use the *gayatri mantra* was a desperate effort to gain control over my distress. It was not my usual mantra, and I had never before repeated it silently. The choice was spontaneous, and without any self-consciousness.

Savoring the sounds *Om, bhur, buvah, svahah*, I visualized the meaning, "Oh earth, space and galaxies…" As I silently began this repetition with a plea in my heart for relief from emotional pain and confusion, I fell deeply into myself. It was like soaring on a swing; the swing went up farther and farther until I felt my boundaries merge with space. The freedom of my spirit was complete. This was perfection and clearly not of the things of the world. Resting in a timeless place, I felt relieved of my assumptions of how life ought to be. After a while I settled back into the body—satiated with a pure connection. All ideas of salvation through people, things, ashrams, and teachers had dissolved. I sat with mantra, breath, and self.

As I sat quietly, I remembered something Guruji said:

"Suffering is one of the greatest boons. Suffering prompts us to search for true relief from pain." Now his words made sense, and all the months of labor and confusion seemed worthwhile. Without occasion to seek, or the conviction that there was something worth seeking, I would not have found those few moments where there was no struggle.

All was perfect as it was.

I revisited the same perfection I had felt before.

This time it felt completely my own.

24

Walk. Don't run.
Swami Bawra

When Bill and I had this confusing time of harsh feelings that came
between us and our Guru, we realized that we could not detach internally
from our feeling of oneness with our teacher. No matter what the
arguments, we remained as if one soul, one awareness. Thinking about
detaching from him did not create separation. Our disappointment and
anger created a distinction and a boundary between our culture and his,
but his presence continued to give us a feeling of peace and profound
expansion. Within a year he had returned to visit and teach. The quiet of
the meditation practice that was the quiet culturing of milk into yogurt
was long gone; the churning and heating of the yogurt to make butter and
then *ghee* was our stage of purification.

"Purification of what?" was the question. Was it ego? That did not
make sense to us. Maybe we did not understand the ego. We were not
working for self-interest. Purification to remove attachments seemed a
better way to say it. Maybe attachments were rooted in ego. Releasing any
sense of pride or specialness because we had a guru was a possibility.
Learning to exert energy and not expect any particular outcome was
another benefit.

I regretted spending so much time away from the children to help the
mission build the houses and to care for our teachers. We had invested
enormous time and energy. We had felt exhilarated even in the midst of
fatigue, but Bill and I questioned our judgment. I wondered how our
children were faring. What would be the long term effects of our choices
on them? There was no way of knowing. After the pain of my sciatica
reduced, and I could walk with some strength, the first step Bill and I

took to feel our independence was a hiking trip to Oregon, without the children. We needed time together. The boys stayed with Bill's mother.

Our travel plans did not go smoothly. The airline lost our luggage, but it did give us a hotel room for the night to recuperate from our flight and time change. The car rental did not have our reserved car, but we got an upgrade. We drove an enormous luxury Crown Victoria around the dusty desert mountains. We felt cared for. We realized that a degree of separation from our teachers would be healthy. We worked to sort out the teaching from the teachers.

Hiking in the high desert plains of Oregon, the air was clear and the nights were below freezing. Ice crystals coated the outside of our tent in the mornings; we built fires to warm our hands before a day of hiking. The lakes of the region were so pure that I soaped up with a mild cleanser and brushed my teeth before swimming—rinsing my mouth and body in one cool plunge that filled my ears with the familiar sounds of water.

It was there I first noticed twisted trees—lying on the ground, their bark having long rotted away. The growth pattern turned steadily as if on a lathe of time, making the inner cambium distinct from the missing outer bark. The drying trunk laid witness to a slow dance and a final pirouette into stillness. Often since then I have paused in fascination by drying trunks like these, and only gradually have I understood that I was taught to be like that trunk, twisted inside with unspoken words and unmet feelings, creating a kind of compression inside. Meditation provided release from the tension, but did nothing to straighten this inner core that was as if pressed from above, a steady hand of inhibition that made my growth truncated, shorter, failing to reach its full height. My feelings could not be felt straight—such as "I am angry." Someone had to be blamed for my anger; it had to be put somewhere, and the backlash from that created another layer of complication. Feelings were woven into my mental fabric as suppression, disowning, projecting—my psyche hoping to root into some place of resolution. But projection is never a resolution; the drama of projection merely confirms the existence of the oppressive spiral.

I often kept quiet, and I was motivated to give my children their own inner orientation to themselves so they could grow straight, un-gnarled with emotion that could not be felt directly. Our children were a good test of the teaching. What was useful for them would be useful to teach anyone, and that would not be Hinduism, but a practical philosophy. Our teacher did not encourage us to adopt Hinduism, though he himself was fully Hindu. The culture was his, but he taught that the underlying, timeless philosophy was *sanatan dharma*, realistic idealism. Any culture will put their stamp on the philosophy. The teaching is for everyone, and the culture of India, though it had produced our teachers and preserved the traditions, was not going to transplant to America. I sought to teach my boys and my students what I was trying to hold for myself and what our Guru was encouraging us to have: direct learning within life.

When we returned home, Bill and I continued with the disciplines of chores and rituals around mealtime and bedtime. Both boys had mulching duty when they were old enough to wrap their arms around the plastic tub that held our kitchen garbage and take it out to the mulch pile. After that, cleaning bathrooms, then recycling and trash, then dinner dishes. Each chore was a duty for two to three years.

Occasionally, Bill and I would sit with them in the evenings for chanting and meditation. One time when Paul was eight years old, he did not open his eyes. Bill, Matt and I waited for him. Finally he blinked, and pulled himself out.

"What were you experiencing?" Bill asked.

"I was inside the sun," Paul said.

Proximity to our teacher was potent: We all felt it. His Sanskrit grace was uplifting, but we needed a simpler grace to share with our children, so I adapted the English translation of a Sanskrit mantra:

> *O my Lord, you are my mother, you are my father, you are my brother, you are my friend, you are my knowledge, you are my wealth, you are everything divine. Thank you for this food. May we ever grow strong, healthy and happy in your service.*

Pausing afterwards in silence felt profound. As a family, we shared stillness. I often went more deeply into myself in those few minutes of grace than in a long meditation. I felt gratitude for our children and the teaching in those moments—uncluttered and satiated.

Learning also comes through observation. Bill and I led a disciplined life. Daily meditation, philosophy groups, yoga and a vegetarian diet were the cornerstones of our weekly routines. Bill and I did not drink any caffeine in these years. We never drank alcohol. We tried to resolve all tensions through meditation, work and taking care of others. Unlike myself, Bill's style also was to confront whatever realities he needed to address to clear out confusion. Didi asked us to teach meditation and philosophy at the ashram when she left town for India. Bill refused because of the confusion at the ashram. He decided to teach at our home. We gathered a group for meditation and the study of Patanjali's *Yoga Sutras*. The boys were ready for bed when everyone came. They watched a bit of TV while we meditated and partway through our discussion came up for hugs and went to bed. Our meditations were good, the house was calm and we could carry on our work.

I was able to pull away from my sense of obligation to the teachers in orange cloth. Their need to have us take care of them was real. They were dependent on the good will of others, but I began to be more protective of my children and my time. When Didiji returned in the summer, I spent less time with her. It was a challenge to resist her, and I had to argue with myself to stay away. Her presence had a kind of magnetic pull that I attributed to her daily chanting of mantras, creating a spinning vortex that spread out around her. When I rode my bike I struggled not to turn the wheel toward the ashram. I argued with myself, with her, the whole time. She adjusted to her solitude by planting a small herb garden, focusing on cooking, eating less Indian-style fatty foods, and taking short walks. I finally relented and told her that I needed her to learn the degree to which loneliness is a problem for us in the States. Taking care of her aloneness was not my sole responsibility. It was unrealistic. Learning to deal with aloneness is learning to live in America and part of understanding who we are. Taking advantage of my feeling of aloneness was not fair of her either. She agreed. I was seeking to put boundaries on what I could give.

My boys needed me. Bill and I both tried to witness them closely, see who they were and mirror them back to themselves. Teaching them to believe in themselves was our main focus. I was also determined that they like one another in spite of the differences in their personalities. Our older boy, Paul, was energetic and forceful. He had a stronger build and could easily dominate Matt. Matt was quieter and never displayed aggression unless he was pressured, but he was slight and quick, and he tried to outwit Paul. Before grade school, when Paul overpowered Matt and made him cry, I would tell him, "Go back to your brother and make him happy." Before long Matt would be giggling in their bedroom.

As they got older, the conflict shifted and included their friends. Matt would feel picked on and teased. He was clever, dominating with skill, but it did not always work. I would listen when he ran in the house upset, let him wipe his face on his sleeve, and then send him back out to play, saying he had to become stronger. Talking with Paul, I would explain that he needed to become more sensitive. I explained that they were a perfect complement for each other—each other's best teacher. I could not change them. But I could teach them to watch themselves from the light of their own awareness and find the wisdom to guide themselves. I repeated the lesson often.

Describing differences in distinct ways to highlight awareness was a practice they began to develop on their own. In grade school, Paul told me that he watched the teachers isolate one African-American boy on the playground as the troublemaker. "He always gets blamed just because he's black," Paul would say clearly, with a sense of inner affirmation rather than with judgment. He was sure of what he saw. In grade school, Matt went to a basketball workshop in a neighboring town that was known for its program. By junior high, their teams excelled because they stressed the sport at early ages. He came home and said: "The coaches there use shame to push the kids to perform. In our town they encourage us." I asked him which he preferred. His answer was certain: our town.

Both boys were learning that action and behavior can be clearly defined, their own and others. And they can make distinctions that bring clarity, helping them feel secure in their perspective and in themselves. This was Bill's strength, and I tried to support him in raising the boys to be conscious and flexible because of their awareness. They did not expect life to treat them in any favored way, but instead, with their own perception and sense of self, they could find an inner security that would always be with them. I did not have that inner security.

25

Possibility is the secret heart of time.
John O'Donohue, Anam Cara

While raising the boys, I sat for long meditations late into the night or early in the mornings, stilling the restlessness that continued to plague me. I loved the new meditation room. It was my inner work space, seven feet wide and eight feet long. Bill had put a casement window in the window well for light and air, and added a fixed pane of glass by the entry door so light could come in from the adjoining room. The main room was an addition we built for the boys as they got older. The sounds in the meditation room were buffered by the thick walls, sunk deeply into the earth on the lake side of the house.

I tried to keep the restlessness in check with exercise, diet and especially by watching my speech. With Bill and the boys, I was careful. I measured my words because Bill and I could argue quickly. And I did not want to dominate the boys with language. I tried to use language to communicate clearly, and keep my frustrations to myself. This room was for that—silence, regrouping, finding a depth of calm that might finally free me from myself.

While studying for my degree in counseling, I tried to take what I learned into my marriage with Bill. When Paul was in middle school and Matt in late grade school, Bill and I found time for each other. We began taking walks around Brady Lake, talking, sorting all that we had gone through together. The most powerful tool of counseling is active listening, a way of allowing a person's speech to flow, encouraged by comments that reflect understanding. Summarizing, nudging towards an insight, occasional self-disclosure, these are all tools of active listening. Clients can begin to hear and see themselves. I was good at it, but Bill was better. He could listen to me; I felt agitated letting him speak without interjecting.

While walking together, Bill and I had plenty of time to process the details of our relationship, review our fights and differing communication styles. We often responded to what we thought we heard, rather than to what the other intended. Slowing our speech helped, but I carried anxiety that made my need to speak overwhelm my ability to listen.

It was becoming clear that while meditation had created a spacious sense of inner freedom, deep meditation also lifted me away from my embodied self. It was as though I was lifting above the twisted truck of my psyche, attempting to leave my old self behind. I was developing an expanded feeling of self not unlike the diffuse openness of a child. I felt softened and glorious, but not grounded, a term I failed to understand. When I did more fully enter my body, I felt a manic force that was agreeable to working alongside Bill, tolerating all the physical labor we had done in the name of service. Finding ways to heal is trying and subtle. Finding the wordless place and letting words touch there requires diligent patient effort.

I felt confirmed over time that my wounding started when I was a baby, because there were no words, only body memories and intense feelings. My earliest memory before the age of two years was a dissociated state of floating on the ceiling looking down at my mother and brothers.

I had to piece together some hypothesis so I could begin to hold my feelings. I alternated between work in the world—cooking, painting, remodeling houses, raising children, setting up lectures—and work in meditation going inward to a dim threshold of awareness of memories, places, and events that stunted my feeling life. I had needed to be held, and it was becoming clearer that the intimacy I had with Bill was fraught with the tension of my unmet needs. I approached these feelings very slowly. I cannot say there was any healing—maybe just some honesty. Swimming helped. Immersion in water felt like a kind of gentle holding that was missing in my body. Meditation could bring that same diffusion, as could a round of yoga postures, but after intimacy with Bill, which also calmed me, I was triggered into more restlessness. Diffuse feelings were palliative, making daily life easier, but what had never resolved in me from a young age was carried by the marriage.

Bill tolerated my early depression, the agitated states of manic restlessness, and sometimes a balanced state that he knew was not likely to last. He would tell me openly that he feared our happiness, because he knew I would sabotage it somehow. That was tough to accept, but I agreed. He withdrew and waited for me, while at the same time giving me all that he could. His love was a substratum that I could take for granted. When he went out of town, his absence was palpable. Alone with myself and the boys, the air was less substantial. At that time in our marriage, Bill was a man of few words—he spoke as needed—but he had a presence. Sometimes I wished he would speak for the sake of entertainment, distraction, just for fun, but fun with language would not come until much later after the boys were adults.

I was with an unusual person, doing unusual work, with few friends, and with children I adored and did not want to hurt in any way. I understand that we all balance many parts of our lives, but the subtle nature of my distress set me apart. My Guru set me apart. At the same time I wanted to enter life fully.

Quiet had been part of my life as a child. It felt alive. My mother used to go upstairs in the afternoon, especially in winter, to sit and say her rosary. If I were home sick from school, I'd find her in the chaise lounge in front of a window in her bedroom, her fingers moving over the brown beads. I would stand apart in the sunlight and watch the silent dust motes as I had gazed at the fleeting crayfish in the small stone pump house with my brothers. The dust motes were alive—glorying in orbits of space.

The anxiety of my childhood showed up in what my parents called "hysterics." "Night terrors" is a more current term. They started when we lived in the farmhouse, so I might have been three years old. I walked and talked in my sleep, and had a recurring dream where the thump of heavy footsteps became a large man coming up the stair outside my room. Terror would rise through me with steps that fell as certain as heartbeats. The man went from room to room and made my brothers and parents disappear one by one. I boldly pounded him on the back. The dream with its intolerable pressure ended abruptly, and I would wake up screaming uncontrollably until my mother came.

"What is it?" she asked.

She spoke quietly in the face of my hysteria. She didn't hold me, but sat on the edge of the quilted bed with her bathrobe held tight around her, her brow wrinkled.

Her presence quieted my sobs. Looking at her face in the light from the hall, I could focus on the tight curls she pinned in front of her ears each night. They were neatly contained, and safe until morning, when she would brush them out. I could not tell her the dream.

I was not more than six when I saw the forms of snakes hanging from two walls opposite my bed. I held quiet at first, and slowly determined that I was awake. Then I shrieked. My mother appeared in the door, the light from the hall framing her.

"What is it, darling?" She sat on the edge of my bed.

I pointed. She looked and turned back to me. "There is nothing."

"They are there."

"There is nothing there."

"But I see them."

"What do you see?"

"Snakes." She did not turn to look again. Then I saw a large mouse, the same smoky gray color as the snake, under my dresser.

"There's a mouse under my dresser." I felt the bed shift as her weight lifted. She went to the dresser and turned her head sideways to look underneath it. Her night robe fell open. She pulled it shut, and leaned in to sit again.

"No, there is nothing there."

Her voice began to soothe me, although my vision was unchanged. The snakes were cloudy with long mouths and tongues. They were draped over nails, or perhaps impaled, many together in clumps.

Another time I awakened with my father roughly holding my hands under cold water running full force from the bathroom faucet. I was screaming. As I watched my hands and the water, I felt calmer and became quiet. My mother stood watching from the side with thick wrinkles in her brow. My quieting was a kind of submission. I think that when I was with Bill, the quiet in our house was a mixture of comfort and repression. I called my mother and questioned her.

"I let you cry yourself to sleep when you were a baby. It tore my heart out," she finally admitted. "I would sit at the bottom of the stairs and cry with you."

"Why? Why did you do that?"

"It is what the doctors told me to do."

That was the end of the conversation. Many mothers followed that advice.

As I grew into school age, I would awaken pressed to my bed with the familiar fear, and, after waiting, it would lessen enough for me to walk to my parents' room. I'd knock lightly and then open the door, the dream compelling me to see if they were there. My mother lay nearer to the door. My father was a large hillside of blanket that never awoke or shifted. I would feel a sense of complete dread that made me stand still, but Mom would speak some word softly to help me approach the bed. The horsehair mattress sank with their weight, leaving a narrow rim on the edge that was set firm by the mahogany bed frame. I would lie flat on my back, perched on the wood and horsehair, and draw the edge of the sheet over me. The compressing hair made a tight sound. The wood squeaked. I moved little. It took an effort not to tip in and touch her, and not to fall on the floor. Poised there, I tried to relax. I felt the unspoken rules. Do not touch her, and do not awaken him.

Decades later, I have traced my distress back, hoping that understanding its origin would help me be free of it. With no comprehension of what *karma* I had incurred, I have only the bittersweet assurance that it was exactly *mine*. I assured my mother that my *karma* was mine so she could lessen her guilt when she saw me unhappy. The pulse of the monster's step was the pulse of the heartbeat in my ear. My worst fear walked in my own heart.

When my father separated from my mother, my brothers had already gone to college. My childhood nightmare of the loss of my family became a reality. I was left alone with my mother. Even though my parents' relationship was tenuous, we had a family structure. When it was gone, I felt abandoned, unmoored, untended. I could not perform well in school. I had no sense of purpose. I missed my father. His leaving triggered the release of a backlog of unfelt feelings that capsized my sense of self. There had been a small box of acceptable behavior: Be cheerful and stay busy. Become accomplished and show others you are worthwhile. When my dog died, no one helped me mourn. When my middle brother Chris went off to boarding school at age thirteen, no one asked if I missed him, or if he missed us. When my parents fought coldly or loudly, I carried the shame of incomprehension. Nothing was explained, as if nothing had happened. Emotional neglect destroyed my ability to cope; I entered adult life crippled with anxiety and fear.

I have read recently of Siberia, where the mouths of the rivers are in the Arctic. When the spring thaws begin south of the Arctic in the Western Russian Republic, the frozen mouth creates a backlog of water, turning Siberia into a soggy land. I was like that land. I was shy and emotionally boxed in. Twelve years after my father left, my Guru opened my inner life and helped me thaw. In the beginning with him, silence was enough—mantra, his voice, the sounds of Sanskrit spoken in lecture, rang inside, softening me with quiet implosions, waking me from the inside. As I thawed from the inside, my mouth remained as if frozen and my emotional life waterlogged. Eventually I would have to integrate my feelings with language, but it was a long, slow process.

26

The sun is the power of the center.
Deng Ming-Dao

"What do you think of that verse? All is painful or not-painful? *Klista aklistah?*"

Kanta Didi was a good teacher of the *Yoga Sutras* of Patanjali. She was patient with us and reviewed the verses from the previous sessions thoroughly. We used a version with commentary by I.K. Taimni, a Quest Book publication. Kanta Didi's explanations were helpful.

"Why would he say this? All experience of the five modes of thought is either painful or not-painful?" she continued.

She had been teaching the first few verses of the first chapter for months. Bill and I met with a small group and had long, deep meditations after which I kept my eyes closed while she spoke.

"Okay then, why do we need to detach?"

I wanted to hear her answer. She put things simply.

"Because pleasure comes from the self, not from experience." At this point she lifted her brow and smiled. Of course we knew the answer. But it felt like a harsh teaching.

"Didi, I understand," I finally spoke. "This is really difficult to comprehend."

"Yes," she agreed. "You see how intelligent Patanjali is here. He gets our attention. The truth needs to be understood. This is why we need detachment to practice. Detach from the sensual experience that will end in loss. Nothing stays the same forever. Seek inwardly to the stable self. The self is the fullness of knowledge, consciousness and existence."

The first chapter was challenging. I was baffled by Patanjali's list of five possible modes of thought. I did not understand the relevance. The five modes were right knowledge, wrong knowledge, fancy, sleep and memory. Didiji reviewed them again and again until I had them committed to memory.

She would visit other communities throughout the States and use our ashram as her home base. We met as often as three times a week. Sometimes I went alone and Bill stayed home with the boys.

Bill and I met with other teachers at this time. It was part of our continued need to keep some separation from our teachers. We had been hurt by the problems at our ashram. One swami, introduced by yoga friends in the nearby town of Hudson, offered a message of simple observation. I hoped to gain help from a different approach to practice. I needed more than a blissful diffusion of spirit: I felt caught between heaven and hell. I needed a middle ground that could place me lightly in my life. This teacher's basic message was beguilingly simple: There is nowhere to go and nothing to prove. Simply witness, accept, and notice how all things change.

My plan was to enlist his help resolving the tension I felt with Bill, so I cooked the swami elaborate Indian meals with fresh ground spices and *ghee*. I chanted mantras as I stirred the pots, careful to include all the details of not tasting the food before it was offered, estimating salt— always more than you think. Vegetables soak up salt the way our skin loves the sun. I rolled the *chapatis* perfectly round and puffed each one, coating them with fresh butter. The swami was the only guest. In saffron robes, he sat on the floor. He tasted the selection of the aromatic food, leaning forward, making small animal noises of pleasure, and then looked at me.

"What do you want from me?"

"I want your help."

I was heartened that he caught on so quickly. If he could read my food, maybe he could read us. He did. He taught Bill to observe, slowed him down and helped him feel more. With Bill's innate capacity to focus and execute whatever he willed, he understood and applied the process. He was capable of feeling the emotion prompting his actions. Bill's intensity coupled with mine made me feel unsafe. So this helped. I pleaded with him to be the first one to change, because he could. I was going to be slower. I thought that if I could feel calm and safe with Bill, if we could avoid escalating, then I could heal myself.

In retrospect, I can see we were sorting out right knowledge, from wrong knowledge, fancy, sleep and memory. The teaching of witnessing pain without reacting was valuable. Knowing deeply that all things will change is a helpful way to hold the difficulties of a marriage. Discerning when the memory of events is more powerful than the event at hand and overshadows our perception is extremely valuable and tough to discern. I could see that anxiety was a partner in clouding my perception. Anxiety made me seek out the comfort and ease of meditation and the release of a good hatha practice so I could lift the cloud cover that descended upon me. Fancy or imagination did not seem to be a problem for me. Or if it were, I was unaware of its power. Sleep is obvious. We need it, and it comes by itself to help us restore our equilibrium. Guruji told us frequently that the deep meditation stage of *samadhi* was simply the stage of deep sleep but with full wakefulness—a profound restoration of the memory of our real self.

Eventually, this swami proved to be quite different from our Guru. He revealed himself as someone who practiced self-forgiveness, rather than discipline. We saw him accept generous donations for preaching an easy path. My most profound experience came from learning to sit more lightly, with less emotional investment. During one of the swami's lectures, after I had gleaned the essence of his talk, I let go of the meaning of his words and felt consumed in flames of heat. Rather than going beyond the body, the body itself felt transformed by a roar of light. I could barely hear his voice which had become wordless, as if he were sitting on the far side of a bonfire. After the lecture, he and Bill debated a point.

"So, Margot, what is your opinion?" the swami asked me.

"Of what?"

"Our argument? You can share something with us?"

I had none; I could not distinguish between their positions. The fire had been purifying, somehow an embodied experience, but nothing else. Nothing compared with the careful way Kanta Didi was teaching us verses.

At this point, I was teaching a few yoga classes a week and lecturing in the community, as the opportunity arose. I was one of a handful of teachers in the area. We still saw our Guru annually, but building temples and schools throughout India and Ontario eclipsed the small activity of our ashram. When we were together, he lowered his voice and spoke with me.

"Do not expect others to do what you have done."

I waited for him to say more.

"Teach *satsang*, not an actual practice."

I understood. *Satsang* was the inspiration we feel in good company. *Sat* means pure or truth. *Sanga* is company. On the paths of Buddhism and yoga, pure company is a key to changing one's life.

"Make them feel some upliftment in coming together with you. They will find their own way. They will be inspired."

In these few words, my Guru affirmed me, and placed himself squarely as mine. As I would expect from a good father or mother, he was observing my changes. He was not restricting Bill and me from seeing other teachers. He approved of my personal practice, which was gaining ground, and he supported my attempts to teach others, even though I was not yet stable in my own self. He was leaving room for us to develop without restraining us. He would also say:

"You will teach what you are, so become fully established in practice, and then you will give divine radiance to all."

Bill's process was different from mine. I tried to find a way to move on, without friction. My inner friction was enough. Because he felt secure in himself, Bill had no hesitation expressing frustrations. He was disturbed by how finances were handled at our ashram and rejected the pressure to find another building that would include a temple. Our teachers favored including the Indian community, with the idea of a larger building that would house worship. They were used to living upon donations that came naturally with deities and worship. Guruji and Didiji flatly refused the idea of fee-for-service, implying that they did not see how meditation, philosophy and some hatha classes would elicit sufficient donation. Bill as an accountant was conscious that their style meant that a few would be burdened. We had been asked to donate money in addition to our hours of labor—somehow always overlooked. Bill wanted a place for meditation and philosophy, without a cultural or religious focus.

Rather than sorting out our differences and finding ways to move on, Didiji blamed numerology.

"The ashram house number of 1246 is a number 'four,' a 'hot' number that causes disputes," she said.

She told us this more than once as a way to summarize our problems. "Okay for Will." Guruji and Didiji called Bill, "Will" when they wanted to point out the power of his will. They used this nickname with a knowing smile.

"But not our mission." No community thrives on disputes. Clearly that is the case.

Our Guru sent this letter in response to Bill's confusion about how to create a healthy separation from his teacher. How does one not fuse with the will of the teacher if you feel as if you are one soul?

Feb 1 1988

Dear Bill with love and affection

Father and mother are eternal and not changeable. Wherever you will be my blessings will be with you in this life. There is no question of guru or ex-guru. Son and disciple have the same place. Son is the projections of body and disciple is the projection of soul.

I have an inner inclination to spread divinity in the human world. Then according to that divine plan, many seekers will get benefit from my service. The world is very vast, not small, not just Ohio. People are eager to know about and to achieve divinity everywhere and this is my vision and the aim of my life: to work for God and to spread divinity amongst mankind. I will offer my last breath for it. If you do the same thing wherever you are, even in your own house, you are fulfilling my wish.

There is one sun, one moon, one space. Whatever is one is absolute, not confined to East and West. In the same way divinity is eternal and not related to one country. Just as material science works universally, so spiritual science works everywhere. I wish to spread divinity in a scientific way and remove all barriers created by selfish people. Truth cannot be bound or limited.

If you teach even part of whatever I taught you this is my mission. Mission means idea. It is nothing but a divine idea. Its only purpose is to spread ideology. It is not to collect money. I want to spread ideology, not collect money. You are free always to come and go. I am installing a beautiful idol of Lord Rama in a temple on the ashram at Virat Nagar in India, and naturally I would like for you to be here. If you came and you wished to visit other places too that is fine. It is good to make many friends, not harmful.

So Bill if you are teaching people, you are fulfilling my wish and it is enough. My heartiest blessings are always with you and I would like to see all of you when I come in the summer. Convey my love and blessings to Margot and the children, Matthew and Paul. Remember, my boy, you will always be welcome here. Always. Please convey my love and blessing to all my nearest and dearest ones. I hope I will see you all in summer. Rest is okay and blissful.

May God bless you all; it is my heartiest wish.

Yours own, V. Bawra

So that was it. He was ours and we were his. All of us the rays of one sun—inextricably linked.

27

Now, the removal of suffering in nutshell form.
Kapila

"Come to India. I'll give you a name there," he said, as if continuing an earlier conversation.

It had been a few years since Guruji had invited me to make a trip to India. Bill had gone soon after we met our Guru. The children were too young for me to leave them. Matt and Paul were now ten and thirteen. This trip would require a separation of five weeks—a big leap forward to overcome my fear of loss.

I had been feeling comfortable with him, as comfortable as I ever felt. Entering his room in the afternoon at the Kent ashram, I found him with the thick English encyclopedia open on his folded knees.

"What does 'numinous' mean?" He peered at me over his reading glasses.

I was flattered and surprised each time he consulted me. I did not feel expert in English myself. I did my best. "Well, it's a word meaning pertaining to spiritual feelings of expansion."

"Let's see." He turned the pages slowly finding the 'N's. I listened to the rustling. It was quiet in the ashram.

Our ashram was quieter than those in Canada or England, where the Indian community was more involved, but he kept returning annually and delivered his series of lectures. Without an endless stream of visitors, Guruji had time to study in the afternoons. I was able to observe his habits. When he first arrived, I would bring over my dictionaries, an English encyclopedia, a Hindi/English dictionary, and a Sanskrit one with partially blurred type that made it difficult to distinguish among the Sanskrit letters of the Devanagari script. Guruji studied mostly English texts while he was with us.

I had not been to the ashram in India. I wasn't thinking about it. I wanted a new name.

"'Nu-min-us,'" he began slowly, reading. "'Pertaining to a numen.'" He smiled at me. "Not helpful. Second one says, 'Spiritually elevated or elevating; mysterious and awe-inspiring.' Okay."

"Guruji?"

"Yes." He looked up at me, hearing a shift in my tone.

"Can I have a new name?"

Five years ago, he had answered me with, "Well, I have given that some thought, but I am not satisfied."

He sat forward so that he was no longer leaning against the wall and shifted his legs as he turned to face me. I was sitting with my legs folded off to one side, leaning on my hand.

"The only name I have come up with is 'Gargi.' You know the story in the *Upanishads* about her?"

"No."

"She was a great thinker. In old India, people debated about spiritual matters and whoever won the debate was the one the others would follow. She could out-debate any man. Only one time was she defeated in argument, and that man became her husband." Pausing, he looked at me and wrinkled up his nose as if smelling something sour. "I don't think that is a good name for you."

I felt flattered because Gargi was smart. But I could feel Guruji's implication: I argued with Bill. I did not want to be dominated by him, even though he saw more clearly and argued more rationally than I could. I had married the one man who could defeat me in argument, but, unlike Gargi, I could not admit it. Bill and I were in a stalemate. I wanted to argue with him until he was defeated—a decidedly irrational problem.

I agreed with Guruji, but I had no reply. I refrained from further conversation with my Guru, retreating to my safer habit of silence.

I had not spoken with him further about my name. Other, newer followers were getting names without asking. He had an easy time changing one woman's name from Mary to Mira, a poet and a mystic. It occurred to me that maybe my name could be changed from Margot to *Marga,* which means "the path." But the drawback of that was obvious: I might remain on the path and never reach the goal. I was on a trajectory that seemed not to end. The psychotic break I had in early adulthood had a nice ironic twist to it. I feared not being normal, and yet I'd set out with

158

extraordinary determination on a non-ordinary path. Adding an Indian name might help shore up my identity.

Getting a new name was a crowning idea for me. So much of what I had done to help myself felt piecemeal, but with a new name I expected a smoother ride, a more stable identity and a kind of erasure of the past, as if the blackboard of my childhood could be neatly cleaned with the fresh water of a new vibration. As part of seeking a spiritual identity, I wanted more removal from my family of origin. My father had little good to say about his mother, my namesake. It was my mother who preferred the convention of family names. I was the only granddaughter on my father's side. I received my heritage through my paternal grandmother's full name, first, maiden and married, French, Welsh, and English. A new name might help me escape my legacy.

India was an appealing destination. In India I could go to the main ashram at Virat Nagar, north of Delhi, in Haryana. An ashram is a place of rest, a shelter, but also a busy place, with a schedule of prayers and meals. Virat Nagar was a large campus of residences and meeting halls.

Most of my experience with Guruji had been at our modest Kent ashram. Because of its location, we could never advertise properly since the house was not zoned for education. Parking was insufficient and the addition of handicapped accessible washrooms, handicapped access and firewalls was beyond our budget. So the house became more of a rectory. Our Guru continued to make annual visits from India. He would stay at our ashram, and lecture there or at nearby churches. At the homes of people in the Indian community, Didiji would offer *puja* or *hoven* before Guruji's discourse, or before recitation of the *Ramayana*.

To further complicate the settling of our ashram in Kent, it had been established in 1986, the same year that a murder took place among the Hare Krishna group in New Brindaban, West Virginia. The suspect was said to have fled to Kent. For his afternoon or evening walk, our Guru, who had a long white beard, would stroll the sidewalks near the high school wearing an orange skirt and top. We heard later that his unusual appearance had prompted the children to tell their parents who had demanded formal hearings with the staff regarding potential threats to their children.

To bring people to see Guruji, I made a phone list and drew up flyers to post around town. These efforts produced varying results but the work continued. The Hindu culture could be disarming and confusing with unspoken rules, first felt, later clarified, such as acknowledging the altar with a bow, not sitting with one's back to the alter, not placing holy books on the floor, even if you are sitting on the floor, bowing *pranam* or touching the feet of the orange-robed swamis rather than shaking hands, not straightening one's legs toward a teacher in lecture, or the altar, because it is a sign of disrespect. Those kinds of things were tricky to catch onto and were not given out as typed instructions. There were hints, mild admonishments, and a kind of breaking in period where the uninitiated were brought into the fold or not.

Our center ran more smoothly when Shivdas came to live there in 1988. He shared the cost with others who occupied the larger two rooms upstairs. We were able to make the ashram self-supporting. Bills, insurance, and property taxes on our mortgage-free structure were easily covered. Shivdas was a devotee as well as a resident, so he took care of our teachers, fetching vegetables and fresh *chapati* flour, chauffeuring them to the functions outside of the ashram. Shivdas also cut the vegetables so that Didi could easily spice and cook them.

By afternoon, Shivdas had the vegetables chopped and rinsed, ready for the hot oil and spices. Didi had the *dal* simmering on the stove for the evening meal. The thump, roll and dry-frying of *chapatis*, done just before eating, had not yet begun. Didi and a few visitors were studying or resting.

Returning home, I told Bill what I had in mind and asked him to remain home with the boys. Then I could concentrate on my practice in India in peace, knowing the boys were cared for. Bill was listening.

"I hear you," he hesitated. "Are you stable enough?"

He supported my decision, but he was concerned that without my routines, I might feel unstable in India.

"I have to go. I need you to stay with the boys so I can concentrate on going inward."

Bill complied.

The next day I returned to our little ashram ready to tell my teacher about my ticket date. Inside the back door of the kitchen, I kicked off my sandals alongside others randomly scattered under the flour bin. I walked onto the sky-blue carpet of the living area, bowed on my knees at the altar of pictures of deities, some pressed at odd angles into donated frames, and tucked my legs under me while nodding greetings to a few disciples seated in the room. They had come to share in the afternoon meal and would stay for the evening lecture.

160

One of them, Evelyn, turned to me and said, "Margot, I heard you are going to India this winter! Well, so am I!"

I looked directly in to her blue eyes and tried to hide my real feelings. "Oh, when are you going?"

Evelyn was full of joy at her news, just as she always was, whether about her children, or her husband's job, or their new house. She failed to notice my flat tone. She went on with complete enthusiasm, "January!"

My first experience of Evelyn had been back in the early days of hosting in our small home by the lake. I recalled her request for salt for her children, used to TV's in all their rooms, and for peanut butter and jelly, instead of the rice that serves millions of the underfed—blessed by the guru and sufficient for my boys. Yes, my lofty resentment had not suffered any diminishment. My life was about work, not play. Frank and Evelyn had bought new living room furniture and donated to the ashram their old popcorn-butter stained set from their family movie-viewing room. She would ask me why I had not asked Bill for new furniture for our house. I did not think about new furniture. I was not an only child, as it turned out Evelyn and Frank both were. I was the youngest of three in close successions and used to hand-me downs of boys' clothing. They treated their three children like three "only" children. I was impatient with Evelyn. And I had been enjoying the idea of going to India!

I took a slow breath. "Wow, that's great. What dates?"

"Well, just in time for Guruji's birthday and then the traveling that he does with the group afterwards."

I calculated. That gave me barely one week to adjust to India and the ashram without her. Evelyn continued talking. I decided to adjust but I retreated inward, nursing my conundrum, silently talking to my God, my soul, my nameless one, saying, "How could you? This is both incomprehensible and perfect. Could there be a more perfect unsolicited way for me to confront myself than by sending with me the one person in the world with whom I am happy to spend three seconds before finding something else to do? It is not possible she holds up a mirror to what I cannot see in myself. She is foreign." That was it—a pure unexamined prejudice.

Over the next week, Bill observed my preparations closely. I needed some clothes for India. He watched as I sliced the blue material with the loud crunch of sewing scissors, crawling on the floor as I made my way around the pattern from Jo-Ann fabrics, shaping my own version of a

161

punjabi suit: a long top with loose pants that pulled in at the ankles. My head was bowed in determination, and some blocking of him. He was still not sure I should go alone. He knew travel in India was overwhelming. He finally spoke:

"I'll come too."

"No, I need you to stay with the boys." Going between the sewing machine and the ironing board, I worked methodically, and stubbornly refused to shift my position.

"I've earned time with my Guru."

Bill relented again. He agreed.

The *punjabi* suits were important to me. Guruji had asked me to wear a sari for the occasional celebrations in America, but I found I did not like them. I am almost six feet tall. Indian women are closer to five feet. A sari consists of a length of material six feet long by forty-five inches wide that is wrapped and folded around one's middle with one end tossed over the left shoulder. A blouse of matching color and a plain cotton skirt with pull ties at the waist are worn underneath. Shorter women have a good eleven inches of material to tuck into the cotton slip that is tied securely about the waist. With my height I had maybe an inch and half of tucked material at the waist. A reason not to wear a sari—though I was told I could put an "extension" on the top where it tucks in.

Early on with Guruji, as a young nursing mother, I had agreed to wear one. An Indian friend generously offered one of hers, holding it to me in two arms as if in sacrament. She showed me how to measure the wrapping and folding using hands and arm lengths, tucking and lifting. Once robed, l had three options for sitting on the floor: knees wide, knees to one side, and knees up. Legs could never be pointed out when in the presence of the teacher. But with a wriggling baby in my lap and an active toddler tugging at me, I had to move. Every time I left the room to nurse Matt or check on Paul playing in another room, I had to negotiate with the sari. I found a pushing-off technique: rear end up first to lengthen the sari and then untangle it from the feet—often with the toddler on my hip so he would not fuss while waiting. Then straighten up and walk.

By the end of the evening, fatigued by these maneuvers, and intent upon putting the little one to bed, I pushed off the floor with my hand, catching one end of the sari under my ankle. Standing straight would plunge the sari to the floor. So I crouched and clutched the bulk of the great unraveling, shuffling to a back bedroom.

162

This experience became the foundation of my personal code of "no saris." Then I made it a principle that was good for me and for other American followers. That unyielding side was like Gargi.

I had a strange kind of pride. Call it reversal, stubborn refusal to conform in ways that were unique to myself. A kind of identity woven with threads of rebellion, but in this case a position well-bolstered by men like Gandhi who wore hand-woven cotton from India as a boycott of the British stranglehold of India, and my Guru himself, whose concession to civilization was to add a simple rectangle of a skirt to his loincloth.

Living with Bill, I rarely shopped for clothes. From childhood, I disliked shopping, and I was not good at finding bargains. I found myself failing to even buy boots for Matt when he was two—I awoke from my self-denial suddenly appalled that I had been remiss. Wandering into the lingerie and nightwear aisles at Dillard's I found myself sobbing dry tears of longing while handling pastel fabrics. I turned my unyielding nature into a personal ascetic code. Getting a new name in Sanskrit would be a way of discovering more of who I was or could become as I continued my self-denial and practice.

I had often wondered about the didi's names, like *Pragya*, and *Divya*. What was the difference between the layer of truth that shone like light, *pragya,* and the lamp of devotion, *divya?* Both were light. What was it like to feel the vibration of those names? Maybe it was the philosophy again calling me—my true love of ideas. What meaning was yet to come from my adult life choices? My sense of pride in treading any ordinary path was gone when I bartered cigarettes in the mental institution, where the symbol of a glass house and throwing stones was lost. The experience cemented a commitment to create a life on my own terms. I entrenched myself in a pride of living with less, and in wanting something more that may mean nothing to others.

Bill was not getting in my way. He supported me and he had patience with time resolving most things. He was not seeking a name. Bill had received his name in meditation on his first trip to India. He received personal teachings in meditation because he had the capacity to hear the inner teachings. Ironically, it upset him. He wanted his teachings from the mouth of the guru sitting in front of him.

Lacking a strong sense of self, I wanted a name that might sustain my link with the sublime. I wanted a name that might shine a steady light on my path within the ineffable grand scheme of things. One Indian man

163

told me the reason a name can take a while to come forth is that the guru has to see one's inclinations after they emerge through practice. Well, now it was time to go to India to receive one. I must have reached the necessary spiritual maturity and readiness to blossom into the full-bodied soul I hoped to become.

28

The birds have vanished in the sky,
and now the last cloud drains away.
We sit together, the mountain and me,
until only the mountain remains.
          Li Po

"Do you want that jelly?

"Can I have that sugar packet?"

Crackers, butter, cookies sealed in cellophane all disappeared into Jyoti Didi's widening orange-cotton shoulder bag.

While on the transatlantic flight to Holland, which was the longer stretch of our journey, the shorter was from Holland to Delhi, Jyoti Didi kept leaning forward and turning her round face to find her traveling companions.

"Didiji, what is this for?" I thought the amounts were small, the trouble of carrying them a nuisance out-weighing value.

"You never know what we will need when we travel in India," she said, taking the packets gently from my hand.

I settled in with yet another cup of hot coffee that sent me chanting every lengthy Vedic mantra I knew while heaving my body forward to ease my back, and back to ease my legs. I had left the boys with Bill and with the jubilance and constancy of many years of mothering trailing behind—no regrets. I had left my graduate studies, all completed except an internship.

I met up with Jyoti Didi and other friends of the Canadian Mission so that we could arrive in Delhi together. Traveling north from the airport toward Chandigarh was tiring. Now there is a fast train, then only buses and taxis for the last swerving five-hour journey on the ground. The road north from Delhi had no center median in that year, 1992. So the Indian tendency was to use the whole road in both directions with a hand on the horn at all times—calibrating acceleration and braking within the breadth of the road, avoiding the space taken by slower water-buffalo carts and bicycles, swerving past non-moving obstacles of potholes, piles of rubble and resting cows, leaving just the passage needed for pedestrians and on-coming vehicles.

My teaching would begin before Evelyn arrived—the teaching of the ego. I had experienced in meditation that it is possible for the ego to let go of its attachments, rest in reflection, and know itself as *aham*, pure I-am. Mostly we do not feel our I-am, we experience ourselves in constant thought and miss the feeling of resting in our simple existence. I tried to find that safety within myself, and despite my residual fears, I tried to be a haven for my children. A word in Sanskrit that I loved hearing in my teacher's voice was *dhaam*. When he said *dhaam* I felt its meaning, shelter, a place of rest. More than ashram, the campus of buildings and fields where I would visit, *dhaam* is a place where the soul sinks into rest, as I felt when my children were asleep, and the air in the house was still, rising and shimmering with dust motes. If something besides a new name called me to India it was the hope of deepening that feeling.

I arrived at my Guru's ashram shortly before the afternoon meal, served in a room outside his sleeping chamber. Near the entrance, I found a place to sit cross-legged between two didis. The women monks were dressed for the cold, bundled in assorted orange sweaters and orange coats. I have longer legs than most, so I tucked them in tightly. I was in my homemade, light blue *punjabi* suit. It seemed to be a quiet color back in the States. Here it felt very blue. I also wore a blue fleece on top. Everyone was wearing orange, except the men, the temple priests called *pundits*, who wore white with gray wool shawls. About fifteen people were seated on the floor around one wide square of cloth. Guruji was ladling my food. He was used to me, thank God. He raised his eyebrows.

"Enough?"

"*Bas tikhai, anji,*" I replied almost inaudibly. "Enough, okay, yes." I had spoken all my Hindi.

Looking around the room, I saw that the chamber was set up for small audiences. Guruji had a daybed behind him where he could rest or sit. Along one wall were two bookcases with glass doors, books neatly lined and piled askew behind the dusty glass, and behind me a boxy TV set on a narrow wooden table. A straw mat barely disguised the cold concrete under my ankles. To conserve a little warmth, I flattened the tops of my feet, and tucked the soles under my calves.

"Yogurt?" he then asked. He was wearing an orange wool ski cap and an orange sweatshirt over his cotton cloth.

I nodded again and shifted my weight forward up on my knees to take the plate he was holding out. After passing it into my hands, he then carefully replaced the lid on each of the pots. I had been one of the last to come in.

Guruji sat at the edge of the length of the cloth with large pots widely arranged around him. To see into a pot he had tilted forward, lifting his spine, bowing his eyes. Barely within his reach was a pot of rice, one of *dal*, two *subjis*—mixed vegetables—and *chapatis*. Out to the sides beyond the pots were spread additional dishes, bowls, and spoons. Whoever sat near him passed the dishes or held the plates as he ladled carefully to each person's taste. On the mat, in front of the didis, were more pickle jars that seemed to belong to them. The didi next to me dug with a small spoon in a dark, unlabeled pickle jar, her little finger stuck out to the side. She motioned to me with her elbow while holding the spoon and the jar, a way of asking me if I wanted some. I nodded yes, feeling profoundly shy, which made me serious. Accepting a piece of pickle was monumental.

When I was through eating, I waited—my best manners. My mother taught me not to get up until everyone was finished. It had slipped my mind that Guruji liked us to rise when we were done and go wash our plates—always making room for the next person to eat. While I was sitting quietly, he motioned to me with his head. I reacted with a jerk and a lift off the ground to look for a washbasin. I followed a man down a dusty cement walkway, under the overhang of the building past a large dog lying in a corner, with a lassitude of Indian dogs that soon became familiar, and then out into an open courtyard. At the end of a gravel yard enclosed by a tall, faded-orange adobe wall, near a gate to the lane in front of the ashram, was a long washbasin with a row of seven small spigots. A soap container sat above the basin on an adobe ledge—the base of a plastic jar, cut off to make a dish, filled with dense blue soap. I watched the man near me clean his dish. I did the same. Prying soap with my fingernails, I applied it to the plate and swirled my fingers around under a thin stream of cold water. Next, my bowl and spoon. I had started to enjoy the view of the fields and sky from this vantage point when, seeing the man move away in the corner of my eye, I swiftly turned off the spigot and again followed him to a door. Inside the light was dim. Copying him, I placed my wet stainless steel plate, bowl and spoon on a drying rack below and outside a serving window to the kitchen. The kitchen was dark. The floor appeared to be thick with dust and grease—disturbingly unclean. I tried to suppress the surfacing of fear and repulsion. I knew I could be overwhelmed, so to calm myself I looked around with a curiosity that might shift my feelings.

We were standing in a dining hall, adjacent to the kitchen. Two long, narrow woven mats were laid out for sitting. The concrete floor served as the table. All of it felt foreign. The wood shutters were closed to keep out the cold. But the cement building was colder inside than outside, where the waning afternoon light had warmed the earth.

Wrapping my arms tight around me, I returned to Guruji's small bedchamber behind the room where we took our meal. Wearing his reading glasses, Guruji was absorbed in a newspaper. I settled my body on the floor by his bed, but I was not settled inside. It had been a long journey—the caffeine was still pushing me. I began to speak while he read.

"I'm not satisfied with my practice," I began. "I need to deepen, but with the demands of my children, Bill, and school, I can't maintain a deep state of meditation."

He did not look up from his paper.

"So I have left them at home and come here. What can I do?"

He remained silent, reading.

I sat waiting, not sure he had heard me.

Finally, after another minute, he looked up over his glasses, and said clearly and slowly, "Give me time," and went back to his paper.

I sighed, waited for a few breaths and decided that the time would not be that evening. I went out.

No one was around. Not wanting to return to my room, I set out on the dusty lane to the main gate where we had entered. Our car had passed a temple area by the entrance, about a quarter of a mile from the rooms and kitchen. The lane went straight between large garden plots. Long white radishes grew on one side, their tops pushing out of the soil. I had seen them at dinner, thick as carrots lying lengthwise off the sides of the plates. On the other side of the lane, wheat grew catching the breezes off the high plateau where the ashram stood overlooking the dried riverbed of the Saraswati River. The lane was lined with slender eucalyptus trees, providing shade in the hot summer, but in the cooler air a romantic feel of height and shimmering light. At the end of the lane were the aging buildings of the original ashram, rusty red with dirt, a display of the blotchy weathering of many rainy seasons. The larger buildings of the old ashram housed an orphanage.

A few days into my stay, I set out in the morning for the temple and found that I was following behind Guruji. His morning ritual of *samadhi* and bath ended before breakfast with a walk to pay his respects to the deities at the temple, where he bowed down in *pranam*. I stayed behind him, enjoying the sight of him walking swiftly in his wooden sandals. I focused on them, placing his feet firmly in my mind—a brisk, moving meditation practice. I walked freely a hundred feet behind him as he strode the quarter mile to the temple, both wanting his attention and not wanting the intrusion and confusion of my shy feelings. We passed the orphanage school, where the dirt yard was filled with children in burgundy and white uniforms. Guruji paused at the steps of the Sita Ram temple without turning, which let me catch up with him. He began to address me.

"There is a difference between *aham* and *aham-kara*." I was startled to hear him speak as though we were in mid-conversation. It felt as if he had been more aware of me behind his back than I of him in front of me.

"*Aham* is the pure I-am." He continued. He slipped off his sandals and bounded up the steps. My shoes took longer to slip off. The marble was cold under my feet.

"*Aham-kara* means the I-am has fences." I followed him as he walked rapidly to the left of the idols. I wanted to linger there and observe their unnatural state. The life-like Greco-Roman style of drawing had made it to paintings. The picture of Rama as a deity was rife with human muscles and bones, though his skin was blue. The monkey-god Hanuman was convincingly life-like as a drawing, a human body with monkey whiskers and round devotional eyes. Not so with the idols. The proportion of the idols' heads to their bodies matched those of a toddler or an upright chipmunk—credibly not adult and inhuman. They were stiff, very convincingly marble, and perhaps that was the idea—these were self-conscious representations of the abstract formless eternal divinity that expresses in life and in all form. The formless God incarnates into human form to teach when the teaching is needed. Sita and Rama were displayed in a curved enclosure within the temple. As we went around behind them, we rounded the wall. Coming by the front, we passed the temple priest sitting on the altar, three times, circumambulating with Guruji in front and myself behind. Rama and his consort Sita stood with their right hands open in blessing. The temple priest's duty was to bathe and dress the idols each day. They were fully dressed, *dhoti* and sari, in bright shiny blue and silver cloth; white marble faces blushed with paint, unblinking eyes, lined in black, looking straight ahead.

"*Aham-kara* and *asmita* are the same—the ego is bound in identification."

Identification is how we are bound in ignorance and pain. We have a small identity that feels as if it serves us but it truly limits us. Guruji was giving me a teaching to guide my inner work. The time had arrived.

We stood in front of the idols and cupped our hands for the temple priest, with the left palm held under the right. The priest dipped a tiny spoon in a copper pot of water within which yellow and orange marigold petals were floating. He dropped a spoonful of water in Guruji's palm first. Guruji sipped it. When I received mine, I quickly decided that it was not fit to drink—not worth hazarding dysentery for a blessing—and dashed the cool water over my third eye and into the hairline. We held out our palms again, and in them, with two fingertips and a thumb, the priest popped a few balls of white sugar the size of wild blueberries.

I walked away and stopped by the sidewall of the temple to look back at the idols. Guruji stood praying in Sanskrit with his hands folded. He sounded his prayers quickly and in high pitch. My legs felt weak and I slipped onto the floor. Closing my eyes, I sank in to a deep meditation. I felt safe, all of a sudden, sinking into the shelter of the temple, the teaching, finally arriving within myself.

I did not hear my teacher come near, only his voice next to me.

"I'll be going out. You stay here and have a chat with Mum and Dad."

29

Eventually the chickpea will say to the cook,
"Boil me some more...I can't do this myself."
Rumi

Guruji began lectures. The first, before breakfast, was in Hindi for the whole community. It was held in an underground hall, a round room sunk in the earth to keep it cool in summer. The lecture given after breakfast was in English, given in the room where we ate, adjacent to Guruji's sleeping room. A few others joined us, but the discourse was for me.

The underground lecture hall was called the *pravachan mandir*. It was a temple for meditation and philosophy; there were no pictures of deities or idols. The only allowable ritual in this setting was the twenty-four chanting of the *Ram* mantra done as a way of honoring the inspiring force of knowledge. The inspiring force is the place from which all life comes; we can understand it as the heat, light and power of the sun. There is poetry from Tulsidas' *Ramayana* that describes the sound: "The vibration of *Ram* is like a lamp in the mouth that lights the inner and outer worlds."

The corridor into the hall sloped downhill, and daylight diminished as the space opened into the round chamber, large enough for hundreds, but we were only twenty or thirty. There was ample room near the back where I could sit inconspicuously against the wall. The blue walls were streaked from leaks during the rainy season. My feeling, sitting there, was that the earth was cradling us. In the dim light, the walls appeared to be a deep earthy hue, as though night has fallen and the dome of the sky would soon light with stars.

Guruji sat in the front, the farthest point from the door, closely surrounded by a group of didis with notebooks and tape recorders. As I meditated during the Hindi lectures, I heard the devices stop and click as the tapes ran out and they flipped the cassettes. I was surprised from time

171

to time to hear Guruji speak a few words of English. I was starved for English besides "have you taken something?" a polite phrase that means "have you eaten?" I was also greeted with *Jai Virat*, meaning "all glory to the divine source."

I was on a fast from my language. I had practiced fasting for ten years: on Tuesdays, even when we traveled, I refrained from all food but fruit and milk. While restraining from eating normally, I became more aware of boredom, needs for distraction, of fatigue, which muscles were used to complete tasks. I was acutely aware of the focus of mind required for action. I learned to confront myself and my cravings, and to observe my struggle. Here in India, my practice yielded a different kind of fruit. I took my skill in fasting into fasting from language. Other than Guruji's one lecture a day, I heard a few phrases of English as people spoke with me. During the Hindi lecture, I relaxed into the sound of Guruji's voice, which put me into deep meditation. When he chanted any Sanskrit verses, or verses from the *Ramayana,* the vibration of his words sent me almost beyond the realm of hearing, a profound response to words that conveyed no meaning to my conscious mind.

After a few days of coming to the hall and sitting quietly to meditate, Guruji sprinkled in a few words of English, "The *brahma chakra* at the top of the head is actually a few inches above, and it is very tiny, like the eye of the needle. Focus there." I knew from his teaching that this place was above the ego. It was the source of the ego, the place where our inner father and mother, or consciousness and energy, sit together. He had worked these two sentences into the flow of knowledge offered in Hindi. The meaning seared through me. It was as if he had poured some experience directly into me. The subtle *brahma chakra* in the space above my head was suddenly as clear as if it were in front of my eyes, having definition, shape, and feeling. At a point about six inches above me, I found the eye of the needle and placed my mind there, an absorbing focal point of concentration.

Each morning after breakfast in the small room where we gathered near his bedchamber, Guruji gave me my personal English lecture. He started by carefully asking me to review what I had learned the day before. The first time, I replied with a quick summary. He scolded me saying, "Not like a schoolgirl, what did you learn, really?"

On the second morning I had prepared myself for the question.

"What did you learn yesterday?"

Once again I recited a summary, just as I had done the day before, but I had prepared myself by saying the verses over and over in my head until I could feel something. I had no idea what the something was.

"Very good," he said, clearly acknowledging the difference, and then resumed teaching me from the ninth chapter of the *Bhagavad Gita.*

"This is the royal knowledge, the royal secret, *raja guhyam,* easy to practice and imperishable." The sound of the word, *guhyam,* vibrated in my chest, creating ease, which inspired a love for the teaching to come, as though expecting a friend to visit.

"This knowledge is for great souls." With these words, I was flattered even though I knew they were Krishna's words to Arjuna. My teacher spoke them softly, with affection.

The next day, after a chilly January night, I sat in the sun on Guruji's back porch, enjoying a moment of warmth. The porch was a small slab of concrete covered with woven straw where I was sitting with my elegantly folded ankles pressing into the floor. The concrete felt completely smooth through the light cushion of my socks. A few local visitors were sitting on the porch with me. Educated and well dressed, the men wore Western style pants and coats, while the women were dressed in saris with decorative borders on shawls over their winter coats. They were speaking in Hindi with Guruji, who suddenly turned to me and said in precise English:

"You must stop blaming others. You have your own that you must take care of. Be aware—it is up to you and you alone."

As he finished I saw a look of surprise intermixed with pleasure on the visitors' faces. Clearly, they understood that I had been shamed.

Yet, I felt fine—shocked, but somehow happy. I knew he was showing me something I could not see myself. This was the burden I was holding onto with Bill. I could never set it aside. I carried a tendency to blame. It was a momentary accounting. Bill was not there to stimulate me to place the burden on him, so I was free for the moment. My attention went immediately to sitting with the additional challenge of feeling okay in spite of the opinion of others. I had been busted.

A moment later he was scolding the others in Hindi. Their look of pleasure vanished.

I returned to my room, where it was colder than outside. By then, my bed had a feeling of home. The bed consisted of a wooden palette layered with several cotton pads, covered with a cloth and a quilt made of cotton batting. The pillow was unyielding, thick with more cotton batting. I had found an extra quilt to keep me warm. Setting under the covers fully clothed, I lay my head back in order to rest with what had happened. Lying there, accepting my admonishment, which, though vague, felt sharply accurate, I felt a deep trust, a powerful acceptance that built into a feeling of energy.

Suddenly waves of energy began to move through me, from my toes, up through my torso and out my head. Wave after dark wave passed though me—my *prana*, my life energy was somehow freed and coursing, let loose from my usual patterns of thought and behavior. My body twitched uncontrollably even though I felt profoundly calm. Finally I settled into a deep peace.

Coming to India had meant leaving my boys with Bill. I was very attached to them and the routines that surrounded their care. I loved cooking for them and helping them bathe. I loved the sweet smell of soap, and their slippery clean bodies as they jumped out into the cold to be rubbed with a towel and hugged. In India, I had no children to touch, no husband to speak with. I felt a kind of detachment that is normal among travelers. Sometimes it's called culture shock. In this situation, with my Guru, it was called *vairagyam*, detachment, essential for practice, but I had never experienced it to this depth. With my trust in him, Guruji could take advantage of my shedding the familiar and could lead me to a place within, beyond the ordinary shapes of my daily life.

The *pranic* waves had completely subsided, and I was still drifting in a sense of deepening peace as the light in the room faded to the dark of evening. It was too cold to sit in meditation. Instead I returned to focus above my head while lying under the cotton quilts, in my fleece and a shawl. I located the thin eye of the needle, and a feeling of open space began to spread out from my head. It felt wonderful, and I was prompted to speak aloud to myself, or to the room, to God, to whatever listens in the dark:

"Give me *moksha.*"

Moksha means liberation; I wanted liberation from my struggle. The word just came to me. I was not expecting an answer, but a voice spoke clearly in my head.

"Can you leave everything?"

My response came as naturally as the request for *moksha* had slipped into words. In my mind's eye appeared the face of my younger son, Matthew. I felt his innocence.

"No, I can't leave Matt," was my silent answer.

And from the silence I gathered a reply, "Well then, you are not ready. *Moksha* is not really what you want."

I did not understand then, nor for years, what Matt carried of me. I knew that Paul felt intact, sturdy; he had a kind of fearlessness and a sense of self that was similar to Bill's. Matt felt young, unfinished, and mutable—more like me. Really both were children, but Matt reminded me of the young part of myself that waited to be raised from childhood. The significance of seeing his face was not something I could grasp, I just knew that seeing him in my mind turned me back from wishing I could find complete release. I could neither leave my work, nor my children, nor the part of me that still needed a name.

30

Meditation is simply to sit on the ground.
Deng Ming-Dao

I started a daily practice of walking in the dry riverbed in the afternoon. There was a path down behind the cowshed adjacent to the kitchen, a descent over rocks that jogged through a pivoting metal gate that served as a cow fence, preventing their wandering. The metal ends tugged on my shawl as I went through the narrow opening. The riverbed filled with runoff during the rainy season, but in winter it was a quiet refuge of tall grasses and prickles that caught the pant leggings, and groves of spindly trees, stunted by the long, hot dry seasons.

The protracted dry heat pounded the gravel and rock, pulverizing the earth into a dust that penetrated and covered all surfaces. Marble floors of the temples, cement floors and metal armoires were all subject to the dust of the out-of-doors. Socks worn in the cold quickly turned a familiar brown. I was adjusting to the ever-present dust of India that was part dirt and part cow dung.

In the evening, the sun enlarged over the flat plain beyond the riverbed and among the low mountainous foothills of the Himalayas. The mountains appeared closer in the orange light of dusk, the tall and wide shapes backlit by the deep blue hue of the evening sky. The dawning of the stars and the lights of houses and villages in the low mountains combined in a seamless canopy of twinkling lights to the north.

Out of sight, up in the cradle of the mountains was the famous British enclave, the hill station of Shimla, now the capital of Himachal Pradesh. The hill stations were established by the British, conveniently located in the foothills of the Himalayas where the summer heat could be escaped. The higher Himalayan peaks required weeks of travel on rocky and crumbling roads with multiple switchbacks. The town of Shimla was near the plains although perched along twelve kilometers of mountain ridge; lanes running along the ridge, switchbacks and steep ascents all combined in narrow grids, lined with wooden buildings and their windows with many panes of glass opening to the views—very different from the thick brick and adobe buildings of the sweltering plains.

Before Shimla was settled by a Scottish Civil Servant in 1822, there was not a passable road through the jungle of leafy trees and roaming wildlife. But by 1864, Shimla, a shortened version of Shyamala, a name of the goddess Kali, was the summer capital of the British Empire, sporting Victorian architecture. By 1903, the whole business of governing India went in boxes of forms and accounting books up the Kalka-Shimla railway, a more efficient way to traverse the terrain than the twisting road. It was a narrow gauge rail, two feet, six inches, that ascended precipitously to what became India's premier hill station. Indian children were schooled there to join the cadre of civil servants. They were taught English in nursery rhymes before they learned their sums, and then sent to serve in the over-populated growing cities throughout the sub-continent.

Here I was, an American of British descent living among Indians below a city that spoke of how the British had dominated the land while keeping themselves removed from its discomforts. I was raised on British nursery rhymes. I learned to harmonize to Protestant hymns sang during morning assemblies at my all-girl's preparatory school. My mother served tea in the late afternoons, a British habit. Our family laughed when we found a bottle of "Colonel Biddle's Indian Curry," an import began by some distant and forgotten relative. But I felt differently. The details of the college course in History at Brown University I refused to parrot into my blue-book and failed to complete was the colonization of South America during the age of exploration. Spanish, Portuguese, British galleons of men, with Catholic and Protestant clerics and monks, landed in foreign countries as the superior race and failed to see the cultures they were annihilating. Zoological gardens and arboretums in Europe and England proliferated as displays of curiosity, in appreciation of oddities from the colonized world. Museums were filled with the fine pillage of the ancient and the primitive cultures. I was grateful that the British had brought the English language to India, but ashamed of its imperial dominance.

The Kalka station of the Kalka Shimla railway in the Panchkula district of Haryana was a few kilometers from the ashram at Virat Nagar.

Kalka is also a name from the goddess Kali, and, ironically, my Guru instructed me that in his Vaishnava tradition, Kali was not honored. She is the black-faced red-tongued fierce incarnation of the Mother, destroyer of sins and harbinger of *karmic* travail.

Closer to the road to the ashram, was the famous Mughal Pinjore Gardens. Before the British, the Mughals had overrun India, devastating the culture and burning libraries. The most famous library was at Taxilla University, an ancient place of learning where centuries of the aural tradition of India had been preserved in Devangari script on large banana and palm leaves. Pinjore gardens was in the 17th Century style of cascading terraces, topped by a small palace, typical of Islamic symmetry and style— fountains to cool the air, varied plantings on each descending level replete with fruit trees, archways, climbing vines and wide blooms. The lavish Mughal appreciation of the Indian climate was intimate to their downfall. Weakened by a lifestyle of ease, they were subject to final domination by the Colonial British in 1858.

Indian independence was not secured until 1947. My Guru's interest in reviving ancient Vedic thought, the unique crown of Indian culture and the substratum of Hinduism, was taking place in this amalgam of culture that left the English language the currency of a modern business economy gradually encroaching on the old way of life.

Each morning, I was awakened at four a.m. by the sweeping sound of the Islamic call to prayer coming from a small mosque on the main road to Kalka. The loudspeaker amplified the sound across the plain and dry riverbed of the Saraswati into the small window of my washroom. This sweet sound brought me floating out of sleep into a semi-wakeful state. The recording echoing within the cement walls, "Allah u-Akbar," same voice, same inflections each time, ended after fifteen minutes. Then at four-thirty, *Sama Veda* played over the loudspeaker of what I would come to find was a small white-washed Hindu temple bordering the narrow cul-de-sac asphalt road that took us from the main road to the ashram. The sound came to my room from the opposite direction, from the door to the outside. Another fifteen minutes of this growling, guttural rhythmic sing-song was followed by the sounds of our ashram waking for practice. Water would run into buckets from outside spigots set in the corners of the concrete walkways. I would hear splashing and then coughing, gagging and hacking as the men prepared for the day with *kunjal kriya*, drinking

178

water and then vomiting it to clean the stomach. I was up then, mildly disturbed, and would begin my own morning routine.

My routine in India formed around meditation practice. I washed myself—and my clothing—in one bucket. First me, then the clothes. Asana practice was minimal. The floor was cold and dusty, and I had no mat on the floor. I always did some breathing to clear my head, and a few poses to shake the dross of sleep off my body. But hatha was not important. There were no classes to attend. There were no evening prayers at the ashram in those years.

Soon after I had arrived, a small group of us were crowded on the floor in Guruji's room after the morning meal. He was reading and apparently listening, as he replied intermittently. I was adjusting to Hindi with its phonetic bursts and repeated phrases. There was banter back and forth, and then one didi held forth in Hindi, trying at length to get Guruji to reply and comply with her. She appeared to be talking about the cows, their health. Her dark eyes were full and moist. She spoke with passion. I understood one cow was sick, but she was neither getting the attention she wanted nor the help she requested.

I was familiar enough with Guruji's detachment, though I had often been puzzled by his simple disinterest. At the time I did not understand that he was leaving her to make her own decision. I did not have enough maturity to see how he was mentoring her by not answering her question. What I did understand is that he could sit within himself and be okay no matter what the circumstances. He had told me once at my house, breaking the silence of his morning meal.

"I am like that milk." He had waited for me to look at him before continuing.

"When you put me on the heat, I become hot. When I sit at room temperature, I become cool."

He paused. Clearly I had not understood his point.

"People are the heat. When I am with them, I heat up. Alone, I become cool."

Then I understood that alone he was content to be quiet, unanimated. I was witnessing his quiet state when we were together in my house. I also understood that I might learn to be more indifferent to the opinions of others.

Guruji had told us that when the Macedonian conqueror, Alexander the Great, came through the Hindu Kush into India in the year 326

B.C.E., he met a saint. He expected the saint to cower at the mention of his name. The saint was indifferent. India was India. The fatigued ranks of Alexander's army were prepared to mutiny in India, so Alexander waged brief imperious skirmishes along the Indus River from riverboats, and then left the sub-continent to conquer Persia, ordering his men to take Persian wives. He died three years later.

Maybe in this case, my Guru's indifference was because there was not enough money for medical treatment for the cow. Maybe the didi was simply too emotional, overinvested, and he wanted her to calm herself. Before long, I lost patience with my incomprehension of their exchange, or lack of exchange. My impatience was layered with my own wish to feel comfortable with my new sisters, the group of didis, but I did not. I felt awkward.

I pushed off the floor and bowed *pranam* to my Guru's feet. He held up his hand with an open palm of blessing—very different from when he touched my head with affection. His open palm spoke of recognition of my respect and the bond we shared, but without intimacy.

I wandered to the wide metal gate at the courtyard of the cowshed. The cowshed at the ashram is a barn, but with open air—more like a line of stalls. Cowsheds are attached to village homes in India the way we conveniently attach garages for our cars. The family cow lives under a small shed adjacent to the home, close by for feeding and milking.

This cowshed near the kitchen housed about thirty-five cows, and their stalls formed a perimeter around an open courtyard. "The *gaushala...*" mulling the sound of the word in my mind, I discreetly entered and found the cows in their stalls, waving tails, chewing hay. The courtyard was clean of straw and manure.

No one was around. A lone cow clopped over the round cobblestone to greet me. I ran one hand over its coarse hair, feeling the warmth, the sleek oils of her hide under my open palm, and spent a few moments imagining what it would be like to have cows and milking as a duty—hay, grain and water as daily chores.

I wandered out of the confinement of the courtyard and back onto the open path lined with waving eucalyptus trees and strolled toward the temples.

Seeing the cowshed sparked a memory I had completely forgotten. When Bill and I first knew Guruji, we went with our small boys to someone's home to visit him during the day. I assumed he would continue to teach us philosophy. Instead, he patted the seat of the couch next to him.

"Margot, come here." I was surprised he called me by name. My name sounded differently from his lips. "Come and see pictures of my *gaushala*."

"What is a *gaushala?*"

"You know...a *gaushala*...a...how you say...a cowshed!"

I walked on my knees across the floor to the couch. He was smiling. His limbs were relaxed and he seemed personal and friendly. He began to point to the pictures, one by one. With an open hand he indicated, "This is the *gaushala*...oh, the cowshed, and this is..." and he went on to name each cow, with increasing enjoyment. He beamed like a child. I relaxed, in spite of myself. His presence was like the warm rays of the sun in the early morning. A mist cleared effortlessly from my mind, one that I was unaware had been clouding my consciousness. I felt his regard and realized he was offering me something more than ideas of an eternal self that I had listened to in his talks. He was describing feelings of trust and affection.

In India, the fresh milk served each morning was an experience of milk I had never had before. It was unlike milk in the States or Canada; you could taste the affection the cows received, or so it appeared. They were loved as part of the family. That was the only explanation I had. Milk became a metaphor for affection. And the love of the cows—the purveyors of affection—was a love for the traditions lived in this country for so many hundreds and probably thousands of years. My teacher's fondness for the cows and their milk was a feeling he carried into his philosophy and his care in serving our meals. It was a simple intimacy with life. I was trying to learn the philosophy before I came and now here.

I was getting in my own way.

The teaching was waiting for me, like a cow ready to amble toward me, simply because I approached.

31

This air is like honey for all beings, and all beings are honey for this air.
Brhadaranyaka Upanishad

My first few days in India, I'd spent much of the time in my room, meditating on verses from the *Gita* that my Guru had assigned me. My room, where the temperature was 50 degrees most of the time, was lit by one overhead bulb. During the day, the warmth of the sun was faint and barely penetrated the walls. The thick brick walls coated in cement sealed the chill in. To study or meditate, I lay under the heavy cotton quilts, stilling any movement to allow the warmth to gather close to my body.

One morning after breakfast, there was a small knock on my door. A woman entered without waiting for a reply.

"You want anything?" she asked.

She sat on the edge of a second wooden bed by the door. She tucked one leg under, having slipped out of her sandals, and sank onto one hand.

"I am Janiki. I knew Bill when he traveled in India."

"Oh," I replied. "You knew Bill. Yes, he told me how you helped him. But no, I don't know of anything I need."

I was happy to have a visitor.

"You'll need drinking water. We have to boil it every day."

She said "boil" with an extra puff of air that made me feel a boiling down in my belly, a faint recognition. It is always interesting how we recognize a new friend.

I settled into my brick and adobe room, a few days ahead of Evelyn. The room was equipped for Westerners, with a Western toilet as opposed to a hole in the ground with metal stamps for feet molded on the sides. The room also had a geyser for hot water that was broken. The ashram staff who came to look at it agreed it was broken, and did nothing to fix it.

A space heater did work against the January cold, about 45 degrees in the mornings. My early ritual was to jump out of bed, turn on the space heater, jump back into bed and meditate with the blanket around my nose while the heater ran for ten minutes. Then, jump out of bed and use the toilet that stood beside the sink. The water that drained from the sink ran underneath the showerhead. The whole room was cement: walls and floor, with no special alcove for the shower. Next, I brushed my teeth with bottled water and washed off in a bucket of cold water—I was free to splash everywhere—and then washed my clothes in the same bucket. Dressed in clean clothes, I wrapped myself in a wool shawl and went out the back door to a clothesline. There I hung my clothes in the pre-dawn light, before the others came out with their clothes, and the line filled up. Back inside, I moved around in hatha yoga practice. I turned off the space heater, got back in bed and under the blanket to meditate. Then it was time for Guruji's morning lecture, in Hindi, in the underground *mandir* with its blue and water-streak stained walls.

A young woman came to stay in another room for a night. She spoke English well. As we walked she complained about her life, her marriage, and why she had come to see Guruji. I was happy to listen, but later in the day when I was alone, Guruji told me to paste a note to my mirror that said, "All people are empty vessels." I did not understand why I should follow his instructions to the letter. I did not even understand what he meant. I spent little time in front of the mirror. Secondly, we would soon be traveling away from any particular mirror. I felt I was adept enough to post the warning in my mind and see when I needed. Besides all that, the advice seemed to be a heartless and cold, moral reminder to not get infatuated with anyone other than God. The same God is in all beings. It is God we seek, not a person who can save us. I did not see any trouble ahead for myself. I set the advice aside.

After a week, Evelyn, my new roommate, arrived from America with her hair dryer and adaptor. She unpacked her clothes to show them to me, lining them up on a clothesline that she rigged along the wall. Evelyn had shoulder-length, platinum blonde hair and, with her fair skin, she looked well in light blue and greens. She had managed to find real *punjabi* suits in the States before coming. They were tailored to fit the curves of her body. The sleeves fit neatly, the leggings were sufficiently long and tapered that they layered on her ankles, and her suits came with *chunis*. *Chunis* are flowing, long scarves worn backwards in front of the chest and throat for modesty—an alluring distraction from the female anatomy. I listened patiently as she gave me a tour of each one, where she had bought it, how much it cost.

Early the next morning, I followed my routine, mostly in the dark, and left for the *mandir* as usual. Evelyn murmured a question about the hour from her bed but did not rise. Returning from the lecture, I found her waving her hair dryer around. "I can't believe it. A fuse blew when all I used was the space heater and the hair dryer!"

I refrained from commenting, left the room again, giving her time for practice. I went over to the kitchen for hot milk and a plate of vegetables fried with spices in *suji*, what we call "Cream of Wheat." Finishing the savory food, I returned to find Evelyn on the bed painting her nails in the sunlight. She was reciting the long prayer to the monkey god, Hanuman, the *Hanuman Chalisa,* from a little book. She interrupted her prayers to tell me about it.

"Elliot made this little booklet for me." Elliot was her eldest son, the one in pre-med at Northeastern Ohio College of Medicine. "So I can chant the *Hanuman Chalisa* every day." She looked back at her nails and inspected them.

"So what is your practice?" I could not help myself from asking, politely.

"My practice is to be happy, to be myself," she said smiling.

I noticed her coiffed hair. This did not fit with my idea of why I was in India. I quickly made a plan and muttered to Evelyn that I would spend the night with friends, a little sleepover. I could not see how my dislike of Evelyn had anything to do with me, anything to do with how I had a hard time loving myself. I simply made plans to act out my aversion.

I knew Janiki would not mind if I slept in her room. She and her roommate were Indian, and they had a "regular" room. It was smaller, the ceiling lower, and their laundry was slung from lines that crisscrossed the beds. Janiki's roommate took in laundry to make a few rupees; she was standing in the cement bathroom plunging her hands in the bucket and then hanging out the cloth across lines in the room. I was happy lying under drying cloth listening to them speak in Hindi, back and forth over the sounds of sloshing water. I said my mantra inwardly. Guruji had told me not to learn Hindi because it would distract me from practice. Janiki, whose spiritual name was *Ritam Bhara,* the one who sees the truth, explained Guruji's instruction: Mostly what is spoken in Hindi is gossip.

That night, Janiki and I slept end to end in her narrow bed, holding each other's calves to avoid falling onto the floor. The next morning I returned to my room. As usual, Evelyn was happy, her very blonde hair mussed in a sweetheart sort of way. She said cheerily, "You want to see my carry-on bag for traveling?"

Evelyn held up her one carry-on bag. She was so proud that she could fit everything in one bag; not that it was a bag that would pass an airline's carry-on status. It was the gym bag of a Sumo wrestler, packed for Arctic weather.

"Evelyn," I said politely, "There will be lots of us traveling on small buses and trains, and we'll be carrying sleeping bags as well."

"That is precisely why I am so happy to have found one bag for all my stuff!"

All the subsequent nights I spent with my roommate. Tolerating and adjusting are the great virtues in human behavior, Didiji had told me. And Guruji's lesson to me from the ninth chapter of the *Gita* was:

As the mighty wind, going everywhere, dwells eternally in space, so all beings dwell in Me, consider this!   *Gita 9/6*

Our group was preparing to travel the morning after Guruji's birthday celebration. I planned to travel lightly, leaving behind most of the books I had brought to India. As I sorted my extra belongings to the suitcase I would leave in my room, and packed a nylon red carry-on, without warning all my anxieties surrounding separation vomited into my psyche. I fell into fear. The trap-door opened. All feelings of security disappeared as if I had never known safety. For survival, a need for contact, I decided to practice relationship with Evelyn, to talk about myself somewhat honestly. I was hoping she could tolerate touchy-feely stuff, and that she would listen long enough to advise me more than just to say my mantra, which I suspect is all the comfort my teachers would have to offer. My deep, long-term fears had followed me to India.

"Evelyn, I can't help it. I feel terrible, so incredibly insecure I want to hide in my room and not travel."

Her gaze relaxed as she prepared to listen. I spoke for a while about early trauma—unknown stuff, known stuff, guesses and hunches. After she listened appropriately for some time and made nice animal-sympathy noises, I felt more comfortable with Evelyn. It was time to lighten up. I relaxed some.

"So," she asked, "Do you want to see the Taj Mahal?"

"No, not really."

"I do," she said. "We'll have some extra time at the end of the journey before returning to the States. Don't you want to travel?"

"No, I just want to sit with Guruji. If I have any extra time, I'll stay with him and listen to his lectures. While I'm here, I want to learn as much from him as I can."

"I don't really need to sit with him," Evelyn said. "I'm already in *Brahman* consciousness."

The spell was broken. All my open-hearted, loving kindness evaporated in an instant. She had broken the rules. Telling someone you are in *Brahman* consciousness is not a news item such as how your son got into medical school. I was floored. How could I possibly correct her? Miserable, I had gone from the bliss of surrender during my first days in India, to junior high school emotions with a roommate, to high anxiety about traveling on crowded little buses to places with questionable sanitary facilities. And now Evelyn was labeling a simple-minded, albeit real, happiness, as "*Brahman* consciousness."

"I'm going out for a while, Evelyn." I said.

I was distraught. My pride was shattered. I wandered off, ungrounded. I felt abandoned. My effort to gain something through practice had gone on its own separate journey. I went toward Kanta Didi's room and found her closing her door while throwing her sari over her shoulder, her usual way of announcing a quick change into her sari after completing her long morning prayers.

"Didi-jeee," I started to sob shamelessly.

"What happened?"

"Nothing happened," I forced myself to speak evenly. But I could not control myself for long—I had to blurt it out. "Evelyn thinks she is in *Brahman* consciousness!"

"Tch, tch tch."

"She can't tell me she is in *Brahman* consciousness! I don't want to hear that she is in *Brahman* consciousness!"

"Sometimes, people have their own explanations for their experience." Didi consoled me by putting her hand on my arm. It was obvious she would be happy to see me get a grip on myself.

"Can I sit in your room for a minute?" I felt better asking for something specific.

Didiji unlocked the padlock of her door and went with me back into her room. There I felt her soothing patience and the lingering effect of the many hours of meditation I had shared with her. While sitting next to Didi in the quiet of her room, I turned my attention inward.

"What's the heart of the matter? How can I solve this? Certainly I cannot change Evelyn."

Clarity followed. My anxiety settled. After a few minutes, I got up with a sigh, thanked Didi and returned to my room. Evelyn had gone out. I savored a few minutes of calm within myself and within the room we shared. Writing a letter home helped.

January, 30, '92

Dear Bill

I am making sadhana my primary focus here because there is no capacity to help others without realizing the source of life within myself. This I knew but I was not aware of how close it was within my reach. My burning desire has always been to help others but God has to be first. Guruji has bestowed much grace. I dove higher and higher for a week—now my job is to stabilize higher—not so difficult. What this means is that what used to be experience becomes the norm for me.

Manishi Didi is sweet, very supportive. Kanta Didi continues to be "my didi." Yogananda is also sweet. Bhartiji is also most supportive. Janiki has been looking out for my welfare. Today she'll take me to do errands in Pinjore. I have done little. Guruji does not want me to even look at the scenery—just look inside and I have. We will travel to Jagganath Puri in two days—stay five. Guruji has an eleven-day program in a city. I will stay with him with a few Didis. I could go back to the ashram but I want to continue to learn from him. Evelyn will tour. She is a trip. She frequently refers to her Brahman consciousness and her happiness. She spends her mental energy taking care of God's lipstick, God's nails, God's laundry—etc, etc. So my practice is to see God taking care of herself—dancing with herself. Truly she is Narayana. She is here to tour India with herself, not to see Guruji. You are all wonderful to give me this time. Take time to go inside, more and more, and you will receive many blessings I am sure— all of you! Love and hugs—wish it were possible to be two places at once. Love, margot-mum

There was no sense in worrying Bill with my inner collapse. I managed my discomfort with myself by making fun of Evelyn. That is never fair, but Bill would most likely disregard my frustration with her. With any luck my discomfort was momentary, and I could resume getting ready to travel with the group and with Evelyn. When Evelyn returned to our room I calmly explained there is a rule around subtle experience: We do not talk about it because people like me might become jealous, something that would not help anyone. She nodded, smiling, as she looked down at her nails. She was humoring me.

The next morning, the day of the birthday celebration, while passing by the main courtyard, I heard singing—one didi was singing while others stood around her. Her voice was loud in *bhajan*, and she clapped with large arm motions. She wore an orange sari and had a print scarf tied under her chin like a Croatian babushka. I guessed she was not really a didi, but only pretending to be one. She scowled slightly with eyes wide, which made me guess she was mad; it would be lunacy to mistake her for a *sannyasi*.

At midnight, we gathered for Guruji's birthday celebration in the lecture hall near the Sita Ram temple. The Sita Ram temple anchored an area under development near the main gate of the ashram. Across from the temple stood a statue of Hanuman, the monkey god, painted in full color, its height dwarfing the tallest of the other temples. The statue was almost completely enclosed by scaffolding—long irregular poles and small trees lashed together with hemp rope—somehow sturdy. Builders were adding a roof over Hanuman's ninety-foot high figure. Nearby, another temple was also under construction. It had two levels: one for Lord Shiva downstairs, and one for Mother Goddess upstairs. To enter the stairway to the second level, you stepped through the mouth of a tiger, the fierce vehicle upon which Mother Goddess rides. The tiger's head, as yet unpainted, was an ashen color, reminiscent of a Disney icon that had yet to have color added. Crossing this threshold was an inspiration to master the senses, not glory in them.

The hall for the birthday celebration had been built prior to the temple campus. Its exterior was plain, a faded rusty-orange adobe, marked with water stains. I slipped off my sandals, noting with a sense of futility their location among the mass of shoes and sandals, like marking a car in a huge, full lot. From the hall's main entrance, I could see the stage at the far end. By the time I arrived, a mass of people had already crowded in, most seated across the width of the hall leaving only a thin aisle in the middle, the remainder standing along the back wall. On the right were women with the ends of their saris drawn up like veils over their heads, with embroidered wool shawls over their shoulders to protect against the cold. On the left were the men, mostly in pants and coats, though some wore the traditional white *dhoti*, or pants, with long white tops and dark wool shawls.

I did not see Janiki at first, until she lifted up on one knee and waved from near the stage. Self-consciously, I walked down the narrow aisle on the dusty woven mat that lay between the masses of seated men and women. My height and pale skin drew stares. When I neared Janiki, she pulled my arm, squeezing me onto a small piece of ground, a movement that brought the knees of my crossed legs to rest in the laps of two women. Their saris were bright blue and green. Janiki wore white, a striking contrast to her dark skin. The women next to me smiled, nodded, and said a few words in English. "How are you?" I smiled and nodded back, knowing their English would be exhausted with "Fine, thank you." In this part of Northern India, the people were mostly from villages. "How are you?" was sung out whenever someone wanted to practice their English. The extent of their English was like my Hindi.

I looked at my knees resting in the laps of these gentle and polite women. I hardly recognized myself in the white sari with the red border that Janiki had given me. I suspended my resistance to saris for my teacher's birthday. Janiki no longer wore anything but white as she prepared for a life of renunciation. Even a cheerful border of red contaminated the pure white. I was wearing a wedding sari. Because of my height, I had tied the slip tight to secure the long wrapping of cloth.

Guruji was sitting to the left on the stage, surrounded by the monks, most of them women, who had taken their vows with him. The taking of vows is called "taking *sannyas*," after which the monks dress in orange, the color of the rising sun. They sat in a cluster, some meditating or staring in reverie. Their various sweaters, coats, shawls, and hats were all orange. The didis had the ends of their saris up over their heads like the other women. Guruji had on a bright orange knit cap, the color worn by hunters. He fingered his *mala* while his lips moved slightly with mantra. I realized he was placing himself apart from us, even as he was our focus. Though his ego might be the center of the celebration, the object of the love, and reason for the joy, he remained intent upon enlarging himself with mantra, upon becoming our shelter, like a second roof, or even the space beyond the cold night.

On the stage in front of me, the performers stayed seated as the microphone was moved around, and as various instruments were passed

189

forward hand over hand: a harmonium, *tabla*, a flute. The songs began, one artist at a time sending their lilting chant of *bhajan* through the loudspeaker system. A handful among them were truly devoted vocal artists, and the subtlety of their melodic phrasing, unique to Indian music, silenced the low chatter that ran incessantly among the crowded audience like mice in a barn. The more distinguished vocal artists never sang more than one song. They were trained in humility as well. I wanted them to sing more. They may have wanted to sing more, but they left encores for the more common singers. The very best bowed their heads after one song, looking vaguely disappointed. They seemed to expect appreciation for their restraint, even if they could not indulge in more beauty.

After a few acts, a man stepped forward on the stage, towering above the seated figures. His suitcoat buttons barely contained his belly. He made a short speech in Hindi and, in conclusion, shouted and threw a scattering fistful of money. All the orange-capped heads looked over. Even a few of the didis who had been catching up on their sleep, with heads sunk into their chests, looked up. The stout man, bowed *pranam* to Guruji, and returned to his place behind the singers. I pulled on Janiki's sleeve in front of me.

"What did he say?"

"Guruji was sick last year, so we had no celebration," was her hushed reply.

I guessed the rest. The shouting man was trying to inspire extra donations this year.

There were more heartfelt *bhajans* from the less refined devotees; they were so exhilarated by the crowd that they sang a few encores. The more refined singers looked down in their laps, their shawls neatly tucked off to the side like their tilted heads. It seemed a shame they refused to be immodest. Every so often, the man with the coat buttons would jump forward to fling another fistful of money and shout once again. After a few more such displays, the monks scowled, and another man in a wool shawl held the overly enthusiastic man back by the scruff of his coat, almost tearing off the buttons. It was then that I noticed, among the orange-clad people, one slightly odd woman. It was the woman from the courtyard, sitting among the didis, scowling from under her thickly draped hood. The other *sannyasis* tolerated her as they would a stray thought in their meditation. They sat with Guruji, who was still quietly fingering his *mala*, his lips moving, his eyes focused inward.

190

After a few hours, another man came forward from the back of the stage. He arrived late, but men standing or seated nearby reached out to touch his arms, gently encouraging him to take the microphone. By his long, matted hair and dusty, browned shawl, I guessed he was a wandering *sadhu*. Gripping a one-stringed, single-toned instrument, he kept rhythm, shouting a monotonous melody of two tones. Thrilled by chanting to the crowd and to the guru, he began an encore. The man in the wool shawl came forward to pull him off. The *sadhu* had little clothing to pull, so the man in the shawl tightened his fist around his arm. The *sadhu* stiffened, and twisted his thin body around, making his way back to the front, until two of the better male singers stood up and escorted him off. His resistance, given his vows, seemed comical, but I was coming to understand tolerance in this culture, and in my Guru.

At four o'clock in the morning, people began to queue up. Several women were handing out garlands of marigolds. Then I could see nothing, except the mass of dancers that rose between me and the stage, accompanied by the sound of the harmonium and the clapping crowd. Janiki leaned back toward me and yanked at my arm—pulling it upward.

"Go dance!" she shouted.

I shook my head "no." I felt indignity. I had never seen young girls dance for the guru, their arms out to the sides as their bodies twirled around the center like a maypole.

As a line of bodies developed out of the mass, I caught sight of Guruji's cheek. He was disappearing into an orange ring of marigold garlands. His head was bowed. After placing the flowers carefully on the rising ring, each person dipped a finger into a small container of red paste passed from hand to hand. Then they each painted over the thickening line between his brows, from lower to higher, a deepening flame over the third eye. Then each devotee bowed. Guruji placed a hand on their heads. This was the sweet part: a simple garland in exchange for the gentle touch of grace that opened the top of the head. I remembered his touch, how the energy of the body would soar out as grace poured in. I stood up to join the line, carefully, making sure my feet did not catch the hem of my sari. I looked around for Janiki. She must have already gone forward. I followed.

Walking back from the ceremony at around five in the morning, I realized we had about three hours to rest before the bus took off. As I walked alone, I observed the state of my body. There appeared to be

191

nothing between my thoughts and my feet. I could feel the feet touching the earth gingerly, as though they were smaller, and the earth more yielding. The starry night was moonless, and the penetrating cold made me draw the shawl tighter.

Just outside my door, I fished the key out of my fanny pack, opened the padlock, and stepped into the space Evelyn and I shared. She had not returned. The wood door scraping over the cement floor sounded loud as it shut. I lay my body, fully dressed and warm, under the pile of quilts, and closed the eyes. I felt complete and expansive. It was simple. When we are free inside, there are no attractions, no aversions; we are what we are and the world is as it is.

32

The man of restraint is awake in that which is night for all beings;
the time in which all beings awake is night for the sage who sees.
Gita 2/69

I was right not to worry Bill in my letter. After a week at the ashram, my practice had deepened. Sitting in meditation was easier. I felt elevated, oriented to my routine, happy with my new friend, Janiki, and somewhat adjusted to sharing my room with Evelyn. But it was time to adapt again. The bus tour began.

The bus parked in the lane outside Guruji's courtyard. It was white and silver, with narrow blue stripes much like our city buses in the States, except it sat on the chassis much like a truck so there was no room for luggage underneath. The bus was clean of the thick layer of dust that would likely settle on the back and sides as we traveled. We hoisted luggage up the narrow steps and settled our things by placing bags above our heads and at our feet. Damp towels and laundry were tied onto hand stirrups, placed over the poles of the overhead racks and laid out over the backs of our seats. People settled into twos; husbands and wives, and couples of didis who were close companions. I sat with Janiki, even holding hands as we set out. She was yelling jokes in Hindi over my head.

I relaxed somewhat among the bustle of travel. Moving helped me. Just as settling onto a plane with a group of strangers brings with it some sense of belonging, I felt suspended. My inner dialogue quieted. I could feel my human existence as another body among bodies, needing to eat, going somewhere, all the while breathing. A sense of space opens. Moving through space inside a vehicle without needing to move my limbs opens my mind to space.

Traveling in the car with my father, I'd look at clouds and enjoy the silence or his talking. We used to sail in Maine on chartered boats—same thing there, the press of the winds and the sound of the water opened up a large sky. We followed a charted course, but it was an excuse to feel this open place of space around the body. Here in India, I understood that my consciousness was freed to expand with the space moving around and under the bus. I had no control of where I went. Like a child, I could just be.

Guruji was first taking us to Kurukshetra for a dip in the Yamuna River. We passed close to the modern city of Chandigarh, which was only 22 kilometers from the ashram. Chandigarh is the most famous modern city of India, designed by the Swiss architect Le Corbusier, built as recently as 1956. We passed through its traffic circles with orderly planting of shrubs, banks of flowers and topiaries. The city is organized into an expanding grid of tree-lined boroughs and parks and lined with streets and buses that come at almost regular intervals, since the wide avenues prevented the absurd traffic jams of congested older areas found in nearby Ludhiana. Ludhiana is a textile city; the wares are piled and wrapped impossibly high and wide on small carts and bicycles, the drivers dwarfed by their loads. They make their tipsy way through narrow lanes, littered with plastic, rubble and garbage, and lined with small motorbikes, cars and sometimes cows and pigs. The modern shift from bicycles to motorized rickshaws added only a thick aura of pollution. Chandigarh, the "city beautiful," brought a new degree of serenity to the Indian concept of city.

On the ride south of Chandigarh, I had my first experience of using the open field as a toilet. I discovered why the back flap of the *punjabi* suit is so practical. It provides privacy in the open fields.

At the battlefield of Kurukshetra, I first witnessed bathing in the rivers of India by the Yamuna River, where the outdoor temperature was about 50 degrees. A few of the didis, determined to celebrate their *sannyas* day, eagerly changed into their floor length swimming gowns with buttons down the front, orange like the rest of their clothing, and went to the shallow water at the edge of the *ghat* steps. I watched them giggle and splash their faces, the wet gowns revealing more than concealing. Guruji had given several didi's their vows of *sannyas* at this site of the battlefield of the Mahabharata War. This was where the famous teachings of the *Bhagavad Gita* were spoken to Arjuna over 5,000 years ago, a relatively modern yogic teaching that summarized the ancient Samkhya principles and the knowledge of Vedanta into the yoga of skillful action supported by knowledge and devotion.

Then I found myself on a train, traveling economy class. The others might have been informed of our travel plans, but not understanding Hindi, I was the child, unaware of details. Whenever I asked a question, even of Janiki, the answers were brief as they hurried back to their mother-tongue, in which they teased jovially and in rhyme. So I returned to my contemplation.

The deities all ride vehicles, too. We ride in trains, buses, planes, rickshaws and bikes. Shiva rides Nandi the bull. Ganesha, a rat. Mother Goddess, the tiger. Vishnu, the eagle of Garuda. All the vehicles had a kind of meaning, but that was not important to me just then—the meaning was that the power and consciousness of the deity was riding in a vehicle. I got it! The body is a vehicle that our consciousness just rides around in, and the comfort of the vehicle helps us understand that we are more akin to the space of consciousness than the vehicle itself. The elephant-headed god of Ganesha should be scared of mice and rats. Elephants don't like small creatures. This deity has overcome the fear prompted by living in a body. He rides comfortably, transported hither and thither on the rat.

The train toilets were made of stainless steel, molded like a kind of inverted bubble with a hole in the bottom, edged with ridged rectangles on either side for feet. A water tap was near the floor, beside which sat a plastic cup with a handle for rinsing instead of using paper. The compartment was wet with urine and water. I had to wrap my loose pants and hanging flaps of clothing over one arm, hold my breath against the fumes, while gripping the pole on the side. I swayed with the train. At a morning stop, a man drew a long green hose into the stainless steel room and hosed it down. The smell was repellant. It made me gag if I was not careful.

Members of our group purchased snacks at the stations, mainly roasted peanuts in the shell, served in a cone of newspaper. They tossed the litter on the floor of the train without hesitation. At the next station, a little girl boarded with a small broom of hay strapped with twine to a wooden handle that swept neatly on an angle. Almost unnoticed, like a small animal, she moved the broom under our legs and in and out of the stalls, sweeping up the litter to earn a few *paisas*. She was off at the next stop. I could see the balance: the litterers created a job for someone, a child who lived in poverty and did not attend school. I was uncomfortable with it.

The confinement of the train and lack of privacy unsettled me. I sank into a dark cabin—the only one in the train car with doors that closed, the rest being open to the hall. Janiki noticed my discomfort and encouraged me to take a turn in Guruji's stall, to be near him. There, the talk was in Hindi, so I remained isolated in my mind. But then he turned to me, asked me if I wanted my lecture in English, waited for me to get my notebook, and commenced to speak. Receiving his offering of knowledge, which mingled with the knowledge already swimming in me, I finally could breathe freely and relax.

His teaching began to work. The sense of freedom that grew inside could not be explained by any improvement in accommodation. It was the same dirty train traveling at the same miles per hour with everyone speaking in Hindi except Evelyn, who was off on her own somewhere. Janiki explained to me later that when Krishna speaks with Arjuna on the battlefield at Kurukshetra, it is not normal speech. It is speech that fills Arjuna with realization. That is the power of the guru, she told me. If we can empty ourselves, he pours his knowledge into us. I began to understand why my teacher had wanted me to come to India, and why I was mostly glad to be there.

We made a few stops in villages. There, we would be fed in someone's house. Guruji would lecture outside in Hindi. Sitting on the ground or on a concrete floor covered by large straw mats or wide canvas sheeting, I became quite adept at tucking my ankles under and letting my hips open for his two hour speech, during which I meditated. Each time, I adjusted to sitting with more ease. Janiki sometimes leaned against me to ease the pain in her back, which brought my focus to the body. Her leaning would increase the pain in my ankles or the ache in the hips. My mind would wander. I gradually lessened the time of the distraction and stayed as deep in meditation as I could. It helped when Guruji spoke a few words of English.

One particularly dark and clear night, Guruji's English fragments pertained to the size of the universe, the clouds of nebulas and the numerous galaxies. He spoke of many millions of light years, and billions of galaxies. Sprinkled throughout his speech in Hindi, like stars coming out, one by one, the fragments created for me an interior experience of vast endless space.

When we boarded the train, or later went by car, wherever I sat, I would close my eyes and regain the inner space of clarity and freedom. I was able to focus this way many hours a day. Sometimes as soon as I sat, feeling the swaying of the vehicle, I went deep.

33

The one who sees all beings in the Self and the Self in all beings feels no aversion.
Isa Upanishad

The heat of the plains stirred a haze along the horizon. The sky was rarely cloudy as we passed by train going east across the northern province of Orissa. We headed to the sea town of Jagannath Puri on the Bay of Bengal.

The long overnight rocking of the train, the incessant sound of the engine and the simple routines of sleeping, waking, contemplation, a little bottled water and travel food—bananas bought at the station or fried *paratha* with pickle, packed in bags for the journey—had created a feeling of this being the only life I had ever led. The rocking movement on the train was all I had ever done and all I would ever do—through fields of crops, making small stops on the way.

I was here.

The smell of ocean air revived us as we piled our luggage and ourselves into bicycle rickshaws and went to a temple for our lodging. We shared rooms with eight or ten other people, where we set our bags and spread our mats on a concrete floor. Guruji motioned to a room for me where Evelyn was laying out her bed. I ignored him and chose a smaller corner room with Janiki and six other travelers.

The feeling of sky and space had settled in me. An Indian traveler, who was living in Canada, had lent me his headphones to listen to the song that made him feel deeply devotional. It was a song to *Brahman*, the unspeakable immutable source. I do not remember the melody now, but then it was enough to hear it for me to keep the melody going through my mind, awakening a trajectory of timelessness.

If Lord Shiva were to select a bull for a vehicle it would be from Jagannath Puri. The cows and bulls were the color of rain clouds. They were lean, gentle, and omnipresent. With large doe eyes, they tread with a narrow gait, as if walking delicately upon a divine path. Here and there, their slender horns were tinted red with the offering of red paste or decorated with trailing garlands of marigolds. In another town, a large brown bull had paced itself beside me and speared the long cloth of my *punjabi* suit with one horn. Not in Puri.

Non-Hindus were not allowed in the temple at Puri. So I was left behind when the group went off in Rickshaws for an hour of worship. Upon returning, Janiki told me I missed nothing. The worship was a loud waving of arms and shouting.

I had more time for contemplation. Each deity rides a vehicle, as we souls ride in a body. Here in the salt air by the Bay of Bengal, by the sand and among the gentle animals, I wondered if I could solve the problem of deity. Most people worship deity.

Our Guru was taking us to where Christ had studied. "His name was Isau and his visit is recorded," he said. He told me about Puri while we sat crowded into his compartment. I was across from him and had my notebook opened from taking notes on the lecture he had just given in English. I kept my notebook in my shoulder bag, so I was always ready. Gurji had been talking of the intellect as our Mother, consciousness as our Father and the Child in us as the I-am, the ego.

I wondered if he thought I had some interest in where Christ had studied because I was from a predominantly Christian country, and I was raised Catholic. It was a pleasant seaside town worthy of a vacation, but he had no interest in pleasure for its own sake.

"Christ studied in India, you know. A German historian has done the research."

I nodded. I had heard, but I was not ultimately convinced, nor did it matter. During Christ's time the Silk Road was well traveled. People shared goods and knowledge. Christ was seeking knowledge.

"The reason is because the temple in that town was open to all seekers from all castes. It was not the case in that temple that only the *Brahmins* could study. All people could study here at that time."

Christ gave his message for all people. I felt the irony of his conflict with Rome. The Roman rulers of Jerusalem turned against him, putting him to death; later, the Roman Empire adopted Christianity as their faith.

Time reverses history. The dominance of colonial imperialist Britain brought the English language to India, and now the spiritual teachings of India were spreading to the large world of English-speaking peoples. Christian missionaries came to India and now my teachers were calling their work a mission.

As part of my spiritual search, I had come to feel that the teachings of Christ and the yogic teachings were the same. If Christ had been a guru his message would have been, "Only through I-am can you reach the Father."

I was sympathetic with the human need to worship a personified form of God. It is human nature to want to feel something close. To worship a personified form of God provides a sympathetic object, an approachable focus. With deep devotion, the form leads us to the formless. In this tradition, God as the ever-present source of all is called *Brahman*. To think that Christ studied in India did not minimize his impact in my mind, nor did it elevate the Indian culture in my esteem. It emphasized that the perennial search for truth and shelter belongs to humanity, not to any culture.

I had a problem. From what I was reading in the *Gita*, devotion is the easiest path. Guruji often told us to refine our emotion into devotion. I would answer in my mind with a question: Devotion to whom? Devotion to what? I would look at the altars and see pictures of blue-skinned deities, rivers flowing out of the head of god, and the eight-armed Mother riding a tiger. Janiki told me that if you have a personal deity then you always have god as a companion. You can choose what deity you like. You can care for baby Krishna and enjoy that feeling of closeness a mother has for her child.

Janiki's words made sense, but I felt confused. Was this for me? I understood Christ as an object of worship. I could not be Christian at this point. I also did not feel Hindu.

Before we left on this pilgrimage by bus and by train, at the ashram in Virat Nagar, the symbol of *Ram* was mounted on an altar in the underground *pravachan mandir*. The written script of *Ram* as a mantra or sound was made of metal, and both the stand and the symbol were wrapped in shiny, yellow tinfoil. Around the base, a garland of red and silver tinsel was glued to a board, and a resonant halo came from the reflection of small Christmas bulbs strung above the altar. I was standing before it, trying to feel if this symbol meant more to me than the figure of

Lord Rama, the incarnation of divinity. Guruji came up beside me. I startled, as always. I felt like one of many students, not a close friend, so it always surprised me when he noticed me and spoke with me.

"No deity is allowed in here," he said. "This place is for lecture and meditation, *pravachan* and *dyana. Ram* is a symbol of what is beyond the sun. Seek beyond the sun, beyond form."

That was pretty clear indication that searching for an experience through the form of Rama was not for me. My Guru was encouraging me to seek beyond the solar vibration of the mantra *Ram*, beyond the heat, light, and power of the sun, in order to reach the unmanifest source. In the *Gita*, the path of seeking the unmanifest is described as more difficult than devotion.

I was not ready to listen to my Guru. I was leaning toward a minor rebellion. Presuming to know more than him, I wanted to pursue a tangible experience—something palpable. The experience of some form. I continued with the problem of deity. I had an intriguing experience with light coming from a crucifix when I went to a chapel in Iowa years before. I understood the place of icons. But I did not feel that I could sustain devotion to Christ. Years before when I first knew Kanta Didi, Shiva had come alive in my meditations. I felt I had his topknot of hair, the source of the Ganges, streaming from the top of my head. I was puzzled by it. I was not a worshipper of Shiva, but the experience had started when I chanted the name of *Ram* at a fundraiser for a Shiva Vishnu temple in Cleveland.

Bill and I went with the children to the fundraising event. Community members shared songs and chants and played instruments. The gathering was typical of the Indian community—a comfortable, ceaseless chatter went along with the chants. A friend prompted me to share. My version of their music was different. I did not know the subtle melodic lines of the *raga*. I agreed anyway. Matt shifted to Bill's lap leaving me free to lean toward the microphone.

As I began a simple *Ram* chant, I forgot the verses. I kept repeating the verse that invoked "the Lord as my shelter." In complete union with the sound, I flew into my inner self as in a deep meditation. The room became unusually still; talk ceased. Perhaps the people there wondered who was boldly singing such a simple sound, or, as I hoped, perhaps they felt something of what I was experiencing. I saw the unwavering, seated form of Shiva, with the river Ganges flowing from the crown of his head.

His subtle body was becoming a canopy over the entire group, and then over the building, as if the building itself were an illusion and the body of Shiva was the real shelter. This experience led me to wonder if Shiva was important for me.

Now was the time.

Here in Puri, feeling somewhat liberated inside, I chose Shiva. Shiva's vehicle was Nandi, the bull. Cows and bulls were wandering the streets in the bright sea town the way clouds move in the sky.

Shiva felt approachable to me. I focused continually on the name of Shiva. I carried no other thought. In a bicycle rickshaw sitting up high next to Janiki watching the slender driver pump his legs and body, up and down, pulling us along the flat streets to the hotel, I succeeded. In the warm air, I began to see Shiva in subtle form riding every stray cow and bull in the city. The image stayed with me. To reach over and accept a cup of tea from a vendor in the morning, I had to push away the haunches of a few cows. And there Shiva was, comfortable and indifferent, riding on the sway backs of these mild animals.

While flirting with Shiva I was trifling with my aversion to Evelyn. Both sides of the coin were being tossed. How quickly and effortlessly we can go from a place of detachment to a messy place where likes and dislikes play in the mind. My patience with Evelyn was still only superficial. Janiki was my companion in avoidance. She and I had already begun ditching Evelyn early in our journey among the maze of shops in a bazaar in Chandigarh. At a village lecture where a huge, brown canvas tent served as the lecture hall, I noticed sparkles on her eyelids. I rewrapped myself in my plain, brown shawl and left quickly at the end of the lecture. I looked back and saw in the dim electric light Evelyn standing tall, towering just as I did above both the Indian men and women. I never questioned myself why I had to leave rather than witness her. She dazzled in her light blue *punjabi* suit and gauzy shawl, her pale hair and glittering eyelids. She was speaking about her American children, explaining how proud she was to a gathering crowd of Indian men and a few of their wives. I simply did not approve. She kept approaching me in friendship. We were sister disciples after all. I was the one she asked to hoist her huge bag up on to the upper bunk. It was heavy and could easily have dropped back on her head. As I complied, I accepted her appreciation with feelings of guilt.

In Orissa, I didn't tell her when the group prepared to go swimming. I only knew because Janiki translated the Hindi for me. I avoided sharing rickshaws, leaving her to sit alone and pay her own way. And when Janiki and I went out early in the morning, I hid behind the sacred cows that lounged in the tea stalls outside our temple hostel. I knew I needed to detach from my feelings, but I could not. I did not know what they were, other than aversion. I was not willing to see how she might reflect a disowned part of me. Her self-care had a simplicity that mine lacked. I was stoic, she was happy.

I was sidetracked. I was indulging in some kind of attraction and in aversion. I had forgotten my family at home. I was shopping in India—looking for an experience rather than going beyond and finding the source. I should have caught myself. But I did not.

The day before we were to leave Puri, I slipped out alone to buy some sheets in the bazaar. Normally I shopped with others who spoke Hindi. They always haggled with the seller: Ask the price, listen to the answer, shout a word of disgust, then walk away and wait to be called back to receive a lower offer. Everyone tried haggling prices down, even with rickshaw drivers. Janiki was the loudest and most demeaning of all. I did not like it. My dollars had hardly been used, between the exchange and the prices near pennies, I knew I could afford to shop by myself and pay the asking price. A bed sheet without haggling might cost two dollars, instead of thirty cents. I felt safe, walking around the stalls. I bought a poster of Shiva and his consort united as one androgynous person, a number of lightly decorated single sheets, and a small brass image of Shiva dancing, with a hole for incense sticks at the base. After putting my money away and tucking my purchases under my arm, I stepped into an enormous load of cow dung, the first and only time I did this. I heard in my mind:

"Leave Shiva."

My Guru's voice was in my head:

"Not *Ram*, not the form, the sun behind the form, and not the sun either—what is beyond that?"

Returning to my room, Guruji caught sight of me from his doorway and called me in to speak. Somehow he had found out that I was not staying in the room he had assigned me. I knelt in front of him.

"Margot, why are you not sleeping with your friend?"

"She is in a room of people who snore, Guruji." It was true enough. But he looked at me.

"So she is not your friend, she is your neighbor?"

I smiled and bowed my head. Having seen through me, he was cleverly jumping to the heart of the matter by referring to the Christian phrase, "Love thy neighbor as thyself."

Guruji did not teach us to love, he taught us to tolerate. "All bodies are empty vessels," he had insisted before we had started on the journey. He wanted me to detach from people I both liked and disliked. Both are godly. He wanted me to lose my attachment to form, whether a person or a form of god. He was indicating that my path was to find the one source of all expression. Divinity manifests in human life. The flow of the divine creates the play of love in human life, as well as the play of differences, attractions and aversions. What we see moving and breathing in others is divinity.

The conflict I had with "my neighbor" offered me an opportunity to become more detached and neutral around others. Evelyn provided a litmus test. If I could feel neutral around her and without aversion, then I would begin to feel divinity everywhere.

In the last few days in Puri, I made incremental progress; I gradually felt less aversion toward her. We went swimming in our gowns and splashed around in the sea water. We shared the fee of a bathhouse. My understanding grew as Guruji taught me daily from the verses of the ninth chapter of the *Gita*. I kept searching beyond form.

This whole universe is pervaded by Me in My unmanifest form; all beings exist in Me; I do not abide in them. And yet, all beings do not abide in Me. Behold My divine yoga!   Gita 9/4, 5

Sustaining beings and not dwelling in beings is my Self, causing things to be. As the mighty wind, going everywhere, dwells eternally in space, so all beings dwell in Me. Consider this!   Gita 9/5, 6

I was seeking shelter in deity, in place. I knew this when I first arrived in India. I felt the *dhaam* at the temple of Sita Ram. Guruji and I had looked together at Sita and Rama standing side by side, hands up-raised in blessing. I had walked up a set of wide marble steps past a statue of Shiva, larger than a man, with his topknot of the river Ganges. I had felt my legs melt out from under me. Impatient in my search for an experience of Rama as deity, I could not find it. Guruji asked me to look beyond. Even then, I was impatient. The mountain of Shiva, which I had experienced early on while chanting, was simply a doorway to space. The practice my

Guru gave me was to realize *Ram* as the space beyond the sun. The name of *Ram* brings an experience of the space within, no different from the space around us, within which all life is suspended. Many times Guruji had told us that space is not empty; it is an ocean of divine energy and consciousness.

The night before we left, Guruji invited us to join him in meditation on the sand by the bay. The night was full of stars. We sat sprinkled in a wide group in the sand. From where we gazed at the surf, our band of travelers tossed out jokes in Hindi. I enjoyed their soft laughter. I could hear Guruji reply to their banter in rhymes. The jokes went too fast for Janiki to translate. It was not important.

A slender new moon was rising bright in the sky, the tips of its narrow spears holding a dark space. The group became still, listening to the ocean. I moved inward, content with myself, with nature. We sat for a long time. One by one, members stood, went to Guruji's feet and bowed *pranam* in silence and returned to their rooms. I felt how each person was as quiet and grateful as myself. He was teaching each person carefully and equally.

The next day my poster of Shiva went missing, along with the almonds I had brought with me for the trip.

34

To be sick of sickness is the only cure.
Lao Tzu

I remained cautious around my teacher. I did not speak or joke freely, or cause arguments or cry, even as I observed the Hindi speakers doing so. I meditated. I studied and occasionally joked with my companions when talk shifted to English. One time when I spoke at length, they looked at me strangely. They had assumed I was compliant and lacking in opinions.

Our time by the sea was over. We were traveling away from the Bay of Bengal, back to Haryana by train. The missing almonds were offered to me. One of the men magnanimously held out his hand and showed a clutch of smooth, washed California almonds. It took me a moment. I stared at them. I was not exactly sure.

"No, thank you," I said, waving my hand politely.

I was uncomfortable sitting across from him then, but I did not want to show my feelings. I let it be.

My stolen poster of Shiva most likely went home with the same man's sister, who left the group early to return to the ashram. Neither of these two fellow travelers were normal householders; they wore white, indicating they were in spiritual training. India is a place of shortage. I thought perhaps he was hinting I should have shared my stash rather than hoarding; it was an interesting way to teach me.

The Indians have an identity of being clever and maybe they are. Rather than confronting me directly on my unconscious hoarding, they taught me a lesson that sank in gradually. When I heard Guruji lecture on *aparigraha* as the basis of Hindu culture and not *ahimsa*, it really sank in. Non-hoarding means that if you visit an Indian friend in India, they spend

206

everything they can on treating you, the guest, as God. I had not noticed that I was not sharing my almonds—*a small stash of protein*, I thought, *need it for my health*. But in India, the demarcations between yours and mine are not as distinct as in the States. My first descent into Delhi on the jet from Holland in the dusk of evening revealed small yellow light bulbs shining at all depths and heights with a sepia glow through the thick pollution. There was no grid of street lights and parking lots as when flying over any major metropolitan area in the States, no factories and suburban sprawl with carefully planned houses and drives tucked into cul-de-sacs with their swimming pools. There was just a diffusion of points of light, a constellation of people. These lights turned out to be lit from perpetually unfinished rooftops—always ready for another concrete story when the family needed to expand and the rupees were saved. The bare bulbs dangled from poles lighting laundry lines and straw mats laid out for sunning in winter and for sleeping in the heat. The roofs were of all heights, their random layering creating what would soon be felt as humanity managing to survive and enjoy in a swarming mass of interdependence.

Non-violence was not as important as sharing. Our Western view of the greatness of Gandhi's teaching of *ahimsa* as a way to demoralize the British, show them their own brutality by not retaliating with force, was something Gandhi learned from the Pushtun warriors in Afganistan. It was a powerful passive-aggressive act, and had little in common with the gentle Jain sect who also practiced non-violence. The Jains wore surgical masks so that they might not breathe small, living organisms. Their teaching inspired the establishment of insect houses in India where families could deposit their household pests without taking their lives. The Jain teaching was based on non-violence, but not the culture of India. Guruji was firm in his opinion that hoarding, greed and accumulation were stealing the rights of others. *Aparigraha* was the basis of a well-ordered society, not non-violence. Non-violence is a result of virtue, not the cause.

Even more surprising was the opinion that Hitler was considered a hero for weakening the British during World War II, contributing to their retreat from the colonies. Gandhi was not held in such high regard, due to his negotiation of the partition of India such that Pakistan annexed the breadbasket of the Punjab and forced a separation and exodus of Muslims and Hindus, north and south across the border, which has divided families and perpetuated unrest in the region. Beautiful Kashmir, with its idyllic lakes and long history as a place of wonder, became a disputed territory.

We went overnight on the train through Orissa. At the stops, people would fill the narrow aisles in order to file off quickly before the queue on the platform filed in—all in a hurry. As our time to leave approached, Janiki pressed me into service: gathering up and stowing water bottles, peeling the luggage out of the upper bunks, handing the bags toward the door at the end of the car so that our large party would have sufficient time to press off, before the next group came on. If we delayed, and the newcomers began to board, we would lose our chance to descend. Shifting seats, tangling among bodies, parcels and luggage, we would be stranded on the train as it moved ahead to the next station.

One particular night, Janiki, who was always alert, asked me if I might not sit in a more forward compartment to save our reserved seats. Many of our party had crowded together in Guruji's compartment, so the seats in our reserved cabin near the door were mostly free. "Fine," I said. She explained they expected a large group to come on at the next stop, and there would not be enough seats for all of us. If we did not save our seats, we would lose our bunks for the night journey. We would never be able to get the newcomers to leave the front compartment. Affirming my willingness, I went forward to protect our reservation. One sleepy couple of our party was seated there, and they nodded in recognition. There was room for about eight people to sit, four on a side. I sat with extended arms, feeling like a bird in flight more than an anchor for our reservations. Knowing how futile my presence would be if a group of people arrived speaking Hindi, I spread my palms and fingers feeling the space of the bench. I began to question why we would not share.

The train stopped. From the window, I could see that no one went down to the platform. Then one large piece of luggage pushed past the front of our compartment, followed by a man. Then I heard shouts. More shouting. Five men from Guruji's room filed past to the door near the stairs. One of our compartments had no guard. Kanta Didi, barely five feet tall, rustled past. I quickly followed her. Twenty-five people jammed the aisle between my compartment and the end of the car. They yelled and flailed. Kanta Didi stood on a side bunk of the aisle, hanging on a post. She slipped off one of her little *chappels*. She held it by the toe and hit everyone on the head with the heel of her slipper.

Didi yelled with each whack. The men shoved each other. The melee did not last long. As they calmed, I saw that these people, all thinner than our well-fed group, were leaning to find their luggage at their feet. Some began to sit just as they were, on sacks bound tightly with twine, resignation sinking in as they saw that the night would be spent in the corridor. As our party gradually dispersed, Yogananda, the swami who had come to stay at our ashram in Kent, stood holding out a thick strand of his beard with one hand. Laughing, he pulled it to his face.

"They took off my beard!" People laughed with him. I turned toward Didi.

"Didiji! What were you doing in there fighting with the men?"

"I knew they would stop if a woman joined the fight," she said. "And a saint." The *sannyasis* called themselves "saints." She held up her *chappel* and deftly slipped it back on her foot.

"Like a gun in a holster," I reminisced.

We kept our compartment. The newcomers sat crammed together on their luggage and on the rims of the beds that lined the aisle. They had acquiesced. I listened to chatter from our group coming from their compartments, as they turned the beds down and spread out blankets, readying for the nighttime rocking of the train.

Freed from my duty as sentinel I walked down the aisle. I was not ready to settle. Alone in one compartment was an Indian man who lived in Canada, one who had brought video equipment. He was sitting with his head hanging. I stepped in to speak with him.

"What's the matter?"

"I'm depressed."

"Why?"

"The *sannyasis,* they are the ones who are supposed to be detached. They were fighting to keep what they had."

"Yes. Well, there was a shortage, I guess, and they were fighting to protect their own."

"I can't agree. I can't figure it out," he said, leaning farther into the wall of the train.

I felt wide awake and lively, even hungry for a snack. He made me wonder about myself. The fight was not sad to me; it was human nature. There was a shortage of seats and a need to protect. Less demarcation between mine and yours had a downside. Guruji always spoke of passivism as the great weakness of India. That India had been overrun

209

and dominated by Mughals and the British for hundreds of years was a source of shame. He looked for reasons why his beloved homeland was weak. He had told Bill and me that early Buddhism created a drain of the young and intelligent minds of India. The youth chose to be monks rather than scholars and warriors. This exodus of young minds was not unlike the late 20th Century India when young people sought advanced degrees and careers in North America and in Europe. The mere lack of supplies, the infuriating system of bribery, and other problems that handcuffed professional life made it more attractive for young people to leave India than stay. India is changing now, and young professionals are participating in an economic and cultural revival.

Buddhism was dominant in India from before the time of Christ and for a few hundred years after. The great carved caves of the monastery in Ajanta in central India were built in 400 BCE, occupied and expanded through the next 800 years. The site was an idyllic example of a life perched along a cliff overlooking a river, verdant with natural beauty and wildlife. As in the West, spiritual teaching was the province of monks. Buddhism became a teaching of detachment as *tyaga*, renouncing the world and family life, rather than *vairagya*, a spiritual detachment, possible while living among the world. Lord Krishna taught that the highest form of detachment was an entirely internal state of oneness with the source that could be sustained, even in the midst of the battlefield. The teaching came to Arjuna, who was despondent, because his duty was to protect society at the cost of a civil war. He was enjoined to fight. This was not a virtue of the Buddhist creed. The sons of families across the sub-continent were donning red robes and wandering, begging for their food, practicing their passive religion. And in the mountainous region of Hindu Kush, tucked into the foothills of the Himalayas, Guruji described thousands of these monks rounded up like cattle and slaughtered by invading conquerors. It was not difficult for India to be dominated by the Mughals. She had lost her warrior class and her dignity. Our Guru placed the *karmic* debt in the hands of India, and nowhere else. He said that the rigid caste system was a cultural abomination. The fact that his order of monks was a group of educated women, preachers and teachers reviving the ancient culture within the schools with discipline and knowledge, was a careful choice.

210

His words to us were, "Hoarding usurps the rights of others. So we must be non-grasping. Non-violence does not mean we are passive; we must not allow others to take what is not theirs."

The skirmish on the train broke the monotony for me. But more than that, I was coming to understand my spiritual family.

35

To see essence is called the original face.
The Secret of the Golden Flower

Guruji called me into his compartment as our train headed away from the famous temple of Sharada Devi. Sharada Devi is the goddess of eloquence. The temple rose like a nipple on a large mounded hill reaching up from a flat plain—a single breast of the mother. The hill, like the temple, was hand-made. Centuries ago, baskets of dirt were carried and dumped one atop the other until the small mountain stood ready. To reach the temple grounds, we walked a spiral path up, past numerous vendors of drinks, trinkets, small red-cloth bags of sugar, and souvenir carvings of Sharada Devi. Buildings in India, even tall temples are the work of many hands, but this temple mountain covered by thin, drying grasses seemed to be a work of nature.

In the shade of a grove of trees, as cooling breezes swept up from the plains, Guruji gave me his lecture in English, with a small group watching. Nature comforts me. In this particular lecture, on the hill looking over the plains between Orissa and Madhya Pradesh, I felt a joining of two rivers: my love of the soft lap of nature and my teacher's vibrant voice with his nourishing philosophy. He continued to teach from the ninth chapter in English.

I am the father of the universe, the mother, the establisher, the grandfather, the object of knowledge, the purifier, the sacred syllable Om, and the entirety of the Vedas. *Gita 9/17*

I was dwelling on the idea of God as not only father and mother, but Grandfather. The one who goes before; who holds a vision of the family and what it will need in generations to come.

212

Back in his train compartment, Guruji was writing a Sanskrit name on the inside cardboard cover of my notebook. His handwriting, always uneven because he had not learned the fine motor skill of printing until well in his twenties, was shakier due to the jostling of the train. He handed the notebook back to me.

"Devhuti," he said, "means one who calls God…into her lap."

I was choked with emotion. I had waited a long time for a name. Already, I could feel that my waiting was good. The name meant one who called. That was me; I was always calling inside myself. God come near—right into my lap. His words evoked the feeling of holding my children. I felt seen by my teacher.

"She called God into her lap because she wanted to know about inner freedom. God gave her a son who became her teacher. Devhuti is the mother of Lord Kapila, the first Samkhya philosopher, a great seer."

He pronounced the name clearly: "Dave-hooti."

I looked at his writing of my name, carefully lettered on the cardboard cover. Contemplating the wavering lines, I felt satisfied as I recalled the years of practice it took to arrive at this moment. The name was a vibration of some truth about me, a way to help me continue to evolve into myself. The temple we had just left was dedicated to Sharada Devi, the goddess of eloquence. I hoped it was significant.

"I will tell you the story of your name."

I leaned in so I could hear him better over the loud train. At this moment I felt less fearful. Closeness was not uncomfortable. I did not feel diminished by his power, something he did not want me to feel. The person I was becoming would be strong.

Devhuti chose to marry a hermit who lived in a hut by a river so that she could learn about meditation. She was not interested in worldly life. She lived with him and served him, but she was not becoming free. Because he was her husband, she could not understand how to hold him up as her teacher. As they lived together, she had nine daughters, each one perfect. In time, each one became an enlightened being. But her real learning began when at last a son was born, Lord Kapila, an incarnation of divinity. He taught her Samkhya philosophy, which teaches a vital distinction between nature and spirit.

Although I did not yet grasp the significance of the philosophy, I was well aware of how important it was to Guruji that someone spread the teaching to the West. My dedication had not been lost on my teacher. My indifference to success on the world's terms, my marriage to someone who had a depth of experience, but from whom I was unable to learn, even the many daughters who appeared to be my yoga students, all of these traits of the original Devhuti fit me well. Feeling appreciated, I saw my work ahead of me.

Guruji gave me my name the day before our group of forty traveling companions prepared to go separate ways. Seven of us remained with Guruji for another ten days. We traveled in two jeeps and took turns riding in his vehicle. When I was with him, he spoke in English, admiring the villages through which we traveled, communities that sustain a way of life that is threatened by modern values. When we stopped at the village where he was to lecture in the evening, our group was given one room with a bed for Guruji and open space for the rest of us. For the first time, I slept with his entourage and saw the routine in his room. Living in close quarters made me uneasy. I felt his awareness continually. I was uncomfortable, though I had a sense I belonged with this group. We stayed three days.

On the morning of the second day, I heard a tapping. I quickly looked over at him. While the rest of us were bustling about rolling up our beds, going to and from the bathroom, he was tapping on the bed sheets, as if holding a pulse. He tapped repeatedly with a loose wrist, just the fingertips touching. Observing me, he called out.

"Devhuti, come here."

I was slow to guess the tapping meant for me to come to his side—he had been lying down after his bath looking quite comfortable. I was insecure, feeling others around tending to their bedding or reading.

"Yes?" I replied as I kneeled at his bedside. I raised my eyebrows and felt my breath stop. I felt stiff with apprehension. His skin shone with a kind of early morning light.

"You know..." he began as he continued tapping. I realized that his rhythm also indicated a line of thought. "You remember the Oakland fire?"

I did. The disciple named Mira had returned from India to California and had watched her place burn.

"You know Mira spent eight months with me in India." He looked at me intently.

I felt how short my stay was—only five weeks. But I had to return to my children. Mira had no family and was studying to take *sannyas*. Guruji

214

changed her name from Mary to Mira, after knowing her for one week. I felt dismayed at the time. Maybe she was ready for a new life when she met him. I was not. I was ready for his teaching but I had a family to care for.

"She taped my lecture on Samkhya every day. She was with me eight months, but she only had a few tapes. So every evening, she would transcribe the lecture so that the tape could be reused. A lot of work. She was dedicated. Eight months in India is not a short time."

I was still holding my breath.

"She took all those papers back to America to work on them," he continued, taking his hand off the bed and pressing it into the other, miming a large weight. Then, he released his hands suddenly. "And it was all gone like that—in the fire!"

"Oh." I understood that there were volumes to learn about Samkhya. At the time, I knew only that it was different from Vedanta, and that it was ancient and seminal to Eastern thought, like Plato's thought to the West. Guruji just looked at me to see if I caught his meaning. I was quiet for a minute and then moved away from his bed. Flattered and confused, I really did not know what I was agreeing to.

Guruji watched me the next morning as I wrestled with another didi's sleeping bag. It was blue, overstuffed, and very slippery—any fold unfolded itself immediately. She stuffed it in a small sack each day. I was trying my hand at it that morning, forgetting that Guruji was a few feet away. I twisted my body to get my arm at the right angles to capture the next handful before the previous effort to press the cloth and filling would fail and the bag would come back out.

"Devhuti!"

I stopped. The freedom of losing myself in a task was over.

"I am like that sleeping bag."

I lifted my eyes to catch his expression. He was smiling.

"I am fluffy."

I smiled and continued stuffing the bag, feeling that I was wrestling my Guru, trying to do the impossible task, putting an overfull, excess of softness into a small sack. He was asking me to be less afraid of him. "Yes, your Fluffiness," I said to myself, wondering if I could ever say it out loud to him and if he would catch the allusion to royalty. His expansiveness was confined to a small body. To consider the task of reviving and spreading the ideology of Samkhya, I would have to let myself feel closer to him. Perhaps my task would be to let myself stay large, and stop trying to stuff myself back within the limitations I felt were me.

36

Evolution and involution.
Kapila

On the final train ride toward the main ashram at Virat Nagar, we stopped at a platform after nightfall. We stepped down from the train and checked to see that we had our luggage. I had begun to help my Indian friend from Canada by carrying his video equipment so he would have two hands for the camera. As I picked up his bags, I heard a shout.

"Devhuti! Come!"

I was startled to hear Guruji call out my new name. I apologized to my friend and ran along the platform to the front of the group.

Guruji was stepping between two columns of men, eight on a side, each holding a clay pot above his head. Inside each pot, rags burned with orange flames that threw aloft long plumes of black, sooty smoke. Guruji stepped with a long stride, motioning me to follow. The lines of men began to move forward with him. I stepped in behind.

One man shouted a call, "Brahm-rishi Vish-vaatma Baw-raa Jee a– Kee JAI!"

Others responded roaring the same chant. After a few repetitions, I recognized it as Guruji's full name. They were honoring him.

As they continued repeating the chant, and as I walked quickly along, my feet became small and far away. The heavens as if opened. I had quickly expanded again. The energy in my body was roused by the heat of the lamps, the shouts, and the joy in their voices. The galaxies were turning over our heads. I was not just walking on the earth, but on the earth traveling through space at thousands of miles per hour. Yet we still walked in one small spot—a momentary flame of glory. I felt my name still ringing in the sky with his.

217

This understanding of space was the teaching that he was pouring into me.

During the evening program I sat alone near the door that faced the temple's altar. Guruji was sitting in front, his devotees were gathered close. His face was small, lion-like, orange-gold, framed by his beard and hair. His eyes were deep and dark like the night. Off to the side was a lecturer, speaking in Hindi. Guruji was the witness. Whenever someone entered the hall during his talk, the lecturer would briefly chant the name of *Ram*, leading a call and response chant to settle the vibration of the room. My teacher looked out, as if seeing miles beyond our heads. I felt the roof of the temple dissolve and eternal space open above and around us. Often Guruji had told us: Consciousness is like space; it has no boundaries. You can put up walls, but you cannot divide space. Space is infinite. Consciousness is infinite. "Infinity is divinity."

We continued our journey by train, and it was my turn to sleep on the bunk above Guruji. The same space opened. I was settled into the rhythm of the train, my sleeping bag pulled up under my chin. The window was cracked to admit the cool, night air. I waited for sleep that did not come. Instead my awareness rose above the train, expanding up into the dark, flowing into an immense peace and stillness. I spent the night there, knowing I was inside my Guru's sleep, fully awake as he was.

Then we traveled by jeep. Guruji sat in front with a wet hand towel over his head. He tucked the ends behind his ears. He was trying to stay cool. By the end of February, winter was ending. In the heat of the day, he motioned the driver to stop by a modest roadside shrine to Hanumanji, the monkey god, who is often painted bright orange. I was traveling on this afternoon with Guruji, Janiki and Bhakti Priya. The jeep pulled over to the side, and we strolled back in the shade of some tall eucalyptus to a low stone arch in the bluff of the roadside. No sooner had we slipped the *chappels* off our feet, than Guruji lay on his belly in the dirt, elbows splayed, hands in prayer position over the center of his brow. He was speaking his prayers in a high giggle, as if chatting with a sweet, funny friend.

"He loves Hanumanji," Janiki whispered in my ear.

Self-consciously I sat down cross-legged near him, recalling how Guruji had wandered as a monk for twelve years, enjoying worship the way we enjoy the beauty of nature's rocks and streams.

218

By the roadside, I felt how God was not distant, but lived in rivers, in food, and in statues and in babies. God was seen dwelling in all forms. My path was not this, exactly. I was encouraged to find space of divinity within which all forms dwell.

Guruji explained that if a hair were split on end 10,000 times, one of the 10,000 split-off sections would be the size of the *brahma chakra* at the top of the head. It is the causal pulse of energy in the body. Above my head is where I felt my Guru's spoken Sanskrit dance. The words evoked palpable sensations in the air above my crown. Then, when I contemplated meaning, I could deepen my enlivened feeling. This place is called the *chitta* in yoga, and the *buddhi* in Samkhya; it is the mystic eye of the needle. Here, energy, enlivened by consciousness, gives birth to the ego, a child in the lap of two parents. Our initial sprout of ego is innocent and pure, as yet unattached to its own movements in the world.

After the ego is born, before the mind begins to move, there is space, a subtle element. From ego, space emerges. Simply put, when we first feel our existence, we are aware of space before any other experience. We orient to ourselves through the experience of space. Through space comes vibration. Sound and touch are initial movements of subtle matter, called *tanmatras,* subtle vibrations that the ego can experience directly, bypassing the grasping of the mind. The energetic vibrations of life are alive and awake, independent of mind and the organs of sense.

This was the teaching of Samkhya.

In India, outside the realm of the familiar, I engaged in the practice of quieting the senses and surrendering the ego back to its source. It was for this purpose that our teacher invited us to India. In this environment, he could open doors to another way of being. For him, the non-ordinary was ordinary. The meaning of the word *swami* is one who has self-mastery. A guru is one who is capable of relaying that experience to others, removing their darkness and revealing the vast light of consciousness.

Under the harsh conditions in India, Guruji wanted us to stabilize our inner experience. He wanted to free us of the delusion that sitting quietly in meditation was going to be enough. He wanted us to realize that stability does not depend upon comfort or order. Any meditation can be disturbed. Any ordered life can be disrupted by natural change. Awareness is the self. Movement is in service of stillness. Meditation teaches that everything is within us. We need to shift from identifying with the fluctuating world of energy to identifying with stable consciousness. The real self is independent and unchanging.

Many times Guruji told us: "The problem of how to live a spiritual life has not been solved. The monastic orders take this teaching and live apart from the world. The message of the *Gita* and the underlying ancient teaching of Samkhya can help us bring heaven on earth in this life."

At this point in the journey, most of the forty travelers had returned to Delhi by train. Evelyn had gone with them. She would be hosted by a Delhi family and from their luxurious home visit the town of Agra and the Taj Mahal, the famous Moghul Emperor's tomb built for his Hindu wife—a symbol of the blending of the Hindu and Muslim cultures. Evelyn was seeing India. I was still trying to look inside, not outside, and gain more inner stability by traveling with Guruji.

Traveling with Guruji was an experience of *Bharat*, the name of the motherland of India. The British coined the term India, naming the country after those who dwelled in the Indus River valley. Bharat means heartland. Guruji's India is populated with temples, shrines and stupas, creating the constant presence of divinity within shelters, the feeling of *dhaam*. Temples to the Mother are often housed in caves underground. To enter, one must stoop to pass under a low door and then stoop again in front of a small fenced opening to look into a room, the size of a large closet. The space is lit by lamps fueled with *ghee*, the pure oil made from cow's milk. The images of the Mother are shrouded in bright cloth. The worshippers need to be protected from the full force of the Mother—viewing her directly we risk being burned by her power.

I was surprised to find how small many shrines were—and how crudely made of brick and mortar. On my first trip in 1992, all of India felt hand-made. Stepping out of my sandals, I descended to these shrines feeling the cold earth under my feet. The shrines have a gate you can step past, for a few rupees, and glimpse the idol. Because I was with my Guru, I often stepped into a feeling of expansion. By closing my eyes and seeking inside, I felt an elevation of spirit. Sometimes I was disappointed and felt only the alienation of being in a foreign place, but my Guru's constant presence encouraged my search. He was always asking me to "peep" inside. The outer temple houses the inner experience.

Near the end of the journey, five of us, two didis, my friend Janiki, and a young man who was a temple *pundit*, took a trip to the Yamuna River to find a special stone for the Shiva temple at the ashram. Guruji had suggested I accompany the others, saying a day in the village might be too quiet and confining for me. I went along for the adventure. In the jeep, I should have been miserable. I was already suffering from dysentery, so I was weak. As part of my dalliance with attraction and aversion I had foolishly eaten grapes as the weather had turned warm. There is no way to sufficiently clean grapes. For the dysentery, a local doctor had given me a large and strenuously powerful pill that stopped the diarrhea, but I still felt weak. On the jeep ride, fumes leaked out of the tailpipe into the rear of the vehicle where four of us sat facing each other, two to a side. We wrapped our shawls around nose and mouth. The black soot of the fumes and fine dust from the road coated us head to toe. The driver honked in conversation with the other cars and buses, abruptly braking for pedestrians and swerving around rickshaws. Potholes and speed bumps heaved us side to side, front to back. The slow speed was the only redemption. As I closed my eyes to dwell on my mantra, the jerking rhythm faded from my awareness. Gradually the inner eye of the needle opened to reveal our vehicle moving on the landscape. Closed eyes were no impediment to viewing the details of the outer world. Inner sight provided a bird's eye view of the road, the hills, and the tiny people on the earth. My body was a dot, my spirit as large as space and sky. For hours I flew in the back of the jeep this way. Occasionally apprehension would draw me back in to the jeep. Indian drivers do not leave time to stop when they approach the tail of a slow vehicle. They merely slow a bit before swerving to avoid a collision. They stop only when they are certain there is no room to pass, when going around would mean death by impact.

Our small party split up in the riverside town so we could cover more shops, looking for the *Shiva Lingam*. These elliptical stones are found in the river bed here. The naturally large smooth stones are—in a typically Indian fashion—considered divine. None were found to suit the ashram—all too big, too small, or not the right color. I paid little attention to the search, feeling far from my familiar realm.

In the late afternoon, we made our return trip of eight hours. Most of the journey was in the dark of night. We were hungry; our food was waiting. My Guru addressed me as soon as we came in the door of the thatched building. "Your day was long, and you missed your lecture."

"Yes," I replied. "I missed the lecture but not the teaching. Teacher was jeep!"

221

Guruji laughed loudly, slapped his thigh and kept repeating my words, "Teacher was jeep!"

His pleasure made me feel an illumined strength that mingled in my body with the residual hum of the engine and the lurch of the road. I saw myself watching him in the light of one bare bulb. The teaching cinched itself inside me, shifting into a higher gear. Consciousness is free of the senses. The elevation of consciousness above the *chitta* brings a profound perspective, far beyond the needs of my little ego.

In that moment, I felt complete.

37

All greatness is improbable.
Lao Tzu

We continued by jeep. Our last resting place before returning to the ashram at Virat Nagar was a large home. It consisted of a group of buildings encircling a courtyard. There were two washrooms with showerheads set high in poured concrete chambers. This was more like home—a change from the exhilarating practice of dumping the remainder of cold water in a wash bucket over the head. The kitchen was large and clean, well-lit with a center island just like a modern one in the States. A separate suite of rooms was set aside for Guruji, and the eight of us traveling with him shared a large living room with a carpet where we immediately rolled out our bags to rest. Travel with dysentery was draining.

I lay back with legs crossed and began to drift into a deep meditation and inner expansion. At some point a young woman came in, sat on the couch at the end of the room and began to talk. She let loose a river of words—what felt like a tirade against the fate of young mothers who must deal with isolation. That had been my experience. I understood only her tone. I heard my travel companions around me give occasional grunts of affirmation. Inside myself I was floating in a deep peace beyond words.

After a while, I sat up and focused on the fine quality of her deep green sari that spoke of wealth and privilege. Janiki asked if I was okay. "Yes, fine," I answered. She was checking on me because I had been sick. I was more than fine. I was quietly ecstatic inside myself. My practice was private; I did not want to explain that I was meditating, nor was there any need. Most people were deeply peaceful around Guruji. This disturbed woman was an exception, as I had often been.

An interesting shift in the dynamic of our group was that with Evelyn gone, I had no adversary, and Janiki formed a new alliance with another didi who was having the same difficulty I had with Evelyn. They had to share a room when traveling with Guruji. Observing my own drama played out in another triangle was a good point of self-study. I realized I missed Janiki's full attention. And I understood that it was not all about me, but about her need to ally with the one who felt oppressed by the personality of another person. Justified or not, the drama continues in many forms. I felt a healthy detachment.

I went to the kitchen where another mother had a crew of bright-faced daughters and friends helping her. They seemed content, and the mother, who spoke English well, asked about our journey. She was more typical of the devotees who feel Guruji's grace. I understood this peace now; I could recognize it in others. Dinner was served, and I slept early.

There was always competition to use the washroom in the morning, no matter where we stayed. At this home, I did not know if there were more washrooms than the two I had seen, so I awoke early, alert and ready to begin the morning ritual of bathing and washing a few clothes by hand before I meditated. We had been traveling for days. I loaded two buckets with my garments, soaked, washed, and rinsed them, rinsed them again, chanting a little, delighting in a task well done before the others even awoke. My inner voice questioned me quietly with, "You are going home shortly, do you need to clean all your clothes?" I was splashing loudly and happily. I did not want my flow disturbed. I took my clothes out where I had noticed a clothesline, and spread them neatly.

Returning to the washroom, I used the toilet. It did not flush. I went to rinse my hands under the spigot. Again, no water.

I had a problem: there is a rule in India that after using the toilet, rinse the hands. I opened the door into the courtyard, and saw Guruji crossing it with his hair disheveled and his orange cloth wrinkled from sleeping. He was walking slowly behind a man carrying two buckets of water. I came forward to do *pranam* by touching his feet, another way to begin the morning on the right foot, with his blessing. He motioned for the man to stop and he set the buckets down.

Now another dilemma: I had to rinse my hands to touch his feet. I instinctively reached my hands in one of the buckets to take just a little water. Seeing his irritation, I knew immediately what I had done.

"You have polluted this whole bucket," he said. "There is no water."

I looked back at the direction of the kitchen from where he had come, where they had drawn this water.

"These two are for my bath. No pollution, Devhuti!"

Guilt flooded me. I had practically taken a swim that morning and now there was no water. In this generous and clean home, I could feel how my American tendency to enjoy whatever luxuries I find had ballooned back into place. I had been taking care of myself, with no thought of others. I needed another kind of bathing, the kind that would wash away the glaze that had come over my mind in anticipation of going home.

I went off to meditate. There may have been some trouble with the waterline that was subsequently repaired, or perhaps there was a well in back for buckets because by the end of the morning, everyone had bathed and rinsed their clothes. When I went to check my clothes on the line at midday, several lines stretched above trampled grasses filled with long saris, towels, underclothes, and men's pajamas and tops. Janiki stood checking the dampness by rubbing her cloth between her fingers. Guruji suddenly came through the archway from the courtyard to the clothes lines. He stopped near me and looked in my eyes.

"So, you have taken bath?"

Janiki spoke up in my defense, "She was up first, Guruji. She took a bath a long time ago."

I nodded my head and bowed a little, I did *pranam* to his feet as if we were just meeting on this bright morning.

"Yes, Guruji," I said, and then added in my mind, "Janiki does not know I needed another bath. I took that bath, too."

Pollution has a precise philosophical meaning: the covering of the light of wisdom. If we live in the light of wisdom, our life is in harmony and supports the life of others. If we are driven by impulses and cravings we become selfish and dark. If we find a way to live in the light of wisdom, we serve life.

Returning from India, I was heading straight into an internship for my master's degree. I would need to tend to my marriage and the needs of my children. I prepared to leave for the airport from the small ashram in Delhi. Swami Yogananda brought me a double-headed drum to take home so I could accompany chanting with some instrument. Lord Shiva had played a tiny double-headed drum and initiated the pulse of language, Kanta Didi had told me many times. I had asked Yogananda to find me

225

one and he kindly obliged. Guruji must have anticipated the difficulties ahead. He approached my window just before my final jeep ride, leaned toward me and balled his fist.

"Be firm, be fixed, be determined."

I nodded *pranam* and took that as his final blessing.

On the way home, there was a layover in Kuwait. They had wide curved chairs for sleeping between flights. The airport was an international hub for Kuwaiti airlines. My luggage was with me since I had to change airplanes. I found a seat where I could stretch out with one hand draped over my luggage and my drum. I heard footsteps and voices come and fade. In a light sleep, I felt watched. Occasionally footsteps would pause. As the morning light came through the windows, I raised my head and began to ponder going to the washroom with my luggage. A voice came from behind my back, "I'll watch your bags for you."

I turned to look.

"I've been watching you for hours. People have been eyeing you and your stuff."

I had not heard anyone say the word "stuff" for weeks. I felt more awake.

"Thank you. Yeah, I felt like I was being watched."

The woman was older than me, dressed in black pants and jacket.

"You traveling alone, too?"

"Yes."

"Just passing through Kuwait or on business here?"

"I'm a corporate trainer and I was working here. Educational stuff."

That word again. I sighed. It felt wonderful to speak casual English. A dormant part of me was re-awakening. "I'll take just a minute to go to the washroom. Be great if you could watch these."

When I returned, we talked. She had been trained in counseling and was in charge of developing sensitivity to foreign cultures in the international business community. We spoke in depth. My life in English was resurfacing. I could feel a familiar sense of self in the world, the ego. It was both comforting and exciting.

"This is the most English I've spoken in five weeks. I forgot who I was in English."

She laughed. She understood.

38

We need a knowledge that can free us from peacelessness on all levels.
Swami Bawra

The container of my life did not fit the expansion of my experience. The old restlessness remained. For a while, back in Ohio, I would awaken in the night next to Bill and feel I was still in India in some large room with people sleeping around me. I would not know who Bill was. I loved my children, but not my marriage. I felt constrained by our fraught communication—despite the ease I felt living with sparse language in India. When we traveled on the buses and trains of India, I detached from my life in the States. Bill was naturally frustrated that I had not tried to call or to write more. My excuse was simple: both were remarkably difficult in India in 1992, even finding a post office.

In March, Bill decided to go to India to attend the *kumbha mela* in Haridwar. He needed his own retreat. The *kumbha mela* is a large gathering of saints and pilgrims at the Ganges River, where the banks become crowded with masses of people taking auspicious dips in the holy, moving water. In Haridwar, the river is deep and slow, and there are wide *ghats* or steps for descending and bathing.

The *kumbha* was extraordinarily hot, crowded and unsanitary. He told me about lying on the floor of his room to get away from it all and feel the cool cement on his back. He wanted to go inward and block out the stimulation. He said I would not believe the amount of monks in orange cloth, with shaved heads or matted hair, tucking up their robes or disrobing completely to take a dip in the Mother Ganges and pour her water over their heads. Chanting was everywhere over loudspeakers, flowers and rice were tossed in the water and brass plates of flames fueled with fresh *ghee* were spun in *pujas* over the current. The banks were massed with people. Bill retreated to the shared sleeping chamber.

From there, the group went by bus to a Mother Goddess temple in Vindhyachal, where Guruji had done his first hard practice and gained realization of knowledge. Bill had wanted to return to Vindhyachal, and Guruji had agreed to take him. On the side of the mountain was a small cave dedicated to Ashtabhuja, Saraswati, goddess of knowledge. As Bill returned from the cave of the goddess to where Guruji was resting, Guruji turned to Bill and called him *Yogendra*. Thus, without ceremony, Guruji acknowledged and affirmed the name he had called Bill in meditation during his first visit to India. In meditation, Guruji had called Bill by this name and then turned into a mirror in which the many past lives they had shared were shown to him. Yogendra literally means "master of yoga." Bill's name implied self-mastery and the ensuing insight into truth and life that comes from one who is wedded to his real self. Guruji dictated this letter that came home to me in Bill's handwriting. He began the letter with a prayer.

O my beloved Lord, my divine father, whatever is inauspicious among us please remove and annihilate that and whatever is auspicious for us please bestow that. O effulgent light, o merciful lord we are meditating upon you please direct our wisdom according to your own will. This is our heartiest desire.

My dear Devhuti, may god bless you and your children too. My heartiest love and blessing is always with you. I gave new name to your beloved husband and his name becomes now Yogendra. I was giving him one hour daily for early morning walk. And I was teaching him my deepest and finest philosophy at that time. Whatever purpose he had in his own mind when he came here has become fulfilled. And God will help him, and you and children always. You will be vessels of divine blessings and divine love.

I am teaching daily Bhagavad Gita, and when Yogendra was here I taught some in English. I hope that whatever you are both receiving and realizing and feeling and understanding you will put in your own practice and you will become useful for other people in your own country.

I wish to prepare some divine souls for divine service and I believe that you both are among those and will do some great work for divine. You know that if one person offers his whole wealth to one person that will still not make him satisfied. Divine knowledge can bring happiness and peace to not only one or two persons, but millions of people. This knowledge is the greatest wealth which can give peace

228

and satisfaction to mankind. I know that if you will help and guide those people and put them on the proper path, path of divine, then they will achieve inner happiness and tranquility too.

Try to teach people how to meditate and after that read some holy treatises. Maybe Upanishad, Bhagavad Gita, Yoga Sutras. Maybe that part of Bible called Sermon on the Mount. I like that part of Bible and I think that is nothing but translation of our divine thought. Whatever Jesus Christ learned in India and translated for his own countryman.

If you will study that, it will give inspiration and divine ideas to all my devotees. This is my heartiest, heartiest wish to do something for mankind and create such kind of ideas among mankind. If they will tread on divine path they will achieve peace and happiness and it will be greatest gift for mankind.

May god bless you and convey my love and blessing to my children, Paul and Matthew, and other your friends. Mostly everything is okay except for tube well is not working properly. We have now only fifteen minutes of water and this is causing trouble for the cows and for all of us at the ashram. You know now my orphan children have become fifty-four in hostel and then others in ashram. It is very difficult without water. We are going to try and dig a new well. I called one person, but I was not here so now I will call again and give him contract. How we can achieve water God knows. This water is main problem here and I hope we will solve it so our work can continue more easily.

So God bless you, my dear. Live happily and be happy and do some divine work. I know you are doing that and you will do that for the two of you. Convey my love and blessings to the children and all. Okay now. Yours own, V. Bawra.

After Bill returned another letter came.

July 1992

My dear Yogendra and Devhuti, blessings with sweet love.

I believe you all will be happy and healthy by the grace of divine father. Your inner practice will be progressive and joyful too. My health is okay. I spent one month in Kulu Himalaya. That place is very divine, cool, and peaceful. According to divine plan I bought there five acre land with a good orchard, apple, plum, pears. All about 400 plants. I think that you will like Kulu. I gave new name for that land, Devvan meaning divine forest. That place is 400 ft above from sea level on the bank of a divine Vyas River surrounded by big mountain and those mountains are more than 10,000 feet high. The Kulu Valley is two miles away

229

from the city. In summer that place is very good. I came yesterday from there, now after 22nd August. I will be at ashram and then I will go to Korea.

Everybody is happy in ashram. I am going to install Lord Shiva's idol I brought from holy Narada River, so beautiful like Hiranyagarba (Big Golden Egg), at 9th of July and at there will be 7 days of Yoga Camp with Guru Puja. So everybody is busy in arrangements. Fortunately digging of our new well is complete and ashram cows have water. Holy gathering for installation and yoga camp will go smoothly.

How are Paul and Matthew? Give my sweet love with heartiest blessings. My dears, human is only a good instrument in the hands of divine, but sometimes due to his own ignorance and egoistic darkness thinks that he himself is doer and enjoyer. Due to this he suffers and becomes prey of so many calamities. In the light of real knowledge when he understands his own tiny form and helpless existence he surrenders himself into the holy feet of Godhead. Only in this position he becomes free of doership and become free from all calamites and achieves eternal peace. May God bless you both and may he engage you both and make you happy and healthy. This is my heartiest blessings. Convey my love to all my dear children. Rest is okay. With best wishes and heartiest blessings

Yours own Vishvatma Bawra.

These letters were encouraging, but I was not ready to settle down and teach with Bill. I still had to confront myself. "Not God, no teacher, not a thousand gurus can solve the problem of your own mind," Guruji had told us. Guruji gave me an expanded experience in India. It was up to me to integrate it. We have to solve the problems of our own lives.

39

Fulfilling your talent is doing what you were meant to do.
Like the strong wood at the heart of the tree, it is there for the builder.
Deng Ming-Dao

Teaching yoga after my first trip to India was different. I began to experiment with poses and their sequencing, with breath, and with ideas of yoga in such a way that a great expansion visited me before and after each class. Each session ended with a manifest journey out to the galaxies inside me. The effect of my Guru's teaching was that sound was now a palpable experience—subtle ripples of vibration through space. Hatha yoga was still new to Americans; there were not many teachers or classes. Students came from all over to attend these sessions—rousing poses and *pranayama* followed by deep stillness. I taught a Saturday morning class at the ashram in Kent. A year later, I rented the basement of the Unitarian Universalist Church in Kent. This was my main home for yoga for fifteen years. Although I taught in other settings and communities, in this setting I found stability in the expansive nature of practice and confidence in my approach to teaching *asana*. Our ashram in Kent was up the street. When Guruji visited, I could feel his presence uplift my awareness.

On a sunny winter morning in 1993, while teaching the Saturday hatha class at the Kent ashram, the class returned to sitting on blankets, legs folded, ready for *Om* and a Sanskrit chant that I shared at the end of each class. As I sat, my mind went completely still. I was not able to access the Sanskrit. Instead, a vision emerged of a Western prairie with dried grasses and a Native American chant. The figure of a Native teacher appeared, gazing at me with a long serious stare from under his buffalo horn headdress. The vision lasted for a few minutes before fading. I could not recall any Sanskrit, and the class ended in silence.

231

I went home to Bill and the boys. Sun poured through the windows as Bill sat peacefully reading the paper. He had fed the boys, who were playing in their rooms. I tried to sit and meditate peacefully, but the sound of moaning came from Brady Lake, down the hill from our house. The forty-acre lake was refreezing after a brief thaw, and the enlarging plates of ice rubbed against each other, creating deep pulsing moans, as if the ice were giving voice to some great ancient mammal. I asked Bill if he minded if I left the house again to go skating. I could not speak with him about how compelled I felt to be near the sound.

The air was cold and crisp. A light breeze stirred. It shifted the swirling patches of wind-blown snow on the surface of the black ice. I sat on the bank to tie the laces of my skates tight up my ankle, distracted by the beauty of the surface. Sitting close to the sound was transporting; a trance-like state was growing in me. Finally standing on the thin blades, the black ice smooth and firm, I tested my feet and then picked up speed. Tracing a wide arc, finding a path through the snow patches, I felt my peripheral vision fill with blue sky around and beyond the small wisps of clouds. The bass tones of low rhythmic sounds continued, now under my feet, now around me, louder and more resonant. After a while, I could feel and see in my mind's eye a Native American figure in the sky following me. He wore a white shirt and jeans and long black hair streamed out behind him. When the image did not fade, I spoke in my mind to him, "What are you doing?"

"I am coming here."

I continued to skate, the image following me, then tripped on a divot in the ice and fell on my back. Surrendering, relaxed, I let my mind receive the experience. The sky figure began teaching, and told me that my name was "soaring eagle."

As I skated back, the moans were diminishing. Returning to the house, I wrote up the experience and took it to the home of two Saturday morning yoga students and left it there. They had some affiliation with the Native tradition and I was hoping my experience had some meaning for them. They called later to say the experience had nothing to do with them. It was mine.

Thus began a confusing few years. I knew I needed to become grounded and felt that maybe the Native tradition could teach me. I did some study of the four directions and adopted the "Cherokee Dance of Life," a series of flowing movements between earth and sky and the four cardinal directions. This dance flows with movement and meaning and was congruent with the human need to live close to a source of wisdom. The direction of the East brings the first light inspiration; South is accumulation of resources and people to bring idea into form; West is the cave of solitude and assimilation of learning; North is the distilled wisdom of the experience. Three of these four are introspective. They require quiet and an attitude of listening. Listen for the wisdom that comes when we are still. This was the first lesson Bill had for me in our early marriage. Inspiration can also be unusual. If we truly listen as I was when the Native visions came, then we are not seeking control of life, we are seeking to harmonize with life. Inspiration is not within our control.

I started a women's circle at the Indian burial mound in Towner's Woods. I walked barefoot in the woods of this nearby park. After a few months, I turned the women's circle over to the care of other women. A medicine man named Little Elk did come to town. One woman studied shamanism with him. I was not interested. I knew my spiritual home was elsewhere. I had no interest in continuing with another culture and its spiritual language and practices, except the dance, which helps me to this day.

The ice flow, thaw and freeze, were an annual event. The ice on the lake could freeze eight inches thick. The ice fishermen had special augers to drill into the ice, creating a hole wide enough to pull the catch back through with the line. They set small tents over the portals, added portable heaters, and passed long hours with friends and beer. This was normal; my visions were not.

I had met an acquaintance who told me about Jin Shin Jyutsu, a form of acupressure and a new way of healing. I was ready to hear her, ready to try something that might unlock a new place inside me that could hold expansive meditation and my responsibilities. During the first session, I screamed aloud, prompting her to call her teachers in Arizona. The practice is gentle—almost no movement. The practitioner places her hands on specific, successive areas of the body and holds them for minutes. I opened internally, as if for the first time—an ice flow broke with an explosive crack. While continuing sessions with her, I began training in this hands-on practice.

During this time, I rediscovered creativity that been suppressed by my fear of being myself. I had allowed myself to be dominated by what I should do, as my mother had taught me. Discipline had been her tool for survival. I needed to retain my practice and discipline, while rediscovering my humor and melting into myself. I expressed once frozen emotions: drawing, painting tee-shirts, and making beaded necklaces. I wrote poetry and pieces of memoir. I kept following a vision. The spirit of my father was that life should be lived well, put into expression, and shared. At this time in my practice, I could only maintain the serious nature of my inner work if I created art.

I was resurrecting a place in myself that my father had cultivated, a place of creativity and vitality. We had played games of drawing together when I was a child. He was a sky artist; he painted clouds, birds, angels, people with a spirit of story-telling and humor. He submitted anthropomorphized, whimsical bird cartoons to the Pennington Post, of Pennington, New Jersey for over a decade, which I eventually compiled in a chapter book called, *The Best of Biddle's Birdcage*. On our bedroom wall, I hung a picture of his birds and angels, who look like all manner of people. One angel is without wings but is receiving a new pair from another angel. The caption reads, "Angels and birds both share heavenly space. It is crowded and sometimes there are flying accidents and angels lose their wings. God sees new pairs are promptly provided, for God has an infinite supply of angel wings." The words are instructional, explaining heaven to us, as if taking ourselves seriously is the only possible sin.

My creative process needed to mature. James Thornton was the theatre director of a large program at Shaker Heights High School. Starting in 1993, he invited me to be a movement specialist with a select theatre ensemble. He asked me because I knew movement, but not choreography. He trained me to elicit movement from the students and to watch their play. From their movement, I would craft a longer piece, based on the themes of the times. James taught me to look for their strengths and build on them, while diminishing weaknesses. We worked together for ten years; through his training my creative process was reinforced.

I could no longer tolerate the inner freeze and thaw of my emotions. It was not possible for me to subdue my psyche or defer an eruption of its contents. My psyche was no longer held by the scaffold of duty. Creativity was driving me, but it was a torrent of complication. I had not solved the problem of my own mind.

The specter of abandonment was haunting me. As my boys were older and needed me less, I felt a reverberation of the time when my

234

brothers left home. This time I would leave first, before my sons. I would not be abandoned. Though I knew this plan was irrational, the feeling was powerful. I wanted to hold onto it, knowing it carried the force of an important threshold—a fitful crossing. I did not speak the thought out loud: "I have to leave home first!"—knowing how unreasonable it sounded. If I had spoken it, I would have coldly defended myself against the truth that my sons were not my brothers and that brothers leaving home is not abandonment. My sense of self had formed around a core of neglect long before my brothers, Chris and David, had left.

My family's break-up triggered the first thaw in my emotional life; feelings of anger, fear, and unfairness surfaced. The ice was cracking again and the often-submerged mass of unfelt emotions was surfacing with the discordant tone of my badly traveled adolescence. The common unfairness of marriage was now too much for me. The pressure to give and receive warmth and presence within my family was more than I could tolerate.

Unwanted dissociated visions continued. When I entered any state or county park, lands where the Native tribes had lived and roamed, I heard them speaking with me:

"Why are you wearing shoes?"

I would try to ignore the voice. It was as if they saw me as Native. Perhaps I had been. Sometimes I replied inside my head.

"Why are you angry?"

No reply from them, but a quieting as though they heard me.

"Why did your culture fail to retain its power?" I continued.

Then I would lecture to them, whoever they were, the unseen people who had lived here before, or the unseen specters of my own inner disturbance.

"You lived from the heart center, not the higher centers. Your people fought among each other and that was your weakness. You needed to unite as one people in the higher centers, but you could not leave your passions. Your tribes stayed divided."

The answer was simplistic but it quieted the voices, and my own words would eventually help me find my way back to my family. I felt divided; I needed to resolve the problem.

First, I made my family feel abandoned, rather than feel the loss that lived at my core. I would let them be swallowed by the incomprehensible neglect and shame I had always lived with. I felt I had lost my home once, now the warmth of its containment was a reminder that I could lose everything again. I was driven to leave my home and begin purging the feelings of loss that had overwhelmed me.

I gripped my hard-earned adult skills and tools. I did not want my abilities overtaken by psychosis or depression. I did not want to lose my way again in a flood of aloneness and loss. At all costs, I wanted to avoid the feeling of drowning in my feelings.

I felt compelled to leave my family. I ignored what they were feeling. My boys were silent. Bill was outraged but helpless to stop me.

Overtaken by a manic haze, I sought reasonable tasks. One upper room at the ashram was free of renters. I had begun my Jin Shin Jyutsu practice with clients in the upstairs room. This became my bedroom. The downstairs living room became an area for my massage table. I bought solid wood doors to fit the open archway of the downstairs workspace, installed hinges, and hoisted them into place. Shivdas and the other renter watched me. I painted the interior again, some myself, some by trade with clients. I had clean gravel dumped in the back yard and raked it out myself. I did not want help.

I continued to train in Jin Shin Jyutsu, a four-year process of week-long local trainings with national teachers. I planned to attend therapeutic hatha yoga training in California to become certified to teach yoga in the States. I increased the number of classes I taught per week as a way to prepare myself. I stayed busy. Living alone was uncomfortable.

I got to know Shivdas better by staying at the ashram. Shivdas is his Indian name, "servant of Shiva." His mail came to Tyrone Johnson, and, sometimes, Tyrone Jafar, his Muslim name. He was a pleasant African-American man, tall and slender, with close-cropped hair, who for decades showed no sign of aging. He had once worked at a General Electric plant on the Eastside of Cleveland, painting light bulbs. Given the spiritual analogy of our inner light likened to a bulb that is covered by darkness and ignorance that must be removed so that we may live free from suffering and gain self-realization, his job description was ironic. He covered the light, although in pretty colors and for gaining social security in his old age. Shivdas was intelligent and affable, but he was a loner and occupied his nights with contemplation and late-night radio. Among his intellectual pursuits were Hare Krishna, Radical Christian, Mystical Islam, natural healing and vitamins, the origin of human life in the Pleiades, and water filters in case of Armageddon.

He brought fruit pies home to share with me. It did not take us long to realize we were both happy eating fruit pie for dinner—fresh peach, cherry, apple. Shivdas indulged me because he knew I was troubled. He made himself at home when our teachers were gone. One way was by eating exactly what he wanted. In the Hindu culture it is considered a sin not to offer food to others when you eat. Solitary eating is disrespecting the gift of food. Didiji was always encouraging Shivdas to eat meals with her. And at the events at Indian homes, he was expected to eat well. Shivdas refused food. He was recalcitrant. When Shivdas chauffeured them, he often ran a stray errand when they were supposed to be leaving. He made them tardy. Shivdas managed to hold his own.

When the teachers left, Shivdas took it upon himself to pay their phone bills; this was before calling cards, before cell phones. Didi left some money for water, sewer and heat bills, but no extra. Even though this was one of many international centers, he stopped answering the phone. He believed the CIA had begun wire-tapping the phone lines, back in 1986, when we first opened. I was rebelling against the constraints of a life I had agreed to live. Shivdas was a good companion in my upheaval.

During the separation, I felt more anxiety, which was helpful. I had feared anxiety, thinking it might overwhelm me. I found out that I was stronger than I had been. Anxiety prompted me to work constantly. The Christmas season came and went and I hardly saw my children. I had them to dinner once, and brought out a small table so they would not be sitting on the floor. They had little to say then either.

After they left, I sobbed deeply. Shivdas sat next to me with his hand on my arm and said nothing. He could not help me.

Inside I asked my teacher to let me know when I should return. I spoke aloud to the space around me, knowing that my Guru would hear me. I trusted he would know how to help. After six months of living at the ashram and keeping a busy schedule to fill the hours, I was ready to return home.

In early spring, hurrying to wash the road-salt off my car, I locked myself out of the car, with the engine still running. I called the police. An officer came and jimmied the lock. While watching, I heard in my head:

"Don't lock Bill out anymore—return to him."

I called Bill later. The next day we met at Love Furniture in Akron to buy a new couch for the boys' downstairs area.

"So what are you looking for?" I immediately went to a practical question.

"I am thinking of an "L"-shaped sectional.

"This is for the family room downstairs?"

"Yes, the boys spend a lot of time there."

We began again. I moved back home within a few days. Bill was vulnerable, uncertain about himself. I had never seen him that way. He was less decisive. His depression had compromised his ability to perform at work and attend to our children. Bill felt defeated by my absence. His whole purpose in helping me and keeping the family together was negated by my leaving. He needed me. My children needed me. It was time to return and to heal with them, slowly.

I kept the Jin Shin Jyutsu business, but my non-ordinary experiences were a problem. I could instantly merge with my clients' inner states in their subtle body and speak to their issues as if from inside their own experience. I needed to heal myself.

My skills in healing had been inflated by my expansive meditation and the presence of my Guru, even before I went to India. Periodically a student would indicate that my teaching reached far beyond the physical.

One student said, "At the end of class, during deep relaxation, when you laid your shawl over me, I met with my sister who committed suicide. She had felt lost to me."

When I held someone's toes: "I went out into the universe."

I held shoulders: "I went out into the stars."

From a man who had an intense vision of Mother Goddess during the healing session: "My supervisor says no more body work during lunch hour. After seeing Mother Goddess on my break from work, I was worthless the rest of the day."

I had abilities far beyond the capacity of my wounded self.

I meditated deeply and long into the night sitting on the floor at the end of the bed where Bill was sleeping, achieving a profoundly elevated state. But I knew I remained fractured.

40

Do what you can, with what you have, where you are.
Theodore Roosevelt

I went to the yoga training in Santa Barbara, California a couple of weeks after returning home. A letter home:

Dear Bill,

It's good to dialogue with you again. I missed it. Actually I'm doing most of the talking here but that's okay—I like to talk (joke).

All the meditation I have done has not touched the place in me that implodes. I like the analogy of watering an orchard with a sink-hole in it—does no good. I've found the sink-hole. I had to act out losing everything to want everything back and make it all work. Honestly I did not want to live this out but experience is sometimes the best teacher and no matter how hard I tried, I could not learn what pain has now taught me. I hope you can understand that my lack of regret has little to do with callousness; it has to do with a sense of self-mastery. To move forward, I can't dwell on feeling badly about myself. I have done enough of that.

I'm awed by the incredible accuracy and power of karmic reconstruction or construction of surrounding events, personalities, mutual lessons. I think obviously our souls' dedication to each other is real and perhaps because of that or because of some higher need to breach all delusions, we were given the perfect pain in each other to work loose these blind spots. How incredible. I know we know this but the seeing of it is mind-boggling. I hope we can live in the safe, warm side of ourselves from now on—okay and fun too.

I'm bringing home a fantastic cookbook. She uses soft tofu to make sauces and desserts that are wonderful. Good for you and the boys—tastewise.

Instead of teaching a practice therapeutic class, I may teach a class on sadhana—pranayama and higher meditation. So many of the women here are ready and

239

have no teacher to confirm where they are and take them to the next step. I seem to be able to. We've been very blessed.

Love, Devhuti

Tell the boys to be ready for some new cooking.

I had changed. A lasting thaw of my feelings had begun.

The crux of it was acting out my father's sudden exit from our family and recreating my early adult years, when I had determined not to feel or act "insane." My father could not return to my mother; their differences could not be resolved. I was able to return to Bill and the boys. Bill had changed. He had tempered his opinions and was accepting of whatever it took for me to become more stable within myself.

My Guru was disappointed that I chose Integrative Yoga Therapy in California rather than attending his yoga college in Chandigarh, India. I wanted to develop a method of teaching that was suited to my own culture. I went on to earn a master's certification in Integrative Yoga Therapy with Joseph LePage.

Integrative Yoga Therapy was carefully chosen. Most teacher trainings taught a set series of poses and practices. Josegh LePage taught yoga as a method of healing the feeling of separation, by integrating the knowledge of the *kosas* with the bio-mechanics of movement and physiology. The *kosas* are a Vedantic teaching regarding the layers of energetic experience that we carry so intimately we rarely separate them, and they roughly corresponded with my Guru's initial teaching of body, senses, mind, ego and intellect. When first meeting the swami, he suggested I see in what layer of identification I was bound and gradually move to a deeper layer. Energy expresses in layers from casual, to subtle and gross. We understand these layers of life from physics: We share causal particles that are universal, then shared molecules of undifferentiated matter, then structures of form that are clearly distinct from one another. On the level of the body, we appear separate, but as we go deeper to our foundation in thoughts and values and the appreciation of wisdom and compassion, human experience has a shared platform. Our conscious capacity to witness all levels of our experience is what we are seeking—consciousness itself.

The Native American experience and Jin Shin Jyutsu came in my life about the same time. The Asian philosophy was easy for me to align with. It teaches a "physio-psycho-philosophy" in one gentle healing practice. It

240

uses touch and knowledge of meridians to balance the body. Jin Shin Jyutsu induced a relaxation that was harmonizing and peaceful, simple and profound. Giving and receiving helped me integrate myself in quiet.

The Native teachings were less familiar. As the experiences persisted, I thought more about the land we lived upon. The British occupied the Americas as they had colonized India. Here they reduced the power of the Native population more completely. The early 19th Century Quaker ideal of quietism is depicted by Edward Hicks in his *Peaceable Kingdom* paintings. He portrays a delicate balance of the irreconcilable forces of human nature with the lion lying down with the lamb, the bull, the bear and other beasts. Over time, the paintings ironically expose the dominance of the white culture over the new land, without integration of the cultures. However, some blending was inevitable. Alongside the colonists fighting for freedom in the American Revolution was the Iraquois Confederacy, a nation of Indian nations.

The Great Binding Law of the Iraquois Confederacy has been cited as inspiration for the constitution of our founding fathers. There is no historical evidence that it was. Greater evidence lies in the fact that their ways were admired, and their way of life has survived in Upper New York State and Canada. The Great Binding Law was a constitution for living with peace. There were many Native American dialects. The "people of the longhouse" shared a common language and an intention around speaking and listening—the central method of their union. *Hiro kone*, "I have spoken" sounded like "Iraquois" to the French, who were fur traders in the Great Lakes region.

In the Great Binding Law, the people are the firekeepers who swear to mutual protection, to uphold the rights of women, and observe the welfare of all in good will. They swear to uphold their teaching in the brightness of the sun's light and live together as one tree, the Tree of Great Long Leaves, the Tree of Great Peace whose white roots are peace and strength. An eagle keeps watch above the high branches.

This people's ideal of the equality of speaking and listening was a model of democratic voice. They held language as sacred and the peace pipe was often used as a talking stick, passed from the elder to whoever was ready to speak. The others listened in silence. Peace was upheld by respecting freedom of speech without fear of reprisal or shaming.

We are aware of the Greek model, a powerful, short-lived era of democracy. Likewise in India, Guruji had pointed to a large rock outside a village in India, carved with script.

"Margot, the list carved on this rock are the rules of self-governance. There was a small era in this place in India when government was held by all the people together because of their own practice of restraint. If we practice self-discipline, then we can live well in society. But it is not so easy. The democratic ideal has long been alive in India."

For me, the practice of yoga was learning to listen to myself, to others, and to speak truthfully. I listened for wisdom.

Teaching in the basement of the Unitarian Universalist Church with their footsteps sometimes dancing over our heads, I imbibed the beauty of their phrase, "the interdependent web of life," a motto that fit my vision for how yoga helps us as a community. We feel congruence without even knowing one another's names. Healthy inner quiet and the soaring of the spirit help us to see, to listen and to speak with awareness.

I determined to bring these ideas into my teaching and eventually into my teacher training. I wanted to share a practice that would be true to our need for finding inner freedom. The pursuit of happiness is possible with a disciplined practice and a community of support. This was possible to build here.

For nine years, I accepted donations for my teaching but did not keep them; I re-donated the proceeds to various charities including the mission. A student suggested that my yoga students might like me to keep them. That was when I considered certification. Guruji had asked me to go to India to study at the yoga college in Chandigarh for six months. I refused to go to India and leave my family for an extended stay. Ironically, I did leave my family for about that length of time, but the yoga training was a few weeks.

Confronting myself was best done at home. In India, free from the normal constraints of my life, I would not be able to address what I needed to learn from my life here. Given the length and intensity of my emotional quandary, it was clear to me that I needed to free myself from some impression I carried, some assumption that the spiritual life could be lived without feeling strong emotion, elevated in higher consciousness. My life showed me the futility of that belief. We cannot develop in awareness without integrating all parts of ourselves. Suppression of emotion in the name of peace and joy is a vain effort.

Difficulty with pain in the body, knee pain and sciatica were continually addressed in my hatha practice, but those challenges were of no consequence compared with the emotional struggle.

My Guru was disappointed that I trained within another school, but he was ultimately a simple man. The growth of his mission into so many ashrams and schools throughout India and into England, Holland, the States and Canada, was for us, and not for him. We needed places to study, teach and perform service. His favorite story when he first came to stay with us was about a loincloth:

There was a wandering ascetic saint who wore nothing and carried nothing, and one day while sleeping under a tree an old woman awakened him with her scolding.

"Can you at least wear a loincloth?"

The saint looked at himself and decided that he could afford to change and make her happy. He asked someone to bring him a narrow piece of cloth to wrap around himself. Quickly he realized that while it was drying in the morning he needed a second to wear. So he asked for another. As his loincloth dried on the tree where he rested and meditated, people began to gather as if a flag were announcing his presence. They gathered for his holy company and the chance to be graced with his few words. So he began to teach them, and then realized they might be hungry and thirsty. He asked a man to bring a cow for milk. The cow stayed and the saint needed someone to care for the cow. So a man began to live with him. The man needed shelter, and so it went until an ashram was built. The saint continued to live among the people of his ashram for some time, addressing problems, solving disputes, teaching. He had little rest. One day he came out of his room without a loincloth. His disciples were concerned. "What happened?" they asked.

"I understood something," he replied.

They waited for his words.

"No loincloth, no problem."

When Guruji told the story he laughed and slapped his thigh in delight. Bill laughed with him. Guruji believed in simplicity and truth. He saw where Bill and I were headed and gave us permission to work independently. Building a yoga center for the mission meant that it would include a temple and be open as a place for ritual worship. We could not agree to that.

We comprehended our teacher's need to address the Hindu people. In India, eleven hundred years of domination by foreign powers had only recently ended. Our Guru carried memories of brutal atrocities within his own village. His vision was to revive the underlying teaching of the *Vedas* so that the practices that were central to the culture would not be lost as India made her way forward. Bill and I understood this, but it was not our goal. We wanted to offer a path of meditation and philosophy that was more appropriate for our culture.

We needed to teach authentically. Bill was still working full time. I had the time to teach, to study and develop my approach. My thaw had been painful but essential.

41

Keep your outer life stable. Then you can go more deeply inside.
Swami Bawra

In 1996, a few months after I had returned home, Guruji arrived in Kent. I wanted to air out how Bill and I were doing after our separation.

We sat in the living room, waiting for our teacher to come out, after an afternoon rest. The heavy double doors I had installed were wide open.

"Hello, my dears," he said as he walked in. The windows were open, and a fresh breeze was blowing the sheer curtains, mingling with the sounds of traffic on Mantua Street.

We came off the couch and bowed *pranam* to his feet, by now a familiar comfort. He smiled.

"We are fine. Happy as cell mates, I mean, as soul mates," I said.

Guruji chuckled. Bill did not acknowledge my comment, but it felt good to be together.

The differences between Bill and me were puzzling. We shared a fundamental belief in hard work, though keeping up with Bill was demanding. We gave our boys chores to do, starting at three years old. They carried the vegetable scraps from the kitchen out to the mulch pile. The chores progressed from there. By high school, they each had three years of dishes duty, which meant they did all the dishes, no matter who came to visit. If they complained, I told them they needed to do more dishes until washing them felt like nothing. We would help them, but the responsibility was theirs. Bill and I shared a deep belief in a healthy neutral attitude toward work. That, along with an abiding love for both boys, helped us persist.

I carried a fundamental discomfort with Bill, still. He felt open inside, as if filled with space. Lying next to him I felt comforted by his peace, but

245

I also felt a kind of loss of control. Understanding him was like walking in a deep night with no stars or moon. It is disorienting. When we first met, I lay awake next to him while he slept, feeling a depth in him that was vast. The energy in my body ignited, and I could not sleep. Energy raced in my limbs, unfettered and anxious. Years passed before I learned to channel it, and release it, inward, through meditation. It was then that he loved me—when I found the center and opened it through the top of my head. When he sensed that freedom of energy and awareness, then he turned to me, feeling safe himself, and opened completely to my profound inner containment, his wandering hand capturing my limbs. But the huge space of a star-less night I sensed inside him remained and made me fearful.

I knew things would be better for us when I saw Bill with a rolling pin. After a rare weekend away from him and the boys, I walked through the front door, and found him crawling and using the rolling pin to repair the kitchen floor, pressing down on the new linoleum.

Many years passed before he cooked with any regularity, but when he did, we had split pea soup and apple crisp once a week for two years. His salty soup was delicate with tiny squares of cut carrots that floated toward you like the kisses of our children, followed by sweet crumble packed on top of the sliced apples. Bill was flexing his cooking muscles: pasta and homemade sauce, popovers from the oven, grilled sandwiches and vegetarian burgers, food our boys loved when their Dad cooked. They were in late grade school and junior high when he made cooking part of his fathering. Their friends would come over, sit at the table and announce what they wanted from his repertoire.

The selection of food made a sudden shift in 1996 when the boys were in high school. We made a family trip to Italy and Croatia, the places of Bill's grandparents, who had emigrated here before and after World War I. His father's father had been orphaned, or so the story went, and no one in the family here had yet returned to visit. We had been in communication with his grandmother's relatives by letter, so we had a few phone numbers and addresses. They knew we were coming. Bill and I left the boys by the beach with friends in Ravenna, Italy, and drove along the coast of the Adriatic Sea. To get to the island of Kirk, we crossed a great bridge from mainland Croatia and made our way into a seaside village, where Bill's family had lived for 1200 years. We visited a great uncle and his second wife, and ate their garden produce under a grape arbor next to an open rooftop. They spoke no English. A cousin who ran a taxi spoke with us. After eating, his great aunt sat with her head tilted to the sun in the middle of the flat cement roof under the blue sky. She had a kerchief on her head, and a floral dress faded from much washing and drying in the sun. Her hands rested. They were hands that dug potatoes, led donkeys and tended grapes. She gazed at an open stretch to the sea, framed by tall mountains and, in between, carefully tended fertile gardens that had been cultivated in the rocky soil. The rock walls around each garden were piled high and thick. Behind us a kitchen garden and a small orchard grew.

Stepping up to the roof's edge, they showed us green places cut in the valley that had been divided and sectioned off for generations so that every family had small shares scattered throughout the village. There were small divisions of land along the road and a place on the mountainside for lumber. The mountain pasture was shared by the whole village; sheep and lambs knew their masters by their call.

Before we left, Auntie was settling her frail body onto a low bed just inside a door to the roof. She cradled my hands, pulling them toward her to gaze her blue eyes into mine. Her grasp was firm.

Bill and I had rented a room at a bed-and-breakfast closer to the bay. We went up a set of outside stairs. The room was simple and fresh, one of many rooms along a hallway with a shared bath. We slept in separate twin beds that pressed against the outer walls, and were separated by a tidy window with white curtains. On our second and last morning there, the dawn woke me early. Bill was asleep. In the quiet, with a steady breeze from the sea, I felt the blue sky of the new day spread over my head and inside of Bill. It was a day that never went back to night. I understood him better.

The blue sky stayed in him, and when we returned to our home he began to add Mediterranean elements to his cooking: white beans and feta cheese, fresh oregano and rosemary. It was as if the scent of herbs and sea had blown into him, freeing him in his sleep to be Croatian, to be someone who loved his hands and what they craved to handle.

We healed slowly. "I cook for others," he said, "but I'm nurturing myself."

42

Hold the uncut wood. Need little, want less.
Lao Tzu

Many years before, when I was a teenager still living at home, I came to know Mary. Mary was the eldest cousin of twenty-six of us. As a young woman in graduate school in Princeton, she would drive her VW beetle out to visit my mother in the country, near Philadelphia, after my father had left. I was finishing high school. Mary's hair was pre-maturely white, cut in a shoulder length bob, and she leaned forward as she spoke, entertaining my mother. Her ability to talk without breathing was uncanny. We sat on the back patio in the light of candelabra, under the arbor my father had built, and then deserted—along with everything else. Mary came on a mission to befriend my mother Martha. As the eldest of the cousins, Mary had started life on top, and she stayed there. Her first job out of Princeton was in Brazil in the 1970's, where she worked for four years as a Portuguese-speaking Foreign Service officer. I understood some of what she said, and felt a dreamy, vibrant sense of life around her that was lacking on my side of the table, in the dark, as if the candles lit her and my mother and somehow missed me.

I felt different from the way I assumed other people felt. I was quiet. I had no compulsion to talk. Overtime I had resolved that something must have happened to me because I also felt young. When I lay with a blanket over my head and I fell into a place of no words where I sought images, I could see myself in the front hall of the house in Maine that belonged to my grandparents. I was swaddled and quiet in a bassinette in the front hallway of their three-story wood-shingled summerhouse.

I had a child's love of this place sided with wood shingles, wrapped with porches, and lined with oak-panels. In back, a screened-in porch was

248

stuffed with white wicker seats and green pillows, as if the furniture were the company. Next to it, in a parlor with the piano, inside a glass case set on a tabletop, was a small Oriental palanquin that held a miniature carved-ivory death mask. As a child, there was nothing odd about this ornament—the death mask encouraged me to contemplate what felt unusual and different. There were faded orange life jackets in the front closet, there for children to wear, mostly us, when they went to the docks down at Dark Harbor. When I was older my brothers and I went to find the bulging vests and baskets that held thick twine wrapped around square wooden frames for crab fishing. We would walk to the dock, twist fatty bacon around a sturdy hook with our chins pressed down in the straps of the life jackets, and lean over to troll the string along the rocky seabed into which thick dock pilings had been thrust. We could see best at low tide, and often pulled a crab to land on the weathered boards—our little hands smarting with cold and salty ocean water. We would return the crabs to the clear water and watch them float sideways back to the rocks and seaweed at the bottom.

In my earliest memory, my vision is by the front door looking in and my bassinette is set directly in front of the door—a place that to my adult mind seems more symbolic than actual. I would have been six weeks old in the first summer of my life. In this unwavering image, Grandma Biddle and another shadowy figure are peering down at me in a crib. My mother liked parties. There would have been parties in Maine.

Fishing through early memory is questionable. Its shadows reflect uncertain events. But I tried. My first clear memory is from the perspective of the ceiling looking down on my mother mending by the light of a large window. My brothers and I are sitting near her in the living room of our apartment in Philadelphia. I am in the room too, looking at my body, but I feel as if no one is there. There is no talking, no chatter of small children. We are silent. I am floating above.

I had my own yardstick for research into early years: Real memories do not shift. When we moved from that apartment to the house where I grew up, I clearly recall the excitement in the driveway when our new poodle, Paulie, ran back and forth, and the black kitten, Bishop, was left by "Aunt" Minou in the downstairs toilet room off the kitchen. Those events were from my second year. The images don't change. I checked them all with my mother. They were real events.

I have an even earlier memory from our house in Beacon Hill, in Boston, where we lived before moving to Philadelphia. I checked with my mother about this one, too. I see a small room with one door and one window, the crib set on the inside wall and my head near the door. I feel my father peek in on me; he is headed out. My mother is in the house but not in the room. That is it—nothing much—but I never liked cribs. I refused to put my boys into cribs. When I asked her if the memory were accurate, she agreed. She asked nothing about how I knew. I might have told her. I did not expect her to be curious.

Bill and I often visited Martha and her husband Pete in Philadelphia. She retained a daily habit of quiet and prayer. I sought her out in the mornings when she was resting there to try and enlist her help. She was sitting in a chaise lounge in front of a tall window. A small table by her side had a pile of prayer books and essays on contemplation, and her rosary.

"Why don't I feel like you love me?" I asked.

I wanted one thing of her: When I asked a question, I insisted on an answer. I often pestered her with questions until she furrowed her brow and rubbed it deeply. She often told me she needed more time.

"It is not true," she answered. "I do love you."

My mother was genuinely warm and solicitous. This kind of questioning did not help us heal together. The past was unresolved for her as well. I was meeting my own need for an answer. My mother did not manage feelings well. The older she became, the more she repeated: "I am just an old Yankee."

I thought this next question might be simpler, "Who took care of me when I was small, six weeks old, maybe?"

I was seeking a reason for the body memory that had first surfaced at age nineteen before I went to the mental institution, and returned in my adult life many times on the body work table: hyperventilation and the electric surge that shot from my left leg through my right shoulder, so strong that my body would jump.

I was aware of an underlying panic that took me years to feel directly. I wished I had been routinely hit with a two-by-four; then I could easily account for the feeling of having been wronged. Easier than trolling for memories.

Needing help, I had followed the recommendation of friends in 1995, just as I was returning to live with Bill and the boys after our winter of separation. I went to a Jungian analyst, not a therapist, as she would tell me. The difference was not always clear to me. She was an effective therapist; her training was an intensive study of the writings of Carl G. Jung, a follower of the father of psychoanalysis, Sigmund Freud. Jung developed a theory of the self that was influenced by Eastern thought. His method included a process called active imagination. In addition to recording my dreams, I started to draw pictures to bring her.

The analyst looked among the drawings spread out on the floor. She pointed to the one of the snake.

"What are all those lines just outside there?"

I looked more closely at the hatch work of lines, drawn not on the body of the snake, but in front of him, as though guarded by him.

She was intuitive. I spent the next week drawing a series of sketches of snakes battling eagles over an ocean of stormy waves, snakes guarding eggs, and eggs hatching more snakes. I brought them with me for the next session and spread them out in an arc on the floor. As she attended closely to each image, I began to settle into myself. Only much later did my analyst reveal how the images were archetypal principles of alchemy: the vessel, the dark matter to be transformed, the battle between earth and sky. By looking at my images through her eyes, I felt a kind of intimacy with myself. I had battled a long time against my anxiety without significant progress toward resolution.

So I did the work with her. Other kinds of therapy I had tried were too literal. Reaching into my non-verbal state without becoming overwhelmed by the old feelings was slow. The crux of it was revealed by the serpent. The image never faded. Anyone who remembers their dreams knows that images appear. We don't consciously create them. If we attend to them, they become a kind of language, and the language is personal. My experience of awakening that came through my Guru's touch to the top of my head was the experience of the ascending energy called the *kundalini*, which is represented by the image of a serpent. This is a fundamentally positive image, though a serpent image always evokes a healthy fear and respect for the energy that exists along the spine. When it awakens, it moves upward like a serpent from the ground. My awakening in meditation was an expansion of love and peace, with a diffusion of light. No image of a serpent. My personal image of the snake helped release the primal fear I held tightly.

According to Jungian thought, the most important work is integrating the *prima materia*, the dark primal matter of neglected emotional stuff that requires the alchemical vessel of containment. My analyst's office, her presence and close witnessing were the container. Outside, I could lead a normal life. Inside her office, she urged me to excavate my psyche, the contents of my mind, and look at each image, each artifact. Outside, the drama could dissipate. I could comfortably live the life I had set out to lead with Bill and my children.

She returned from a trip with a wooden beaded snake that she set on her coffee table. In nearly four years of analysis, I had faithfully recorded my dreams, typed them out, given her duplicates, and drawn, colored, and painted from my imagination. I had done whatever I could to avoid confronting my feelings. Her purchase was a kind of gauntlet thrown. Enough dancing, what does this image hold?

I was ready. After stepping into her consulting room and lying back on the short couch, I stared at the colored beads on the snake's back. The multi-colored rows rippled. After a few more sessions, the serpent began to shift shape. Each time I returned, the same thing happened. The wooden object seemed to move. I would watch it. After a few weeks, I began to twitch, and then jerk. From my left leg to my right shoulder, I would feel a jolt of energy push through my body, pulling my head to the right, causing me to hyperventilate. The jerking was familiar. During the hands-on healing sessions, a sudden flailing in my body created a chain reaction in the ones helping me; they jolted back, pulling their hands off of me. I would joke about it: "Like a frog on a dissecting table. That's me." The jerk was involuntary and occurred whenever I relaxed during treatment. I could suppress it, but it lay in wait.

My experiences increased in intensity as the weeks progressed. My analyst, sitting in a comfortable chair on the other side of the coffee table, simply observed. Like a patient midwife, her task was to create safety as I hatched my surfacing feelings. When the peak came, my body sprang up in a full swell of panic, head swinging side to side like the hood of a cobra. The panic lasted a few seconds; I let her voice soothe me.

Over the next few months, as I watched the beaded serpent on the table and felt the intensity come through my body, we edged cautiously toward a gradual release. The symptoms of panic subsided. The serpent on the coffee table no longer triggered me and resumed its normal existence as a beaded wooden object.

"The Native Americans say that those who survive the bite of the serpent are fit to be shamans," she told me, more than once.

Here was a connection with the Native American tradition that I had tried to avoid. A shaman is a healer in this tradition. Somehow I had been "bitten" by some experience that had left me vulnerable, and my vulnerability had led me to grow in unusual ways. I had some gift as a healer, though I was reluctant to call it mine. Perhaps that is how healing works best. She made me understand.

In my own professional practice, when I did hands-on healing, my blurring of boundaries with my clients was distinct. I might have a coughing fit before meeting a new client, and then find that my client had recently quit smoking. My analyst suggested I find another occupation because my skill was based on an unmet need. I had needed comfort when I was small and had not received it. She knew I had an unusual capacity, but she warned me against using it. I was sad and resistant to her advice. I did not know what other work to do, but I was beginning to write. It was during this time in 1996, as I wrote my dreams and felt how language can run through deep veins of my experience, I fell in love with the English language. This was different from my feelings for Sanskrit. This was personal. I was creating a companion in language. Better for me than a deity of Shiva or Rama, I had the company of my own self in language. I could record my own story with continuity from beginning to end. Over the next several years, I shifted to writing and teaching others how to teach yoga, and reduced my individual work with clients.

My analysis gradually tapered off, but I continued to record my dreams and contemplate their meaning. What I gleaned about myself was that I had both the noble and the horrific qualities of the serpent. I could assist in healing, but I also had venomous residual anger that could unconsciously destroy. My disowned feelings would go deep, hibernating like a serpent in the winter. Then, I would grow more distant, and at some point act out. I had more to do, and that work I did with my husband, who, after many years, was ready for me to emerge from my shame and confusion into intimacy with him. He helped me in the last stages of this process to confront my intensity and feel what prevented true intimacy. The need for deep thinking to free the mind from confusion was encouraged by him. It is a yogic practice. Our philosophy determines our psychology, and if we truly believe that all we experience is our own *karma*, perfect for our soul's development, then we need to own our experiences, no matter what players are acting in the drama. I had to believe that at some point it was my mistaken understanding that spiritual evolution might be simpler if I disowned my feelings. In this life, I had no choice but to feel. My un-integrated emotions created too much disturbance.

I had asked Kanta Didiji what she thought about Descarte's statement *cogito ergo sum*.

"Didiji, what do you think? Is the statement in the wrong order? Should it be: I am, therefore I think?"

She replied. "He is wise. Our thought is powerful, and, as we think, so our lives become."

Bill encouraged my search to confront myself. His love was large enough and detached enough to witness the enormous friction and drama of my psyche.

I was learning to witness myself and hold my feelings with greater containment. A few years later, our boys almost raised, Bill and I were again in Philadelphia with my mother and Pete. The first evening, when I was lying on the guest bed after the drive down from Ohio, she entered the room with a couple of letters. Her gray hair was pulled back from the sides of her face.

"You might want to read this," she said. Mary's been writing; she wrote this about a visit to the Brady house before it was torn down. You remember the place on Dudley Road?"

My mother left the room. I sighed and opened the top letter; it was Mary's. The Brady house was where Mary lived as a young girl. In the story, she returned to the house to revisit old memories with two younger siblings, Jody and Jenny. Eventually there were five. Mary and Jody were laughing about the night nurse, Emily, and how, when baby Jenny cried, Emily held her under water. Jenny, horrified, came into the room where they were reminiscing. "Do you hear what you are saying?" she asked quietly. Jenny was insistent but not bullying—her point was made. I was calm while reading it. I assessed Mary's writing to stay neutral and not feel much. She wrote the memory as a prose poem.

I opened the second letter, written by my mother, Martha, back to Mary. Martha must have asked Mary to return her letter so she could save the correspondence—perhaps to show to me. In the letter, my mother wrote about how great it was to read a family story, and then ended with how Emily took care of Margot when she was small and, "I wonder if she did anything to poor Margot?"

I checked the date on the envelopes and placed the letters back in them. The correspondence was from a year back. I lay back to process my thoughts. My mother returned to the room and asked me what I thought—a déjà vu moment of puberty when we touched on my change of life.

"Did you read the pamphlet?" she had asked then. She was trying her best.

I felt resigned. "Mary's an okay writer—good story, sort of. Glad Jenny found out why she felt as if she were drowning all the time."

I handed the letters back and crossed my arms. Mom left.

I suppose my mother was carefully answering my question. I felt let down because most of the work had been done. I had released much of the panic and fear, without knowing how it had come in my experience. I did not know if knowing would have made any difference. I still did not know what really happened—was it a pillow over my head in the small hours of the night? A lack of oxygen can make the body twitch and jerk, like an orgasm, under the sure hand of a night nurse. She said that she hired Emily for the summer when I was six weeks old. My two older brothers would have been there, each of us seventeen months apart.

But I must have waited too long to pursue the topic with my mother.

By the time I was ready to press my mother for more information, she said, "Emily couldn't have done anything. I was there. I would remember."

It did not matter.

I called my cousin Jenny. I could see Emily in my mind's eye. Jenny described her from a photo. The image was clear: sepia-toned, a gray, long-sleeved dress with buttons down the middle, a wide, white apron smoothed over the front, gray hair pulled back in a severe bun, and a face with thin lips.

"She was a night nurse," Jenny concluded.

A night nurse was hired to care for the little ones so a young mother could get her sleep and be fresh in the morning to handle her brood. When Jenny told me the term, I felt as if I had always known it. Jenny is older than me by a few years, but we were both six weeks old when Emily was hired to care for us for a couple of months. Our mothers are sisters, and they must have compared notes. Jane, the elder sister would have

255

advised Martha, my mother, who was having her third child, me. Jenny and I both were third in our family's birth order.

The term "night nurse" rang with servants and privilege. As Jenny explained night nurse, I could see how rational it was from the perspective of another time, to hire an Irish nurse for a job that made your life easier. I knew some of Jenny's story and why she was calling.

"I feel so free now. The program is called Core Mastery. You go back and free yourself."

I had told her I would look into it, but really wasn't interested in Core Mastery. I had my own agenda, told her that I had been picking away at my issues for years, and described my Jungian analysis. Jenny was talking on the phone with me while driving to a meeting. She went back to telling me about her program; her new-found freedom was recent, mine from years before, though, like a birth, I could remember it as if it were yesterday. When I reached my core issue, my body, like a snake caught sunning itself, had flailed in panic. It brought relief to witness the panic and understand it as memory.

I knew from Mary that Jenny's panic came with a sensation of drowning. She would be trying to raise her own children, and would feel a need to be alone to meditate and calm the oppressed breathing and fear. Like me, she had used meditation as a way to calm herself.

"When my boys were small, I would go to the back bedroom and pull a blanket over my head," I shared with her. "I became speechless, non-verbal…frozen for a while. I really had trouble coping…so much anxiety." I had a small checklist of areas I wanted to cover with her. "How did you raise your children? What about at night?"

Jenny was quick to respond. "I held them and sang to them as they went to sleep. I would not let them have any disturbance at night." Her voice was emphatic.

"Same here, I wanted them to have no panic at night. Helped them didn't it? At least we got that right."

43

He who offers to Me with devotion and a pure heart a leaf, a flower, fruit, or water, that offering of devotion I accept.
Whatever you do, whatever you eat, whatever you offer, whatever you give, whatever austerities you perform, do that as an offering to Me.
Gita 9/26, 27

For years Bill and I thought we would find a piece of land or a building where we could live with the mission, giving it a more permanent home. We wanted to be out in the country. Kanta Didi to whom Guruji had given charge of our area, wanted to be near the city. For years we had searched; finally we decided to go on our own, for us, our family.

We bought land, built a home and had the area timbered—all without the mission. We were closer to the two lakes, where I frequently walked. Our road turned off Lake Rockwell, where a home business called "Clyde the Vitrified" sold clay drain tile for fields and roads. Just down from the business was a small wooden gingerbread house with peeling white paint sinking into the wetland, guarded by a white oak whose side branches spread thick like trees over the roof.

An Italian-American family had lived on our new land. They raised a generation of builders who used the land for dumping trash, storing cut building stone, and for fishing in a small lake. We cleared 8000 pounds of steel refuse: water heaters, gas cans, old freezers and barbed wire. Then, we timbered eight acres of woods. At one point, the view from the back windows of our new home was of oak and cherry logs spilling from the woods like driftwood after a storm, tossed from the tips of ocean waves. The loggers took only the logs. The treetops with their wide limbs and spreading branches were downed and left for us to clear.

Timbering left us with fires to burn. I felt that the days of brush fires—the drag and burn, the tired lower back, the bulging arms— were part of my Hindu *samskaras,* the impressions of my previous lives in India, where I had used the *hoven,* the fire ceremony, as an expiation of sins. Living in America I had big sins and I needed big fires. I threw each branch with a *"svahah"* to purify a vague plethora of sins with a heavy weight and a leap of flame. *Svahah* is what you say when you throw rice, *ghee,* or herbs into the flame. Any offering, no matter how small, is a symbol of devotion. I was throwing large, cumbersome branches.

We had a fire ceremony, the *hoven,* at the second house we remodeled to live in. There was a *hoven* for the ashram we remodeled as well. Each time I was afraid the fire would blacken the walls. Jyoti Didi or Kanta Didi had used a square metal box on stocky metal legs and fed the fire with twigs and small chopped fragments of logs. First fire, then *ghee* and herbs, over and again. Rice, flower petals and water were tossed on the fire. The offerings represent the elements of earth, water and fire. The scents, the sounds of mantras, and the heat of the fire enter the nostrils, the skin, and the feelings of the heart, as if every aspect of ourselves is asked to lift, to ascend with the fire toward vast space and vibrant air. From the *hoven* I learned the *gayatri mantra.* "Earth, space and galaxies, may the light that illumines the galaxies illumine our hearts and minds that we may live near to the source of wisdom and compassion." This was my translation.

In the back of the woods near our new house, there was a rise above a beaver pond. In the 1960's, after their celery farms were no longer cultivated, the Italian brothers dredged peat from the edge of the wetland, forming this beaver pond where they tossed old tires. Turtles crawled on the tires to sun in the summer heat. The brothers became land developers and builders in the county. Deep in our woods, at the edge of the neglected marshland, we found a rusted generator, bundles of rusted bailing wire, and clay drain tile, evidence of their celery harvest. From the rise above the pond there is a proud view of tall cattails that create a sanctuary for kingfishers, red-winged blackbirds, mink and muskrat. Deer trails lace the underbrush, ending at the edge of the pond. The beaver left when we logged—chased out by the sound of chain saws and Bill's tractor, or perhaps defeated by the felling of oaks and tall cherries. We heard the beaver's tail slap the water when we first arrived. Only their home, the mound of small felled trees and branches remains, set among a stand of cattails.

Bill and I burned many fires on the rise with a view of the cattails and the pond. Many eight-hour burns were needed after the seven large oaks, leaning with fallen limbs, came down hollow. The large bald trunks of other dark oaks lay slumbering in this area of woods; we knew what would happened if we did not thin the woods. Coming down with storm and wind, we would have not only tops, but trunks to cut and clear. On their sides the felled trunks came past our waists, up to our shoulders. We left a ring of white oaks growing straight, commanding the site close to the pond.

We hired loggers who used horses to pull the trunks. They were careful to fell and pull from the back first, so they would not block their path with tangles of branches. The loggers cut over fifty tall cherries, then the seven oaks whose mammoth trunks had to be cut in half to be pulled by the horses. The horses were Clydesdales, huge and brown. They were harnessed around their chests, which bulged to double their size and broke into a thick sweat when they pulled the oak logs. The driver sat on the high seat of a single-axle rig just behind the horses. To the rig he attached the chains and hooks that snared the logs. There was a light snow on the ground in the woods when they began, but as they worked, dense and soupy ruts of dark mud formed, making the burdens heavier and the horses' footing uncertain. By the time the oaks were down, the mud on the path was knee deep and the crisscross of tops covering the ground made it impossible to walk anywhere on the rise.

When the loggers had finished pulling logs and had lined them up neatly at our field ready to be shipped to the lumberyard, Bill and I started hauling, trimming, and burning the tops for eight hours at a time. Bill moved quickly, tying chains around the large branches and dragging them out of the tangle of limbs. At first he pulled the trailing limbs the length of the woods, all the way to the field by the house. As the space cleared on the rise, we started burning in the back by the beaver pond. This clearing was the site of the original house. There's no trace of it now. The beams had been reused for a house built out by the road. The basement had been stuffed with steel trash that we had cleared and covered. A grassy area was open for burning. Bill would fly out of brambles on his tractor, hauling several long limbs at a time. He'd stop by the fire and neatly trim with the chain saw, while I dragged the branches off to burn.

For hours we worked this way. The pile grew impossibly tall with flame, and still we would pile branches higher. We stopped most days by mid-afternoon so the fire would burn down by nightfall, and we could check it before sleep.

Bill worked at a challenging pace. I had to find rhythms that made it possible to work with him. I would dive into his mind-set, his open space of awareness, where he followed the trail of the work to be done and open his energy to join the task. He would clear his mind, find the next thing to do and do it. This was *karma* yoga, work done without the hankerings of the ego. I'd let the whine of the saw and the puttering of the tractor fuel my inner engine. Occasionally the ego would cry for some attention, and then we would pause and admire our work.

"Big fire."

"Can't believe how much we've cleared."

"Couldn't do this without a tractor."

And we drank long drafts of water.

Virya is the word for stamina or energy. Years of living with Bill taught me to find stable energy, like an underground reservoir that feeds a well. But I craved the silence of the woods. After one long morning of drag, hoist, and burn, I asked Bill if we might line the paths, the logging road and the clearing with brush that I could pull to a fire while he worked at home the next day. I wanted to try an eight-hour *hoven* by myself, back by the pond, under the open sky amid the woodland sounds of early spring. So we ceased burning and layered the area with brush.

These hot fires never die in the night. The coals were ready the next day. I began my long vigil by placing small sticks on the coals, enjoying the crackle of a small fire in the cold. I had a new mantra I wanted to learn, so as I pulled the branches, I paused now and again to take off a glove and reach in my back pocket for a folded sheet of paper, where I had written the words. I needed to check if I had it right.

Sarve svarupa sarve she—I had not been able to find a translation so I had only fragments of meaning. I knew the prayer was to the mother. *Sarve* means "all" and *svarupe* is "the eternal abiding nature" of us all. *Sva* is "self." *Rupa* is "form." I did not know the next phrase, but it mattered little. The first phrase had enough meaning for both.

Sarve shakti saman mite—"All power" is the meaning of the first two words. "That lives in us," was how I finished the phrase. The idea gave me energy after a previous day of dragging and burning. Though the day was new, the flame was already high. The coals were hot and I placed each branch, leveraging my weight to help lift the length of each, and placed it where it would flare quickly.

Bhawai byastraai non devi durge devi namostute. I loved the feel of the first two words, words of unknown meaning. *Bhawai byastraai.* The sound started in the lips and pushed to the back of the throat, like reaching something from the depth. Saying the sound drew a kind of sensual devotion from my heart. Then *non*—I took not as a French "no" but as an emphatic "yes," like the Hindu sideways waggle of the head. *Devi* is "divine," and *durga* is "the mother." I was on the home stretch of translation—*namosthite*, "I bow down to that essence of energy, power, the lap of the mother where I find stability." This was good enough for me. I bowed down to that essence of life that pulses in us all and offered the enormous brush pile and my vigil in the cold to her.

Grateful that the sound of the tractor was absent, the chain saw silent, I could be with the feeling of the land and fire. I became aware of the quiet pond. I lay back to rest on the cold ground. The trees around the clearing were bare, the sky was open, the sound murmuring from my lips was soothing, and as I closed my eyes to feel the chant in my body, I sensed the small pond down the hill reflecting the sky. With my eyes closed, the sky opened. My awareness shifted to the west and north. Not even a mile away were two larger bodies of water, Lake Pippen and Lake Rockwell, on eight hundred acres of protected land belonging to the City of Akron. I rested comfortably with my inner vision spreading over the lakes. Then my awareness took a leap, extended farther to feel the shape of the earth, the curves, to Lake Erie, forty-five miles north, her huge body reflecting an endless scope, the boundary of earth around her border not visible.

I did not know all the meanings of the chant, but the intent had found me. My awareness expanded. Bill came around the path with a cup of hot tea on his morning break from working at home. He was worried that I might be lonely. I thanked him, grateful he could stay only a few minutes. Later he brought me lunch as well. It was not safe to leave a fire in the forest until it died down to embers. Even then, a wind could spread sparks.

At lunch, I told him I was fine. No need to worry.

"Make sure you finish before long," he said.

I understood another layer of meaning in Bill's words: After finishing this kind of labor with my body, I felt ready to work in another way, with my mind and intellect.

44

Be in the tabernacles of my brow.
Stanley Kunitz

On Guruji's last visit to the Kent ashram in 1998, we had not solved the problem of finding a new center. I was going to attempt to buy land, but Bill did not think it was a good idea. Guruji and I resolved between us that Bill and I put our energies into writing rather than running a center.

I compiled Guruji's lectures on the second chapter of the *Bhagavad Gita*, "The Science of Stable Wisdom." I also spent time with personal writing. To write well for him, I strived to find authentic personal voice. I wrote philosophy and wrote for myself. It was a slow process; the book on philosophy took three years to complete. On his next visit to North America in 1999, our Guru did not come to the ashram in Kent, only to his Canadian temple. His health was not good, so we visited him there. When I put it in front of him, he set it aside, and tapped on the cover.

"Nice cover—the spinning finger means the book teaches what inspires the highest chakra. The finger moves like a wheel."

"Oh, I did not know what the hand on the cover meant, Guruji."

Bill and I had nothing to do with the cover art. We sent a donation for the first set of books to be printed in India through the mission's Divine Radiance Printing. I felt satisfied. I had persisted in completing this through all of my troubles with Bill. I kept refining the language so that it would be closer to what we were used to in English, without losing the meaning of the teaching. I called it a lyric style, as compared with the purely philosophical language.

Guruji handed me another book. Across the room, I noticed a man looking pleased. I assumed he was the author.

"He brought this to me today. He has put my complete philosophy into his own language."

The man looked even more pleased.

"He has retired from a career in science, and with his time, he has written a book that compares Samkhya with scientific theory."

Guruji handed me the book. I examined its cover. Clearly my teacher wanted me to keep going. In his eyes, I had hardly begun. I felt mildly defeated, but I trusted my teacher.

"When are you coming to India?" Guruji asked.

Bill and I hesitated. It is a long trip, but one that our teachers had made many times, making it possible for us to study with them.

"I'll go if we visit the Himalayas, Guruji," Bill said.

"Okay, September, we will go."

"Can we have lectures on Samkhya?" I asked.

I needed to comprehend more thoroughly the teaching that my name, Devhuti, indicated was important. Devhuti was the mother of Kapila. Guruji said that he would give daily lectures on Kapila's *Tattva Samasa*, the nutshell version of this philosophy.

Now Guruji hesitated. He tucked his head down. Then he looked at me.

"You know, Samkhya is a hard path. The hardest path."

He said nothing else, but I understood enough. Samkhya is a path of analysis, so we have to confront reality. It does not have the sweetness of devotion. My assessment was that inner freedom, on any terms, is sweet.

Bill and I arrived at the ashram in Virat Nagar in the heat of September, and the next day found seats on the bus parked outside Guruji's courtyard. We were going to visit the Himalayas. I sat sideways. Bill straddled his seat. For the last hour, we had watched a few nimble men pile luggage four feet high, cover the pile with a tarpaulin and lash it tight. Inside the bus, the overhead bins were bulging, and in the aisles, hand luggage was stuffed in at odd angles, making passage awkward. Curtains were pushed back, and wet towels and laundry lined the window rods. A call went out for everyone to get aboard. Now the bus was sitting, unmoving, in the ashram courtyard in one-hundred-degree heat.

No one would explain until later that we were stalled because we had missed the auspicious time for departure.

We had to wait.

With our heads resting on the seat in front of us, we resigned ourselves to India.

Bill had taken this same cramped school bus on a previous trip, and he did not want to repeat the experience. At the first stop in Haridwar, in the foothills of Himalayas, he and a few other men hired a luxury bus, so we could sit in more comfort. There would be more delays.

We traveled north for three days through the curves of the growing mountains across the state of Uttarakhand. Our lodging at night was in government houses. The rooms were airy and spacious. Our crew cooked over gas fires in the courtyard in back. We hung our laundry around a perimeter of lines. Guruji began his daily lectures after the evening meal. Each was under an hour. He was explaining the twenty-two "nutshell" principles of Kapila. The first was that suffering can be removed. To suffer is not our inherent nature. Suffering comes from a lack of fulfillment that we seek to remedy in ways that make us suffer more. When we have fulfilled our inner demand for wholeness, then we are truly free to serve life and others.

Our first pilgrimage site in the Himalayas was Kedarnath. The heat of the plains was behind us, and we enjoyed the dense rain that greeted us at our stop. Our first walk in the village was through a downpour among narrow streets with deep overhanging roofs that mostly protected us. We purchased thin plastic ponchos, available in the small shops on our way up the steep road. Men from the village carried our luggage on their heads. Our hotel was at the top of a hill at the end of town, a Buddhist *dharamshala*, a hostel for pilgrims. The name means "a shelter for those who follow the right path." At the end of the street, people took their daily baths in a square pool in the center of an open courtyard. Behind the hostel was a river that flowed downstream with a roar. Bill and I went up the stairs to the second floor and chose a room where we could hear the water. We were happy to be off the bus. The sound of water was a reprieve from the whine of the vehicle, and the soot and jerky rhythms of the narrow roads.

Our room was dirty, but I had already quickly checked others. They were all black with slime, on the floors, walls, ceiling, bed sheets and pillows. I knew to expect discomfort, but this was an adjustment. We settled in by spreading our sleeping bags over the bed just to sit. The bed sheet was covered in the same dirt as the floors. I dragged a molding, black, stiffened blanket out of the closet into the hall. It stayed there untouched.

We shared our room with Lucy, a British woman who had been living at the ashram in Virat Nagar. We were three Westerners. Lucy and I tiptoed into the bathroom wearing our shoes. Wooden pallets were set on the floor to lift our feet off a layer of mud. To lighten our mood, we decided to inspect the river. Outside, Bill went quickly down, finding his way to the river bank ahead of us. I stepped by his side as he muttered, "Oh god" and backed away.

"Look at all the shit on the rocks. This is their toilet."

The next day Bill was ready to leave on the pilgrimage, the *yatra,* up the mountain on horses. He gathered with the rest of the party, about twenty people, including didis and other Indian couples, all wearing the thin disposable plastic ponchos over their clothing, still visible under the ponchos' tints of bright orange, pink, green and sky blue. Guruji had told us in the evening that we could ride horses to Kedarnath at the peak of the mountain—but I was afraid of the bitter cold and wet rain. I let the large group organize itself and leave. I cried as Bill went off. I did not want to go, and I did not want to stay—a familiar place in me. Four women stayed back: two female monks who were attending Guruji, and Lucy and I. Lucy had a fever and pain in her kidneys from untreated parasites. I wanted to take care of her, but she would be consoling me if we stayed. The inside of the buildings was worse than outside.

Lucy and I went to Guruji and told him we were staying. I was crying. He listened quietly and then insisted that we go. Suddenly, my aversion was suspended. It was not that I believed in the pilgrimage to the summit, he simply tipped the balance in favor of the journey. Neither option was good, but my indecision and lack of control had a resolution: Go.

Lucy and I found guides and horses at the base of the trail. Manure was inches deep around our feet. The guide motioned to a small horse, decorated with bright colorful brocade on its reins and saddle. As I lifted myself up, the horse flattened his ears, bracing himself to haul my weight. I felt certain that my beast, more than Lucy's, was reluctant to go. He lagged behind. My driver kept saying "Ha!" as he planted a stick firmly on the horse's small flank. The horse felt like an extension of my body. The stirrups were short, as if my legs were the wrong length. As in a bad dream, I was having trouble forging ahead. I shouted to Lucy above the splatter of the rain.

"My horse doesn't like this—how are your kidneys?" I knew she was in pain.

"Fine," she replied. She turned back to look at me with a brisk smile, while huddled forward against the incline, and her pain. I knew her kidneys and fever were more important than my horse, but I was mentally stuck in my own experience. I was absorbed with the rhythm of the "Ha!" the stick, and the pinned ears, and could not detach from my helplessness.

Within my distress, I located a fear of horses, though I was more afraid of the cold rain. A long time ago, a friend took me riding. I had been thrown when my horse had galloped under a low branch. I fell to the solid ground. A comforting quiet had come through the numbing cold ground. Images of family and childhood played vividly; I watched with detachment.

The memory of detachment gave me some peace as I rocked on the back of my small horse with the bright-colored bridle in the downpour of cold rain. Heading fourteen kilometers up a cobblestone path, the clouds were low, and the Himalayan peaks were shrouded. We passed a couple of didis, wearing transparent pink ponchos that fit tightly over their orange cloth. They looked like bubbles. Lucy and I wore two ponchos each, a green one to wear on top, and a blue one to cover our legs. I bent my head low and watched the jerking rhythm of my horse's neck, while keeping the rain off my face. We stopped halfway for a hot *chai* and to feed the animals grain. I watched my horse carefully as he ate, finally feeling some separation from him.

"You want to trade horses?" Lucy was responding to my earlier complaint about my little horse, she was trying to help me feel better. In spite of her own pain she was attending to me. I declined. When I mounted again the horse seemed livelier. The clouds were lower and the rain denser but my mind was freer, and while watching his neck and rocking on his back up to Kedarnath, I reflected on the nature of hardship. It was by chance the weather was cold and wet, but Guruji's insistence was not chance. He was encouraging us to face adversity for the higher purpose of detachment. I needed *tapasya,* the heat of purification. He was not asking me to join a horse ride in the rain; he was compelling me to search beyond the experience of the senses.

At the top of the mountain path, Lucy and I found our destination outside a small village. We tethered the horses on the side of the path, along with a hundred other horses, left them in the care of our guides, and set off on foot. We hurried; we had to make the return trip before dark. Following the steepest path, we found wide stone steps that led up to a temple entrance.

Shoes are left outside temple walls. In the courtyard I tucked my wet socks in my shoes and placed them close to the walls, hoping they would not fill with more water. My feet met the sharp cold of the stone. Moving inside, I lost Lucy as I pushed forward to catch a view of the shrine. A crowd was worshiping a wet rock—covered in flowers, and orange and red paste—a *Shiva Lingam*, a primordial image of creation. It was a crude *lingam*, a large stone, silently humble within the noisy worship. The stone was wetted by the sprinkling of *puja* water, colored by tossed flower petals and the touch of fingers dipped in sandal paste. I was disturbed by this image, as if the stone was unprotected like the cold path outside.

Distancing myself, I wedged my body between a marble pillar and a wall just beyond the press of worshippers paying for *pujas* intoned by the temple *pundits. Pundits* were scattered through the crowd shouting prayers. Trays were waved. More flowers strewn. Red marks placed on foreheads. I closed my eyes. A focus developed in my mind that pushed away the sounds; a place inside opened above my head. In a swift shift, I felt a thin thread of connection to my body as the rest of my awareness floated out to vast space.

I welcomed this shift. An image appeared in my mind's eye—a Sanskrit symbol etched in black, as if crafted in iron, placed between my form and the sun. It was my mantra, the sound I used in meditation, as if written in the sky above me. The symbol was a gateway, revealing the place and power of language—spacious and transcendent. I felt complete, distant from the noise and my bare feet.

When I came out of meditation, I returned feet first. The floor was white marble layered with slick, wet black dirt. I had left comfort behind by coming here; I realized how often I let comfort seduce me. The contentment I was feeling now was completely beyond my circumstances, and it appeared to have been waiting for me. When I could let go of my own limitations, I was greeted in the wide embrace of sweet peace. The vision of the symbol was like a party favor I could take back in hand.

Lucy and I found our horses and returned quickly down the mountain. The horses' legs clopped loosely around the bends of the wet cobblestone path. Ahead of me Lucy was silent, her head bowed with the worsening pain in her kidneys. Her blonde hair covered her face. The descent was relentless and steep. Motioning to the guide to stop, I dismounted and began to walk the remaining five kilometers to the base. The mountain pulled speed from my legs. I let them fly, finding their own footing like the horses' hooves. Manure splashed up to my knees as I ran loosely with a freedom of body and spirit that had eluded me on the way up.

Back in the cold *dharamshala*, we changed into dry clothes and wrapped our heads to keep them warm. After our cold ride in the rain, the Buddhist ashram offered no relief. Lucy and I went to see Guruji. He asked me why I had cried earlier. I gave a reasonable explanation—the distress over the human feces on the rocks by the river outside our window. He was never happy with my strong emotions. But I pressed forward.

"Our window is broken so all the slime comes in with the rain."

The roar of the river that had drawn us to our room in the day became a monster at night, lifting molecules of feces into the heavy mist and into our room as we rested.

"Did you hear us hit the floor last night with a stick to scare the rats back out the crack in our broken window?"

Guruji tipped his head down in thought, and lifting up, said simply, "In my tradition the sound of the river is 'hare, hare.'"

Beyond the hovering filth that I was breathing in each breath, the space was filled with sound. I knew that *hare* means remover of sorrows. Closing my eyes, I could hear it, and felt myself riding the horse again, up the mountain in the rain, rocking in the saddle, a small point of awareness moving with vast space around the body, my closed eyes no barrier to the details of river, village, and steep Himalayan peaks. I sat still, humbled to the virtue of *tapas*. *Tapas* is the friction of austerity that purifies us of our attachments. The ride up the mountain had value.

Then Lucy stepped in front of him, and kneeling said, "Guruji, would you bless my *mala*?" She brought out the *mala* beads she had purchased in Haridwar. Kneeling on one knee on the concrete, she lifted them up to his hands with her head bowed. In that posture, I felt how bold she was compared with me. I waited for his blessing—not thinking I had any power to choose when I might be ready.

Guruji took the crystal *mala* in one of his hands and gave it to his other hand, then to both. He sat still for a moment with his head bowed, then twirled the beads around his right forefinger, making a wide chakra

269

in the space above his head. I saw his lips moving as he repeated a mantra. Suddenly his eyes flashed at me. I caught his glance, then looked back at the *mala* and saw sound in the form of light coming into and off the beads. Although the room was dark, light was shedding off the beads as if they had been dipped in water and twirled in rays of sunlight.

I sensed his awareness of my new understanding. Somehow he knew I had met the power of language in space. Any residue of resentment vanished.

I felt free.

For two days after, I heard the sounds of the elements in space murmuring their language. While balancing on my toes on the wooden pallets in our filthy bathroom, water out of the tap murmured. Food said "*garum*," warm. Everything was alive with vibration and meaning—language.

Lucy's illness receded after the ride to Kedarnath. But others developed sinus problems, head colds and bronchitis. Keeping quiet was challenging for me. I retained my opinion that the pain of illness should be prevented, if possible. I learned how to feel inner freedom and adhere to a sense of my own authority. Our buses went south out of the Himalayas into dry, warmer air. Then the gears ground loudly as we shifted to a northern ascent to another site, Badrinath, where we would confront freezing temperatures.

45

Only that day dawns to which we are awake.
Henry David Thoreau

Our buses ascended to Badrinath through familiar winding roads and small villages. The bus would slow for turns and stone outcroppings with barely enough room to pass. Stopping at a village was a lesson in patience. This was India, and there was nowhere to strike out for a walk. A village would have one main road with a descent on one side and a steep incline on the other, at a place where the mountain widened enough for a few dwellings. We would disembark to stretch our legs, find some *chai* and a small bag of chips or dry biscuits, and ask the villagers for the toilet. Sometimes there was one, sometimes a grassy area. Trash was tossed in the street and thrown down the side of the mountain, a scattered area of paper litter and glossy chip bags.

A mudslide blocked the road on our way. Part of a mountain came down and there was no other access to the village of Badrinath. This was like my marriage. I was looking at a big obstacle on the way—this mountain slide was similar to my projection onto Bill. I could not see past who I felt him to be to see who he actually was. Coming to India together had two purposes—gaining the philosophy and finding a better footing for our marriage. Something about the absurdity of the small horse pulling my weight up the mountain's path, along with Guruji's affirmation that I could get past myself, I felt lighter. I started to suspend what I felt and watched Bill in action. He stood out on this trip to Badrinath.

Our bus parked in an area packed with vehicles, mostly buses. Guruji stood at the front of the bus and announced, "Take nothing. No luggage. Just walk and we will catch a bus on the other side of this small mountain." I saw men with baskets on their backs, and watched as a few older people turned to sit backwards, their feet dangling from the men's back as the porters set out to carry them up the steep trail.

I had a tooth brush in my bag. Bill took his in his pocket. But he then questioned Guruji, "Take nothing? Are you sure this is wise?"

"Yes, my boy." Guruji held out his hand, palm facing down, a gesture intended to calm Bill's concerns.

My suitcase was filled with manure-soaked clothes; leaving it for a day would not matter. We set out on a steep, rocky trail. After half an hour, we had reached the summit and were descending, when I looked back and saw my Guru riding in a basket on the back of a slender man. His heart was too weak for the climb. I hid behind a rock and when he passed, jumped out and snapped his photo. He was smiling broadly, holding onto the sides of his basket with two hands.

This was a triumph for me—sharing a moment of pure humor with my teacher, within all the duress.

Once we had descended, we were told to wait in a group, and then to board a battered bus, one of many sent by the village of Badrinath. I took a seat at the rear of the bus. When the bus backed up, I looked out my window and down into space—the rear wheel was suspended off the edge of the cliff. I stood and ran to the front while yelling—sweeping my friends, Bill, Lucy, and our young friends from Guyana and Suriname out the door by the driver. We waited while the bus turned, and my heartbeat returned to normal.

My excitement in dragging my friends off the bus had given me some feeling of control; I settled into my seat and the adventure and another long drive. When we arrived, it was dark. It took time to find a hotel, and once there, we, the Westerners, sat in a small room downstairs and waited—the last to receive our rooms. I was tired and cold, and felt despondent again. Without any command of the language we were helpless to assert ourselves. I felt a profound dismay with this loss of control and could not lift myself out of my feelings again.

Bill stepped outside the cold room where we had been escorted to wait and saw a large pile of luggage pulled out from the belly of the bus. The didis had hired porters to bring their bags over the hill and into the battered bus to Badrinath. He was furious.

"Guruji, how can your didis call themselves renunciants when they have brought everything, and we, the householders have nothing, no luggage!"

Guruji had no reply. Bill was upset by the lack of discipline. These Himalayan sites were holy destinations, considered to be the pilgrimages of a lifetime. These sites held the possibility of freedom from bondage for all eternity—complete *moksha*.

The obvious attachments of the renunciants disturbed him. I did not care enough to be angry, or maybe he cared so much, I did not have to care. I checked my purse again to see what I had. No face cream, and certainly no underwear. I hoped they had some stalls where we could buy a few things, maybe a hat. I concluded that the *sannyasis* had simply traveled more and known better than to suffer without fresh clothing when it was easy to hire a porter. Bill was observant and holding to a principle that everyone was willing to let slide.

Badrinath was set in a wide mountain valley at about ten thousand feet—dry but cold. Early the first morning, I heard Bill shout from the foot of the stairs below our room.

"Come, quickly!" Lucy and I got up, pulling the blankets off the bed to wrap ourselves tightly against the chill. My nose was cold. It was still dark, and I was not happy. Walking out the front steps at the ground floor, I made out a row of figures wrapped and staring up. In the black sky glistening with stars, was a white diamond shape suspended and glowing.

"Bill?"

He answered me without turning his gaze. "It's a Himalayan peak, thousands of meters up—catching the dawn. I've been here for an hour watching it. Lit up out of nowhere."

Bill was awake to what went on around him. I would not have noticed the luggage or the bright peak, but I noticed that most of our group was wrapped in new blankets. We had traveled with dozens of wool blankets to distribute to the poor and the *sadhus* who lived in this high altitude. Bill was awake for the light on the mountain peak. He had strong feelings about what he saw, and now he was wrapped in his own awe, but not so much that he failed to call Lucy and me out of our sleep.

While in our rooms at the village, we slipped under the bedclothes to stay warm. We spent a few rupees to have hot water delivered to our rooms in the morning. Guruji wore his bright orange wool ski cap at all times. He took his morning bath in the hot springs in the center of town. There were buildings covering the springs, but Bill and I were not enticed. The water looked dirty. When Guruji had come here as a young man, he

273

had camped under the sky. There were no buildings other than the old temple, and those who stayed longer found caves in the steep hillside above the temple grounds.

During the day, we sought the sun, and walked the few streets peering into shops for face cream, a few items of clothing, and warm wool caps. The mountain village of Badrinath was above the temple and hotel area, an easy walk through villages of small clay huts and fences, past villagers carrying loads in bundles on their backs. They sometimes consented to be photographed and sometimes shielded themselves with their arms against the camera. We went toward the border with Tibet, controlled by China, on paths kept open by human feet and by herds of wandering cows that followed one another single file. We felt comfortable here. It was sunny during the day and free of cars.

Uphill from the village was the meditation cave of Vyasadeva, a seer from thousands of years ago who compiled the *Vedas* in written form. He coerced Lord Ganesha into writing them down by daring him to write as long as he could speak. Vyasadeva spoke without ceasing. His inspiration was the loud roar of the Saraswati River, rushing above ground in this area, before dipping under the earth for a long journey, finally joining the Ganges in the plains.

The cave's only intrusion was this sound of the mountain river, near its source. We left our shoes outside, and descended through rock walls onto a flat dirt floor under a sloping cut-rock ceiling. Facing a small altar set high in the wall, we closed our eyes to find our inner resonance with the vibration of this holy place. A few other pilgrims were sitting with us. One began to chant, his echoing voice mixed with the rush of the river.

I was peaceful.

The walks into the hills were refreshingly free of crowds and litter. We went every day, one time finding a small boy who offered to be a guide. He showed us trails that went closer to the border with China. Bill wanted to give him a few rupees but had none with him. The next day he took off by himself to find the boy during our lecture time. I went alone to Guruji, who was sitting in his cold room, warmed somewhat by the crowd of his disciples in the small space.

"Where is Bill?" one of the didis asked.

I looked at Guruji when I answered, shrugging, "He is looking for a small boy in the mountains."

"A very small boy," Guruji agreed, looking back at me.

274

I felt a double meaning. Guruji must have known that Bill went off into the hills. He knew Bill was frustrated. The previous afternoon when I was resting, Bill had gone to see Guruji in his room and had aired his concerns with him about our ashram in Kent. Guruji had wanted the discussion, telling Bill that he could never understand why our mission in America had not grown. He had tolerated our independence, but was not resolved. Bill was emphatic that the reason the mission in Kent had not expanded past the small building we originally found, was not due to our lack of devotion. Our need was for pure philosophy, yoga and meditation practice, not a temple for Hindus. We found the mission unable to adapt to the financial and cultural changes needed to reach the American community. The impasse remained. Bill expressed his opinions openly. On the day I was with Guruji, I was uncomfortable with Bill's absence, but I had no knowledge of this conversation.

We left Badrinath. A new road through the mudslide was cleared enough for us to pass—the bus tilting and swaying over the freshly carved bed. The day after we reached the ashram, news came that Guruji's brother, Bhaiji, had died. People sitting around Guruji's room were stricken with sobbing, or just hanging their heads. As the calls kept coming in, Guruji's voice would crack as he talked on the phone. I had never seen him so emotional. Guruji's fever spiked and his lungs began to fill with fluid, yet he needed to prepare for another long journey. Within a day, Guruji and most of the ashram members left for Bhaiji's village to attend his funeral. No one was ready for a twenty-five hour journey so soon after the *yatra*, and the unusual rain and cold. But they went.

Bill and I stayed behind to catch our flight back to the States.

Only after we heard the news of Bhaiji's death did Bill tell me that he was troubled by the thought that our Guru would die soon. These thoughts had plagued Bill the minute we first arrived at the ashram in Virat Nagar. We observed our Guru's disregard for his health on the pilgrimage in all extremes of weather. Bill prepared himself. He felt compelled to settle the issue of our ashram and our devotion. Guruji must have known what Bill was feeling. I had been oblivious. As it was, this was our last visit with Guruji. He died the following year.

I met Bhaiji when I went to India the first time. When we last saw him, Bill and I were together, leaving on the *yatra* to the Himalayas. Most of the ashram members were setting out for the Himalayas, but Bhaiji was not coming. He had been in Guruji's room watching a few didis empty a

275

shelf of its cache of donated shoes and slippers. Guruji's devotees wanted to encourage him to wear shoes in the mountains instead of his carved wooden sandals. Guruji preferred the wooden sandals. He was smiling at each new pair of footwear and the chorus of wise cracks in Hindi. Even without language, it was easy to be amused by the orange and white tennis shoes, embroidered gentleman's slippers, and other less defined footwear flattened with neglect. I wandered out. A few minutes later I saw Bhaiji cross the courtyard, strolling in the hot sun to his room wearing dark glasses. He was also wearing a pair of white canvas loafers, and had a pair of orange tennis shoes and some slippers cradled in his arms. He looked content.

Relationships feel different in India. Independence is not valued. We needed to boil water daily to have something to drink, and we shared small heating coils. On later trips we bought cases of bottled water. As we traveled, I was one of the tall ones who placed the luggage on the high racks. I carried the water bottles. Lacking in language, this was how I contributed. A feeling of being part of the mass of humanity is easy in India. Being with Bill in India was helping me feel the simplicity of our connection in spite of our differences.

The name of God pulsing in everyone's heart creates one flowing river, pulling us into currents that bend and play. Amidst the chaos of the streets, God is present in the tumult. When we leave our sandals outside the temple walls, on the steps and on the dusty earth, it's not uncommon to have someone innocently walk off in yours.

46

Awe is the salve that will heal our eyes.
Rumi

Bill and I caught a flight from Delhi two days earlier than planned. The ashram at Virat Nagar had been deserted for the ceremony in Guruji's village. On the long flight home we sat across the aisle from each other. The two young professionals sitting near me opened their books to read. They were of Indian origin but by their dress, they appeared to have lived in the States for some time. I had time to be quiet and review the last few days of our stay at the ashram.

The last days were comfortable at first. Guruji's driver took us to an outdoor fruit bazaar. We were told he had recently lost his wife in childbirth. She was attacked by a ghost, or so the story went. Bill and I went with Lucy and the three young men from Guyana who had traveled with us. In the bazaar, we searched for fruits to give the driver and his family. We spent half an hour shifting like a loose cloud of birds, looking for firm fruit. We feared losing track of one another in the crowd, so as soon as I wandered, Bill or Lucy shouted my name and pulled me back, handing me a bag, like a weight to hold me close. Krishan, one of the boys, went off to one side. I saw him patting a man on the shoulder. With his other hand, he pulled away a large vendor's basket that we quickly filled with the bundles in our arms. It took two of us to carry. We negotiated with shopkeepers for more bags of apples and Asian pears. The aisles of the bazaar were lit by strings of bare electric bulbs that held the night aloft just above our shoulders. Our burdens were all that held us from lifting off in the darkness. At the end, we huddled around the driver where the ashram bus was parked and offered him our basket.

Bill and I prepared to leave for Delhi. Our drive to the airport was not long, but it is never simple to travel in India. The afternoon he left, Guruji introduced us to his driver's brother, and assured us that the small ashram bus would be available. As we were packing our luggage to leave, this driver's wife went to the hospital. She was also pregnant and scared because her sister had died in childbirth just ten days before. She thought that the same ghost was attacking her.

Rakesh came to tell us. We had no ride.

"So," Rakesh finished, "it is not difficult to find another driver, but this one simply cannot leave his wife. She needs him right now."

Bill and I were not surprised by the change in plans. One thing India teaches is "change is the nature of nature," a phrase our Guru liked.

We had two hours left to find an option, but the choice was clear. Rakesh explained that we could take a train or a Sumo, a jeep, with another hired driver. In India, cars come with drivers. It is not easy to navigate the traffic or the roads. One passage will have bullock carts, bicycle and motor rickshaws, tractors and scooters with whole families on them. Cars and buses travel equally among wandering cows and pedestrians.

Bill went to find Kishore, the ashram manager, to discuss how to get to Delhi before midnight. I knew I was not needed, so I secured the screen door and lay back on the bed to write. I wanted to document an emerging theme. Bhaiji's death came at the end of a series of illnesses and deaths. Aside from the death of the young woman in childbirth, in the next town, two hundred people were in the hospital. The buckwheat flour eaten during the nine day fast of *Navaratri* was poisoned. The preservative that kept the buckwheat fresh for the biannual fast had been ground up in the wheat by mistake.

The reason we had come to India to study with our Guru was that in India the impact of the teaching is felt more deeply than in our familiar life. Away from comforts, the teaching stands on its own. We had said goodbye to him, among a few trees just outside the gates of his dusty courtyard rimmed with stucco walls painted burnt orange. His pet parrot watched from his perch in a cage that hung from a branch. Guruji was about to enter his Sumo with his driver when Bill said, "So now I know it was your brother and not you who was going to die."

Bill did *pranam* at his feet, and as he stood, they hugged. Guruji then came to me and placed his hand on my shoulder. "Give my sweet love to your boys." His hand carried a charge and I felt a course of love rush though my body. I turned away with tears pressing my eyes.

Then the stench of a dead water buffalo in the dry riverbed down the hill from the ashram invaded the entire ashram like an unseen fog. To keep the smell out of our room I had pulled our window shut tight. The air is cooler outside than in our room, but the sun intensified the smell. Death is the greatest teacher of detachment, but the smell of death was more than I could tolerate.

When we first arrived the night air was filled with the scent of a white blossoming vine that climbed the veranda pillars near our room.

That grace had ended. Guruji was gone. There was no reason to linger at the ashram. Bill and I changed our flight to leave two days earlier than originally planned.

I left my room, doors and windows shuttered tight, covered my nose, and joined the group in Guruji's room who were sitting on the floor leaning against Guruji's bed, watching cricket. They were staring at a murmuring television. I chose a rocking chair and, glancing at the television, could not distinguish between the two teams standing upright dressed in white, all eyes on the swinging stick. I looked back at the watching faces. It appeared nothing had been decided about our ride to Delhi.

They probably missed a return call from another driver with a jeep. Rakesh had been on the line with family in Holland. Receiving calls had been interrupted by bad phone service for days. No one was irritated with Rakesh. Bill started discussing the possibility of a train with Kishore.

I pushed out of my chair. With frayed patience, I stepped outside in the courtyard and was the first to see a Sumo and driver pull in. He told us the phone had been busy so he stopped by to check.

We had a driver. We left the Guyanese boys each something: a box of bottled water, extra tapes for lectures, our spoons. They smiled and waved as we passed from the ashram kitchen. Just outside the gates the driver nearly hit two children on bikes. I yelled. He smiled over his shoulder at my lack of confidence; his Sumo had not one dent or scrape.

We came to a high-speed road, Krishan in front with the driver. Bill, Lucy and I were in back. From the first near miss, Krishan soothed the driver in Hindi, joking with him, touching his shoulder, and cajoling him to slow down. The driver smiled.

At dusk, we passed an overturned truck with a bent axle, a spilled load of gravel and a dead cow. Later, coming through a city, we passed another accident lit by streetlight fogged with pollution and dust. A man lay on his side on an out-stretched arm. He was not covered. The rest of the accident was cleared away from him. The crowd pushed back off the road. His limp form was left as a kind of shrine, visible to all from the street and the shops, an unusually wide berth announcing his departure from the body.

"What would you like to drink, Ma'am?" My reverie was broken by the voice of the stewardess. I heard her as if with a delay, past the sound of the rushing air vents.

The woman next to me spoke.

"So what were you doing in India?"

I briefly replied that we had been visiting an ashram. She nodded and quickly turned to her paperback novel. She was dismissive. I felt pegged as an ashram groupie.

"I think you take your culture for granted." I ignored the fact that she had turned away from me. The young man looked over from his seat by the window to glance at my face. He did not want to appear eager, so he sat back.

My Indian dress is particularly odd when I am in transit. In America, no one knows the meaning of my cotton *punjabi* suits. They are made for ashram life. The cut of my dress is all wrong. I am too tall. In India, I am an anomaly. In the airport, people of Indian descent wear tight jeans, black clothing, and have a sleek look. Even the aging grandparents wear tennis shoes and pants. Traditional colorful clothing is rare among travelers, and my kind of cover-the-body ashram wear is peculiar, looking as if cut from bed sheets.

I ignored their opinion of me and forged ahead.

"The people from your culture live all over the world, and they are successful. Besides all the doctors and engineers, when my husband and I travel out West, every motel we stay at is managed by Gujaratis." I used flattery to keep their attention. "Why are you so successful? You take for granted your Hindu culture, the way you were raised and cared for. Although some Westerners seem to have advantages and privileges, many of us begin life without any meaningful connection…it is a handicap."

They were looking at me.

"If you don't value what you have, it will be lost in time."

They both affirmed my point with a brief nod, but I doubted they were convinced, not that I cared. I just wanted to have my opinion, speak clearly and not appear to be someone other than who I was.

47

I dream of swimming and far under the ocean I see a submerged city. It looks faintly orange like the color of your robes. Then I am walking in rusty orange grasses feeling the soft brush of the dried stalks against my calves. All my dreams begin to dream themselves in the color of your robes.
Dream Journal

Home from India in October, Bill and I landscaped an area of grass. In the previous spring, we had laid some rocks as steps and built a small retaining wall near the crown of a hill. Then in the cooler October weather, we got out the tractor to haul over some topsoil from a mound in back. The construction of a new home and septic system had left a wasteland of subsoil. We did not elect to have turf rolled out around the new house. Instead we began to reduce the mound of topsoil that lay sprouting briars and saplings at the edge of the woods, leveling its height at one end as we brought it around bucket by bucket in the back loader of the tractor. The topsoil mound stood taller than a man. I had to scramble a cliff to stand on its crown. From there, shovel by shovel I pressed my feet deep to dig into and release the earth. Watching it tumble down, I waited for the empty bucket to return. Near the house, we cleared out rocks and roots, scattered the grass seed, and raked again with the taut prongs of the garden rake to settle the seed below the top layer.

The pond near our house was man-made; the previous owners had dug into the marshy soil to create a setting for condos. But none were ever built around the acre of water that they stocked with fish. Now rimmed with lily pads, this was a place where I joined the dragonflies for baths in spring and early summer. Later in the summer, the warm water becomes viscous and brown with growing microorganisms. Before we came, a neighbor had thrown in Alaskan carp, bottom feeders, to keep the weeds in check.

My way of settling in to Ohio was to live by water. Before this, we lived in two adjacent houses on a rise above Brady Lake. The lake was ringed with summer cottages from the late 1800's, which had been remodeled for year-round use. Our sons learned to swim in a shallow sandy area, where their feet left the sand as their heads explored the lake bottom. I would not have moved from there to our new place had there been no water.

Our sons, Paul and Matt, are older now, driving their own cars. Paul has a job teaching. Matt is off in college. Bill cooks and fills their freezers with tomato sauce, wedding soup, and chili. Bill also packs his mother's freezer with minestrone soup. Bill is a kitchen gardener. I can watch him from the high window that looks over the garden, bending down and disappearing into the hedge of pole beans, and then up and back down among the tomatoes. After a while, our front door opens as he rushes in with an armload of vegetables to leave on the counter, leafy greens, zucchini, and tubers. His well-tended garden transforms into pasta with Swiss chard, butternut squash soup, collards and fried potatoes with garlic and onions. Olive oil guards the stove, cloves of garlic wait. He has built a cold frame for Mesclun lettuces, parsley, Chinese cabbage, beets and spinach. We eat spring salads into December.

It is not uncommon for Bill to wake when it is still dark, and cook into dawn. By the time I am awake, the counters are mostly cleared. The sky is lightening up. I sweep the corners of the kitchen floor of flour, crumbs, and onion, and wipe the counters clean. We have a haven where I have water, Bill has gardens, and we wait for spring.

Two springs after the *yatra* to the Himalayas, heat came early, and the pond was warm by the rim. I walked around looking at the new life. At the far end I saw a carp, three feet long, belly-up, white. I walked back to the shed and got a shovel. Reaching out past the grasses, I touched her side. She shifted her tail in the hot water, curved her body to the other side and lay still.

When the air cooled down again, I returned to her place in the water grasses. She had never righted herself. Quiet, I pulled her with a shovel and rake into a wheelbarrow. Her scales scattered on the metal sides, large as quarters, as I hauled her back by the old oil well at the edge of the marsh and dug a trench in the dark soil by the cattail reeds. She slid from the metal as I tipped the wheelbarrow, her weight making a muffled sound as she landed heavy on the hard earth. Heavy in death, lifeless as the soil, I covered her side until she was buried a foot deep.

Our Guru was buried that same season, in six feet of salt, sitting in *samadhi*. He had left his body while meditating, traveling on a train in February, 2002. I had traveled with him by train in that same month. The air is cool then, and we had cracked the windows for only a small stream of fresh air as we slept at night. The train rocked in a steady rhythm. Meditation is as natural there as anywhere. The mantra finds its own counterpoint to the rhythm of the train. But on his last train ride my teacher's heart and lungs were weak; the lecture tour was a strain. He cared deeply about India, and the Indian troops were lining up on the borders of Pakistan. War was threatening. He was preaching the glory of the tradition of knowledge, the *Vedas,* as wisdom for humanity.

This article we found later in the On-line Tribune, Saturday, Dec 1, 2001 Chandigarh India:

"The Maharishi with a Message," Monica Sharma

Pinjore, November 30

He hasn't denounced the world. Living in it, Brahmrishi Vishvatma Bawra ji Maharaj talks of bringing about a revolution by creating awareness among the masses through a rath yatra from Vaishnodevi to Assam starting from December 5.

Unlike most religious heads who chant mantras and tell you of the ways to attain "moksh" even though they know little about the materialist world they exist in, he is clear about his mission—to teach the masses the importance of being self-reliant, of being strong enough to defend themselves, of exploiting resources in a balanced manner and of bringing "clean politicians" to power.

But shouldn't a religious leader be talking about salvation and redemption? What is the relation between religion and the economic degradation of a country? "There is a clear-cut relation," he asserts. "If the country survives, religion too will survive. If we succumb to foreign forces attacking our country, religion too will face the danger of extinction. Politicians have failed to bring us out of this menace, but in fact are responsible for throwing us into it. The onus is now on the religious heads."

Our Guru was drawing the saints of India out of their complacency and asking them to help create a spiritual revolution in India. He wanted

India to climb to the status of a world power; her policy reflective of her high philosophy. Not passive, visionary.

Later in the summer, Bill and I visited the Canadian ashram where we see a video of his burial. His devotees, many our friends, buried him in salt next to the statue of Hanumanji on the ashram temple grounds in Virat Nagar. The monkey-faced god Hanuman stands ninety feet tall, painted in bright colors, and looks out over the landscape like a lighthouse. Hanuman was a servant of Rama. The sound of the name of *Ram* in his heart gave him the power to overcome all obstacles. The power of devotion, of surrendering his ego, made him larger than life. Our Guru was often likened to the monkey-god.

In the video, we saw our friends standing near the statue, barefoot with their sleeves rolled up. They passed softball-sized chunks of rock salt in a brigade down to one man below ground, close to Guruji's body, who gradually made his seated figure disappear. Our Guru's body was sitting as if in meditation. They called this ceremony and this place his *samadhi,* rather than his burial. Salt preserves the body. Guruji's body was said to have the name of *Ram* vibrating from the pores of his skin, as a result of the constant whisper of the sound from his lips and in the pulse of his heart. *Ram* is the vibration of life from beyond the light, heat, and power of the sun. Guruji realized truth through this sound and through his devotion to the eternal that lives in life, dwells in our hearts and whispers eternity. The disciples kept Guruji sitting in *samadhi* so his skin might whisper *Ram, Ram* and sustain his spiritual essence in the ashram.

At the ashram in Canada, Bill and I sat on the floor leaning against Guruji's bed. On the film, a man wearing a white *dhoti* was closest to his body and was placing rock salt, finally, by our teacher's head. The head kept falling first to one side and then to the other. Although his soul had left his body, the body was not stiff. Again and again, the man's hand touched his cheek and, with the patience of training a small child, raised the head back up. A few times later, he was more insistent. Each time he removed his hand to reach for more salt, Guruji's head would shift to the side, and lie still.

48

Remember, I am my knowledge.
Swami Bawra

To find a real guru is rare. The moment at the ashram at Virat Nagar, when the cow ambled out to greet me, affirmed the simplicity and intimacy of our Guru's grace. I found out that in the guru-disciple tradition, aspirants who wish to serve are first sent to the cowshed. There they learn simple service, devotion and respect, before assuming further responsibility with the knowledge. Bill and I live where lone blue herons stand to fish by the pond, and green herons visit, occasionally squawking from the low branches of maples and willows that lean out over the water. We teach and write. I had done plenty of hard physical work. I was ready to write.

A white marble temple was built over Guruji's *samadhi* at the temple campus in Virat Nagar. When Bill and I visit India, we bow *pranam* to an idol of his seated form in the center of the temple. There we circumambulate his memory and his place in our lives. There is not a day I do not feel his presence, his words, and his touch that have lifted me into myself. My transformation was guided by his steady witness.

Bill and I finished editing *Tattva Samasa*, the nutshell principles of Kapila while on another trip to India in 2004. We poured over the transcripts in the early spring in the Himalayan town of Kulu, the mountain village Guruji had written about in his letter. A modest Brahmrishi ashram and school had been built on a mountainside. Above the ashram a small temple was visible through the trees, the place where Kapila himself had lived, thousands of years before. The trees were not allowed to be cut; they were protected there, a sanctuary of nature.

In 2004 I realized I could base yoga teacher training on the flow of the knowledge that Kapila presents. I began a local yoga teacher training, Brahmrishi Yoga. Bill retired in 2006 and devotes his time to compiling Guruji's knowledge. His first work was *Kapil's Samkhya Patanjali's Yoga*, a book that explains how Yoga philosophy is based on Samkhya principles. Within the six systems of Indian philosophy, Samkhya is paired with Yoga and Vedanta is paired with ritual practices. Our interest in reviving Samkhya is to make the practices of yoga more comprehensible.

Samkhya philosophy is often distinguished as dualism and atheistic, both of which misrepresent the tenor of the teaching. Yes, Samkhya teaches about two powers, but they come from one source in *Brahman*. Samkhya is not a devotional path, but it emphasizes one spirit, one indivisible consciousness that dwells within all media of nature. It believes we have to do the hard work of freeing our own minds. Samkhya teaches the value of discerning the difference between the two powers as a way of gaining freedom. Bondage is misidentification of our self with things that can change. Loss always comes with change. Freedom lies in finding the self as awareness. We free ourselves from identification with what is changing and find a stable identity in consciousness: an unchanging, eternally blissful and truthful presence. The qualities of energy are form, movement and radiance. By resting in our awareness, what is called the seer and the knower, we can best participate in the dance of energy, free from any need to have life suit our desires and cravings.

As Bill wrote and I edited, we had many discussions as we refined terms and the relative importance of various concepts. I emphasized the balanced state of energy in practice, *sattva*, while Bill emphasized the observer of energy because the seer is more stable than any energetic state. I had needed balance to overcome my anxiety, but now I needed to learn to be free under all conditions without fear of what I might feel. By working on the knowledge with Bill, my practice became deeply embedded in knowledge.

I could finally listen to him.

"You know you only have to do the difficult part once, don't you?" Bill asked. "What you are doing is the hardest phase of practice, loosening your identity with the body and the confusion of the senses and mind. Once it is done, it is done. Freeing yourself from this level of attachment requires the most effort. After that, practice has its own momentum."

It was good to be able to hear him and appreciate how established he had been in himself all along.

The motto of Brahmrishi Yoga is wisdom, love and service, or head, heart, and hands. Our Guru told us many times: First knowledge! First we have to understand, then we can devote our effort and our intention to that ideal, then we can serve. The training includes a manual and primary texts with detailed knowledge of philosophy, anatomy, physiology and method. Each person in the training is encouraged to do a home practice and find a unique approach to yoga. Health issues, emotional imbalance, and mental states are all addressed in a practice. If you can help yourself, you can help others. If you cannot help yourself, then you are of little use for others. If you do not know yourself, you can be harmful for others. Assimilate the knowledge of yoga, process that knowledge, develop a clear intention and then create what you can to serve others. In the training, we talk and listen, write and share our writing. We work in small groups and large groups. Each teacher finds his or her own voice. We learn to speak well, listen well, observe well and witness one another. The teaching we end up sharing is always a very small moment in the long life of these practices.

Union of self with the source of life is like water poured into water. This is yoga. Through our consciousness we are one. Our bodies remain separate entities of nature, a divine power, and our minds orient us to the waves of experience. All parts of us are aligned through practice with the experience of oneness. Our *chitta*, or intellect, holds our learning and practice. It is the subtlest part of us that needs to be purified so a steady state of oneness can be maintained.

The subtle experiences and visions that came in altered states subsided. Guruji told us that intuition is the highest function of the intellect. Once anchored in a higher state, intuition functions in everyday life making it run more smoothly. Intuition is different from getting caught up in subtle experiences, which, in my case, were often a defense against feeling and emotion.

In his retirement, Bill assisted me in a vital phase of healing. Since I had frequently pushed onto him what I could not tolerate feeling, he was sensitive to my inner shifts. He immediately knew when I dissociated or lapsed into resentment that I wanted to disown. He gave me consistent feedback when I could not feel my emotions and projected them onto him. I learned to detect for myself how I project my feelings on my environment. I learned to withdraw them—the true practice of yogic restraint—and be stable within my own flow of feelings. I am grateful to him. My determination to heal filled my meditations with anguish for a few years as I directly felt what used to overwhelm me. It did not seem possible that the blissful state I had often experienced was a kind of dissociation away from these intense feelings, but it was. I was determined that the story end. It did. No longer divorced from my own feelings, I became calm and happy. Anxiety comes now as a simple motivation to act; not a problem for Bill.

Shivdas stayed on at the ashram. Kanta Didi visited less frequently. When she did, Frank and Evelyn made the trip to see her from where they relocated, a few hours away. Their adult children visited with their children. But mostly the ashram sat unused, and, in winter, Shivdas kept the heat low.

Finally the old furnace failed to pass inspection and had a red caution "do-not-use" tag wired to its gaping front. Shivdas lived in the smallest room upstairs, and spent the majority of his time on a sleeping bag rolled out on the floor, a small television and a space heater at his feet. The bathrooms and floors had always been cold at 40 degrees, without any furnace, it was just a bit colder. Shivdas was comfortable enough, until, naturally, the thaw.

About the time this is happening, in the winter of 2005, Swami Raghavananda was headed to our small ashram. Raghavananda is Rakesh, our young friend from India who stayed at the ashram and traveled to Kedarnath and Badrinath with us. He had taken his vows to become a monk from Kanta Didi, and he had moved to Florida to live and work there. The head swami from Florida had brought him to our Kent ashram.

Before he could settle in, the iron water-filled radiators had to be removed, and walls and ceilings repaired and painted. Raghavananda worked hard stuffing water-logged debris in black plastic bags. He cleaned after the fresh drywall dust had penetrated the kitchen and living room. He and I painted the walls and ceilings together. He continued working, raking the gravel drive free of leaf mulch in early spring, buying a pair of Wellington rubber boots to wear instead of wooden sandals. I often arrived by car to find him bent over in the drive with a metal rake, finally tending the ivy border by trimming it back.

Raghavananda had never lived in this kind of isolation. The *hoven* ceremony comforted him. I helped him cut small twigs and branches at our place so he would have plenty of wood that eventually blackened the walls with a thickening charred smell. He stayed much of one year and then moved on. The walls needed to be painted once again.

I was done with this repetitive task. I hired a woman to scrub the walls and another yoga student to paint. This student had made a down-payment for my yoga teacher training course and then failed to make any more payments. I asked why. She admitted that she did not believe in a money economy and did not want to participate in it. She was perfect. She did not have any experience, but she had time, and steadily applied small bits of paint from the roller to the walls.

For a long time, on the back porch of the ashram, filling with rain water, sat the metal *hoven* box with its wet ash and a few floating charred sticks, alongside a pair of Raghavananda's Wellington rubber boots.

Bill and I feel content that the ashram served its purpose. We enjoy the change of the seasons at our place, working outside, pruning and gardening when the weather is warm, burning wood in the winter to stave off the penetrating cold. We often think the same thoughts and share them gently. At night I hear the trains running east and west, their warning whistles and rumbling shaking me lightly out of sleep. Their steady murmur opens up a feeling of the vast diameter of the planet lying under my back, larger in the dark of night when distinctions are blurred. Sound opens my awareness. It is my practice to hear the drone in the air at any time, in the mower while I mow, in the mantras when I chant, and from that drone, birds sing in the early morning, people begin to speak, kitchen noises rattle, and all movement has a center of balance.

Sound is my closest companion.

After the Guru came to our living room for the first time, I had the idea that a story was ahead. I was quite excited and spoke to Bill about writing. He was naturally skeptical. I did not write. I could not sit still. My thoughts were scattered. But I stored the idea as an inner commitment to remember what was important about the story as it unfolded. Rather, because I knew my limitations, I asked God to remember and then to remind me later, so the job would be easier. I did not keep a journal. When the time came, we were living in a quiet place, where I could listen for the stories.

Our children have good careers; they are married with children and live nearby. My mother visits on occasion. My Dad and I became close friends in the last fifteen years of his life. We were able to talk, giggle, and air the hurt and confusion of our early years. He was in the hospital when I called to say goodbye to him, while I still had a chance.

"Dad, you were the best Dad. You know when I was a little girl, I thought clouds were white," I said.

"Yes..." He was impatient with sentiment.

"I saw you painting orange clouds in your pictures, so I asked you why you did that."

He was quiet.

"You just said, 'Look!' So I started to look at clouds more closely."

He was quiet for another moment.

"You know, Margs, you have made a good life for yourself. Your marriage, your family, the way you help people, immersing yourself in another culture—you know that is a sign of someone who is really part of life, of the world. It's wonderful! Okay, now your turn."

I smiled to myself. I knew he wanted more details.

"Dad, that is why I called. You taught me clouds are orange!"

I still laugh when I remember the last thing he asked me before he died. He hung up the phone, before I could reply.

"Is that all you got?" he joked.

I want now to tell him, "Not really."

There is so much more to say.

Clouds are everything.

Space is alive.

Acknowledgements

Anne Brennan is the editor who at the final stage of writing found her way into the heart of the work—jumping up and down, helping me spin straw into gold while demanding the first-born child. She was my Rumpelstiltskin. The child belongs to neither of us, but in the hands of you, the readers.

David Hassler and Pauline Thornton are lifelong friends who helped me enjoy the English language. David is the enthusiastic director of the Wick Poetry Center at Kent State University.

Wednesday Kent Writers that met bi-monthly for a decade at the Women's Center on the campus of Kent State University was the group that got me thinking like a writer, both from reading their writing and their close reading of mine. Their voices are my inner editors. Thank you Kathe Davis, Tiff Holland, Stephanie Sesic, Vicki Bocchicchio, Phyliss Hammerstrom, Eileen Manion and Tess Wolfe.

For a preliminary reading of the stories, thank you Matthew Gregor and Julie Tamarkin. For a complete reading of the first draft with line editing, a special appreciation for Camille Park. For your reading and comments, thank you Heidi Shaffer, Lisa Thiel, Pauline Thornton, Matt Milcetich, and my husband Bill.

For all your help, thank you again, Bill. There would be no book without you.

All proceeds will benefit Swami Bawra's free school in Jabalpur, India.

GLOSSARY

-A-

Acharya	- teacher
Aham	- I-am, pure ego
Ahamkara	- egotism due to *kara*, "fences," i.e. attachments
Ananda	- blissfulness; a stage of *samadhi*.
Anji	- "yes, dear"
Arjuna	- the warrior in the *Bhagavad Gita* who receives the teachings of Lord Krishna
Arti	- prayers and ceremonial worship with fire and sweet foods
Asana	- physical postures; one of the eight limbs of *astanga yoga; Lit:* stable, easy seat
Ashram	- place of rest
Ashtabuja	- the eight-limbed form of Mother Goddess; a name of *Saraswati*
Asmita	- I-amness, egoism
Astanga Yoga	- this eight-limbed path *Patanjali* outlined in the *Yoga Sutras*
Atma	- higher self; soul is free from attachments

-B-

Baba	- old revered one
Bhagavad Gita	- the discourse between Lord Krishna and Arjuna on the field of *Kurukshetra*; it is found within the *Mahabharata*
Bhajan	- sacred song

293

Bharat	- the motherland of India
Bij	- seed, used to describe short *tantric mantras*
Brahma	- deity of creation
Brahma chakra	- the highest *chakra* in the body, at the top of the head; the place of the *chitta*
Brahmacharya	- control of emotion, energy; one of the five *yamas*
Brahman	- the unmanifest; one, absolute source
Brahmin	- the highest caste of the Indian social system
Buddhi	- individual intellect, situated in the *brahma chakra*
Burfi	- a square sweet made from milk

-C-

Chai	- black tea boiled with milk, sugar and spices
Chakra	- centers of energy in the physical body
Chapati	- round flat bread
Chappel	- slipper
Chitta	- the first projection of nature; the medium that adopts and reflects consciousness and functions as intellect; situated in the *brahma chakra*
Chuni	- long scarf worn by women

-D-

Dal	- bean soup
Darshan	- the power of the guru's presence
Devanagari	- alphabet and script of Hindi and Sanskrit
Devhuti	- mother of Lord Kapila; *Lit:* "she who calls God"
Dhaam	- shelter
Dharamshala	- Buddhist hostel
Dharma	- an action that supports the life of all beings
Dhyan(a)	- meditation; a prolonged focus; one of the eight limbs of *astanga yoga*.
Dhoti	- leggings made of wrapped cloth
Didi	- sister
Dvesa	- aversion; see *raga*

Dyana	- meditation

-G-

Ganges	- the largest river in India, considered most sacred
Gargi	- a female yogi from the *Upanishadic* era
Gaushala	- cowshed
Gayatri mantra	- a twenty-four syllabled *mantra* invoking the inspiration of light
Ghat	- wide steps along a riverbank
Ghee	- clarified butter
Guhyam	- secret
Guru	- teacher; one who removes the darkness
Guna	- quality; the three qualities of nature: *sattva, rajas,* and *tamas*

-H-

Halva	- a sweet made from cream of wheat, *ghee* and sugar
Hatha yoga	- postures and breathing exercises to balance the systems of the body; two of the eight limbs of *astanga yoga*
Hanuman	- monkey deity; the power of selfless service
Hanuman Chalisa	- prayer to Hanuman written by Goswami Tulsidas
Haryana	- a north-central province of India
Himachal Pradesh	- a northern province of India
Hoven	- fire ceremony

-I-

I-Ching	- Ancient Chinese Book of Changes

-J-

Jai Virat	- greeting; "all glory to the one soul of the world"
Japa	- repetition of the holy name
Ji, -Jee	- *suffix:* "revered or beloved one"
Jin Shin Jyutsu	- an ancient art of harmonizing the life energy in the body, revived in the early 20th Century in Japan
Jiva	- living being

| *Jivatma* | - the individual soul |
| *Jnana* | - knowledge |

-K-

Kali	- a fierce, female deity representing purification of sins
Kama	- sensual desire
Kapila	- the Vedic seer of the *Samkhya* system of philosophy

Kapila's Samkhya Patanjali's Yoga, B.V. Bawra, edited by William and Margot Milcetich, Brahmrishi Yoga Publications, www.createspace.com (Amazon subsidiary)

Karma	- action
Karma yoga	- the yoga of selfless service
Kosa	- the five sheaths of energetic experience: body, breath, mind, wisdom and bliss; a *Vedantic* system
Krishna	- deity of maintainance; see *Vishnu*
Kumba Mela	- periodic gathering of saints along the holy rivers
Kumbhaka	- a breath hold in *pranayama* practice
Kundalini	- the upward force of *pranic* energy
Kunjal Kriya	- a cleansing exercise, *kriya*, of the stomach
Kurukshetra	- the battlefield where the war of the *Mahabharata* took place

-L-

| *Linga* | - representation of the force of creation in an elliptical stone; *Shiva-linga* |

-M-

Maha	- great
Mala	- string of 108 beads used for meditation
Mahabharata	- historical Indian epic; includes the *Bhagavad Gita*
Mandir	- temple
Mantra	- syllable(s) of sound used in meditation or in worship
Mara	- a Hindu goddess of death
Mira	- 15th Century mystic poet
Moksha	- liberation

Mughal	- (also, Moghal, Mogol) a Central Asian dynasty that ruled India from 1526 to 1858. The Mughal emperors, mostly Muslim, were Turko-Mongols from Uzbekistan who claimed to be descendants of Genghis Khan. Their reign influenced the cultural blending of Persia and India.

-N-

Namaste	- a greeting with hands in prayer position acknowledging our source in oneness
Narayana	- a deity representing the source of life, associated with life-giving water; incarnation of *Vishnu*
Neti	- cleansing practices of *hatha yoga*

-P-

Paisas	- fraction of a rupee
Paratha	- a fried flatbread often with vegetable filling
Patanjali	- compiler of the *Yoga Sutras*
Path	- prayers
Peda	- a round sweet made from milk
Prakriti	- nature; the feminine aspect of divinity; name and form
Prana	- life energy; breath
Pranam	- special obeisance to the *guru*
Pranayama	- breathing exercises; extension and/or control of breath
Prasad(am)	- sweet food distributed as the holy remnant of sacrifice
Pravachan	- discourse
Pundit	- temple priest; one who chants memorized *Vedas* and other scriptures
Puja	- worship with prayer and the offering of a small flame
Punjabi	- relating to the area of *Punjab* e.g. in dialect, dress
Pushpam	- flower
Puraka	- a *pranayama kumbhaka* practice of holding the breath in
Puri	- fried flat bread; a city
Purusha	- spirit; *Lit.* the indweller of the city of the body; the masculine aspect of divinity; existence, intelligence and bliss

297

Raga	- attraction; see: *dvesa*; also, the melodic line and mood of Indian music
Raja	- royal
Rajas	- the quality of movement and passion
Ram(a)	- deity of maintenance; see *Vishnu*; a mantra
Ramayana	- book of devotional poetry and the story of Lord Rama and his consort Sita, sometimes called *Ramacharitamahasa*
Rechaka	- a *pranayama kumbhaka* practice of holding the breath out
Rishi	- seer
Roti	- bread, meal
Rudraksha	- a seed used in making *mala*
Rupee	- Indian currency

Sadhana	- committed practice of meditation
Sadhu	- wandering ascetic mendicant
Sama Veda	- the ancient knowledge in chanting and verse
Samadhi	- evenness of intellect; absorption of deep meditation
Samagri	- spice mixture used in *hoven*
Samkhya	- one of the six systems of Indian philosophy that distinguishes nature from spirit and describes the nature of suffering; paired with *Yoga*
Samosa	- a savory fried food
Samprajnata	- a stage of *samadhi*; *Lit*. with wisdom
Samskara	- impression, memory
Samyama	- focused concentration on one point
Samosa	- a savory fried snack stuffed with vegetables
Sanskrit	- traditional scriptural language of India
Sannyas	- a lifestyle of renunciation
Sannyasi	- a monk
Sanyoga	- to join different qualities together
Saraswati	- a name of Mother Goddess, goddess of knowledge
Sari	- traditional female dress; six feet of wrapped cloth

Satsang	- a gathering for worship; "good and true company"
Sattva	- the quality of light and dispassion
Sharada Devi	- goddess of eloquence
Shastra	- a commentary on scripture
Shiva	- deity of purification and change
Shyamala	- another name of *Kali*
Sita	- consort of Rama; the feminine aspect of the power of divinity
Sita Ram	- the combined female and male aspects of divinity, nature and spirit
So-ham	- *mantra* of the breath
Subzi	- vegetables sautéed with spices
Suji	- "Cream of Wheat"
Sutra	- aphorism; *Lit*. thread
Svahah	- an offering into the fire
Swami	- one with self-mastery

-T-

Tabla	- a set of two drums
Taj Mahal	- the white marble mausoleum of the third and Hindu wife of the Mughal emperor, Shah Jahan, in Agra, Uttar Pradesh, that sits by the bank of the Yamuna River
Tanmatra	- subtle matter
Tantra	- a mystical yogic sect; origin of *chakra* theory
Tapa	- jealousy
Tapah	- also, *tapasya*; penance, austerity; one of the personal observances of *astanga yoga*
Tik hai	- "okay"
Tyaga	- renunciation of worldly life

-U-

Uttarakhand	- a Himalayan province and river source in Northern India
Upanishad	- teachings from the *Vedas* that are dialogues between teacher and disciple; *Lit*: to sit near

Vairagya	- detachment; paired with practice, *abhyāsa*
Vaishnava	- a devotional sect related with *Rama*
Valmiki	- a sage who wrote an early version of the *Ramayana*
Veda(s)	- ancient body of knowledge
Vedanta	- one of the six systems of Indian philosophy; *Lit:* end of the *Veda*; one of the six systems of Indian philosophy; paired with ritual
Vidya	- real knowledge; vs. *avidya,* ignorance
Virat Nagar	- "divine place of the north"
Virat Purusha	- cosmic form of divinity; cosmic soul
Virya	- vitality
Vishnu	- deity of maintenance manifesting as both *Rama* and *Krishna*
Viyoga	- disunion, to come apart; see: *sanyoga, yoga*
Vritti	- fluctuation; thought; modes of the *chitta*, *Lit:* wave

Yama	- vows; self-restraint; one of the eight limbs of *astanga yoga*
Yamuna	- a sacred river in Northern India
Yatra	- pilgrimage
Yoga	- oneness or union of similar qualities; one of the six systems of Indian philosophy that describes the methods of gaining inner freedom; paired with *Samkhya*
Yogendra	- king of yoga; master of the senses

Versions of texts used for quotes

The Bhagavad Gita, Winthrop Sargeant
The Essential Rumi, translations by Coleman Barks
Everyday Tao, Deng Ming-Dao
The I Ching or Book of Changes, Richard Wilhelm, Cary F Baynes
Isa Upanishad: Living in Divinity, Brahmrishi Vishvatma Bawra
Lao Tzu Tao Te Ching, Ursula K. Le Guin
The Secret of the Golden Flower, Thomas Cleary